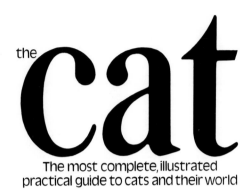

the cat

The most complete, illustrated
practical guide to cats and their world

the
cat
The most complete, illustrated
practical guide to cats and their world

David Alderton

A QUILL BOOK

Published by New Burlington Books
6 Blundell Street, London N7

ISBN 0 948872 09 8

This book was designed and produced by
Quill Publishing Limited
6 Blundell Street
London N7

Art director Nigel Osborne
Editorial director Jeremy Harwood
Senior editor Liz Wilhide
Editor Joanna Rait
Designer Paul Cooper
Illustrators Steve Braund Elaine Keenan
Paste-up Alex Arthur Dennis L. Thompson

Filmset by QV Typesetting Limited, London
Origination by Hong Kong Graphic Arts Service Centre Limited, Hong Kong
Printed by Leefung Asco Printers Limited, Hong Kong

Quill would like to extend special thanks to Creszentia Allen;
Paddy Cutts, Animals Unlimited; C-Vet; Su Gooders, Ardea London;
Rita Hemsley.

CONTENTS

The Cat and Man

The domestication of the cat is believed to have taken place later than that of other animals, which may be one of the reasons why cats retain an independence of attitude not evident in other domestic species. Over the centuries cats have proved increasingly popular as pets; aside from companionship they have also been valued more practically for their ability to control vermin and other pests.

Few other animals have inspired the depth and variety of reaction that the cat has provoked. In different societies at different times the cat was revered as an object of worship, cherished as a guardian of hearth and home, reviled as an instrument of Satan or feared as an intrinsic part of magical or occult rites. Even today, traces of these beliefs persist in everyday superstitions and imagery.

Domestication of the cat probably began in the region of the Middle East at least 4,000 years ago. The African wild cat (*Felis libyca*), reminiscent of a tabby but paler in colour, was involved in this process. The jungle cat (*Felis chaus*) may also have been tamed, since its remains have been discovered in Egyptian cat graveyards. The prime reason for domestication was probably religious, as cat gods in various forms were recognized in many areas of the world.

In the Middle East, where leopards and lions were considered sacred beasts, it appears that smaller cats were initially kept as substitutes for these larger, unmanageable creatures. As domestication proceeded, the small cats ultimately attained a divine status of their own, being associated with the moon and with the cat goddess, known under various names such as Basht, Bubastis or Pasht, from which the term 'puss' may have been derived. Special rites followed the demise of a cat, with a period of mourning and subsequent embalming of the corpse. Each year at an appointed time, there was a ceremony when cats were entombed at a temple of the cat goddess. It is thought that more than 100,000 cats were so buried, in front of audiences numbering perhaps half a million people at any time.

The festival itself took place in the spring, which suggests that Basht was a goddess of fertility. Sacrifices were made and items left for the deceased cats, with the ceremony ending in a large feast where wine flowed freely. The cult of Basht eventually went into decline, however, and it was ultimately outlawed in AD 390 after a period of nearly 2,000 years. Archeology has revealed a large array of artefacts which were associated with this cult, ranging from tomb murals and statues to jewellery.

Cats appear to have played a significant role in the cultures of many different societies, judging from the number of objects which have been discovered to portray them. In Ancient Egypt, cats were worshipped in the form of the goddess Basht, who had the body of a woman and the head of a cat. Basht was probably a goddess of fertility and is shown here with many smaller cats at her feet *(ABOVE)*. Other cat artefacts have also been discovered in Egypt, including this small statue of a cat wearing gold earrings, dedicated to the cult of Basht *(RIGHT)*. In the early civilizations of the New World, cats are also well represented in art and myth. The stylized feline made of onyx *(FAR RIGHT)* comes from Teotihuacan, Mexico.

Few domesticated cats had been seen outside Egypt because their export was condemned for some time, but it is likely that travelling merchants eventually took them to other parts of the Mediterranean region. The Greeks maintained the traditional link of cats with the moon, but never held these creatures in as high a regard as the Egyptians. Aesop, the teller of fables, linked them to the female form as exemplified in the goddess Venus, and this association has remained strong to the present day.

The hunting ability of the domestic cat was not of great significance to the Greeks because they already kept a form of weasel or martin for this purpose. The Romans also considered cats largely as pets, although they were regarded as having a guarding role at the fireside. Pliny the Elder included domestic cats in his work on natural history during the first century AD. Advancing Roman armies introduced the cat to regions of Europe.

In the East, where they were probably introduced by sailors, between 2000 BC and 400 AD, cats became prized for their ability to control vermin overrunning agricultural areas. Ceramic figures showing cats in a seated position had to be displayed in the house to ward off poverty, as this also became associated with their ownership. Cats were similarly valued as protection against evil spirits at night. Buddhists appreciated the cat's apparent power of meditation, while in Hindu areas they were popular pets. The Indian feline goddess Sasti, symbolizing maternity, maintained the traditional sexual or fertile power of the cat.

Yet while the cat was revered and welcomed in the East right through the Middle Ages, periods of persecution and hatred were to follow in Europe.

During the latter part of the Middle Ages in Europe the cat came to be viewed as a sinister creature, linked with Satan. Its important role in pagan festivals, combined with its independent and nocturnal habits, served to condemn it as a symbol of evil. In the early medieval period, faced with hordes of rats spreading plague, people had turned to the cat for deliverance and craftsmen made various cat artefacts for display in contemporary churches. This was an uneasy truce; the Church had always viewed cats with suspicion. The revival of pagan worship, which began in the thirteenth century in the Rhineland, once again featured cats in its ceremonies, and rekindled their persecution by Christians. The Church turned on both the followers of the cult and cats with a vengeance which was to last for nearly 500 years. Many cats became closely linked with the occult and witchcraft during subsequent centuries. This reinforced the notion that the cat possessed a female form, and it was a widely held belief that they could change into women and vice-versa. Black cats took on a particular significance as witches' companions or familiars, and were accredited with mysterious powers.

Legends about black cats have lasted down to the present day, giving rise to various localized superstitions. In Yorkshire, for example, wives of fishermen kept a black cat in their homes until the boats returned. It was believed that

CATS Since its opening in London in May 1981, the stage musical *Cats* has been a resounding success on both sides of the Atlantic. The Broadway production went on to win seven Tony awards in 1983, including Best Musical and Best Costumes. The show, with music by Andrew Lloyd-Webber, is based on the collection of poems by T.S. Eliot entitled *Old Possum's Book of Practical Cats*, first published in 1939. Originally written for Eliot's godchildren, the poems are delightful character studies of such memorable felines as Macavity, Growltiger, Rum Tum Tugger, Skimbleshanks, Mungojerrie and Rumpelteazer. Adapting Eliot's work for the stage not only involved setting the poems to original music and choreography but also meant the creation of special cat costumes for the human actors and actresses, costumes that would suggest the 'personalities' of the characters while allowing freedom of movement. An imaginative set was designed, recreating the world from the cat's point of view, with props scaled three times life-size.

Wild cats have also inspired different types of representation. The Ashanti lion *(RIGHT)* from Africa, is a hollow object made of cast brass which was used for weighing gold. *Tippu's Tiger* *(FAR RIGHT)* from Mysore, India is a mechanical toy made in 1790, which makes growling and screaming noises. Domestic cats have been cast in many roles, but for many centuries they were linked with the occult. Witches were thought to use them in their black magic rites. These witches *(BELOW)* are shown accompanied not only by a cat, but also a dog, mouse and owl — their 'familiars', or demons in the form of animals. By Victorian times, cats were popular pets, beloved rather than feared. The Cheshire Cat *(BELOW RIGHT)*, from Lewis Carroll's *Alice in Wonderland*, nevertheless retains an element of feline mystery, appearing and disappearing at will. The cartoon character, Felix *(INSET)* from the twentieth century, also hints at the cat's natural cunning, an angle later to be exploited by *Tom and Jerry*.

if the cat escaped or was lost, the outcome could be fatal for the men. Cornish custom dictates that whenever meeting a strange black cat, a person should draw a cross on the front of their shoe with a wet finger.

Cats began to achieve respectability again from the seventeenth century onwards and were portrayed more sympathetically in both literature and art. Charles Perrault wrote *Puss in Boots* at the end of the century, which was adapted later to a pantomime, as popular then as it is now. Among the artists of this period, Chardin and Le Mercier featured cats prominently in their work, while during the nineteenth century the forerunner of the Impressionist school, Edouard Manet, was also fascinated by cats. His sensitive portrayals featured in the special edition of the

Champfleury's *Les Chats*, published in 1868. Other writers, such as Victor Hugo, also helped to promote the cat's image in literature.

Interest in cats was by no means confined to France; Gottfried Mind, a Swiss artist, concentrated on them almost exclusively as subjects for his work. Outside Europe, cats and their behaviour were captured by the Japanese artist Kuniyoshi. Cats had been introduced to Japan from China during medieval times, and were treated as semi-deities at the Imperial Palace right up to the seventeenth century.

Distinguished writers and artists who have focused on cats in this century include Paul Galico, T.S. Eliot and W.B. Yeats, but cinema and television have been responsible for the popularization of the cat and its characteristics on a much wider basis than ever before. Cartoon roles of the cat range from *Tom and Jerry* to the adult film *Fritz the Cat*. The sinister image of cats gained a new interpretation in films such as *Diamonds are Forever* while individual cats have found starring roles on television. Jason appeared regularly on the BBC programme *Blue Peter*, while in the United States the NBC *Today* show featured Morris, who achieved a large personal following. Cats have also been used to extol the virtues of many products through advertising.

Within the last decade, two separate representations of cats have captured public imagination, on a scale previously unknown. The adaptation of T.S. Eliot's *Old Possum's Book of Practical Cats* by Andrew Lloyd-Webber into the stage musical *Cats* has brought almost unprecedented success on both sides of the Atlantic. The combination of feline body costumes and characters coupled with human heads was a unique gamble, and yet proved instantly appealing to the public. The production opened at the New London Theatre during 1981; when it transferred to New York advance sales for the Broadway show totalled six million dollars.

One of the most telling modern representations of cats is the cartoon character Garfield, who started life in a comic strip devised by an Indiana farmer's son, Jim Davis. Garfield is portrayed as the typical anti-hero of contemporary life, indolent, overweight and often unprincipled, and yet is completely unrepentant about his flaws. His relationship with his owner Arbuckle mirrors the independent streak of cats, which gives them a certain dominance over their owners. Devised in 1976, *Garfield* now features in 1,200 newspapers, with an estimated readership of 55 million people. Books based on this character have sold over seven million copies, featuring in the *New York Times* bestseller list. Such is the current popularity of Garfield that a complete industry has been built around him, with an annual turnover approaching 20 million dollars.

Today the links between cats and humans have never been stronger. The huge numbers of cats kept as pets all over the world and their popularity in all aspects of art and culture reflects a bond which has strengthened in the face of a rapidly changing society.

Characteristics of the Cat

The cat is perfectly adapted to life as a hunter. Its agility, well-coordinated movements and acute senses make it one of the most successful predators in the wild; the domestic cat retains many of the physical and behavioural characteristics of its near relatives.

Understanding a cat is a question of appreciating the natural instincts which help to direct its behaviour. One important factor is territory. Scratching, spraying and even fighting are all ways in which the cat marks and defends its own home range.

The Origins of the Cat

Fossilized remains indicate that the ancestors of today's cats appeared at about the same time as the dinosaurs became extinct, nearly 70 million years ago. The miacids — climbing creatures which evolved from the earliest placental mammals — had a similar pattern of dentition to that of present-day cats, and may also have possessed claws on their feet. They are thought to have been the forerunners of all the carnivorous mammals on the earth today.

Many of the early recognizable cats were large and dangerous creatures which have now become extinct. The European cave lion was a fearsome example. Perhaps the most notorious of the cat's ancestors was the sabre-toothed tiger (smilodon), which had a wide distribution over much of the earth's surface apart from Australia. These tigers were ferocious hunters, capable of hacking prey down with their elongated upper canine teeth. They are believed to have fed on mastodons, or primeval elephants. Unlike contemporary cats, sabre-toothed tigers used their canines for stabbing rather than biting, sinking them deep through the tough hide of the mastodon. Their line finally died out about 13,000 years ago, which is recent in geological terms, and they left no immediate descendants.

Smaller cat-like animals began to emerge about 12 million years ago; the history of the present wild cats can be traced back through fossilized remains for some three million years. The distribution of these cats was directly influenced by the movements of the various land masses.

From early climbing carnivores, the miacids, modern cats eventually developed. Some, like the prehistoric sabre-tooth tigers, died out leaving no descendants; others continued to evolve into today's family of cats, the Felidae. The Felidae can be divided into three genera: the cheetah *(Acinonyx)*, the great cats *(Panthera)* and the smaller cats *(Felis)*, from which our domestic cats are descended. The cheetah *(RIGHT)* is the only member of its genus and evolved separately from other felids. The genet, a carnivore living in the tropical forests of Africa, is one of the closest living relatives of the cat *(ABOVE)*. The skeletal system of the cat *(LEFT)* is comprised of approximately 244 bones, with over 21 in the tail alone. The tail is, in fact, part of the vertebral column; between individual vertebra are discs which act as shock-absorbers. At birth the bones are not fully ossified, but are composed partly of cartilage which is replaced by bone. Over 500 different skeletal muscles are attached to the bones *(BELOW LEFT)*. Those in the hindlimbs, neck and shoulder are particularly well developed. In addition to these skeletal muscles are smooth muscles, which are involved in the functioning of various organs.

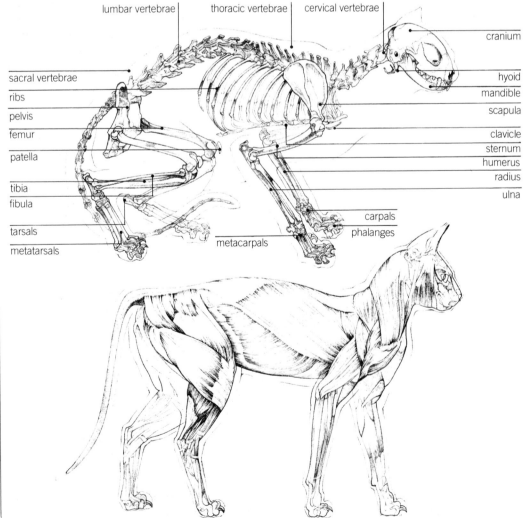

lumbar vertebrae — thoracic vertebrae — cervical vertebrae
cranium
sacral vertebrae
hyoid
ribs
mandible
pelvis
scapula
femur
clavicle
patella
sternum
humerus
radius
tibia
ulna
fibula
carpals
tarsals
phalanges
metatarsals
metacarpals

Australia separated from the major land mass called Gondwanaland about 180 million years ago, which was long before cats had evolved. The South American continent did the same but linked up again with its northern neighbour approximately two million years ago. This event afforded cats on the northern land mass an opportunity to spread southwards into new territory, whereas cats have never been native to Australia. Meanwhile, in the absence of 'true' cats, as they are classified today, marsupials had evolved to fill the same predatory niche in Australia and South America. Such creatures are often described as 'cats', although they differ significantly, not only by the presence of a pouch where the young are reared, but also in their pattern of dentition. The tiger cat, or large spotted-tailed native cat (*Dasywrops naculatus*), found in eastern parts of Australia, is a typical member of this group.

Physical Adaptations

Cats, as members of the Felidae, are adapted to a unique carnivorous existence among mammals. As hunters, their movements are agile and their musculo-skeletal system is adapted both for power and to allow a high degree of maneuvrability. The flexible backbone enables them to swivel their bodies into a wide range of postures, impossible in other species. An arching of the back, associated with stretching after a period of rest or as a threat gesture, is achieved by this means. Cats can curl up into a tight ball to sleep, and then roll over onto their backs before twisting.

Powerful hindlimbs provide the major thrust for running, with the forelegs offering stability and direction. Cats are not suited to prolonged running, but can outpace prey over short distances before launching into a jump if necessary. The claws are held in a retracted position by ligaments.

Kittens do not possess the agility and surefootedness of their elders, but quickly learn. The semicircular canals in the ears are linked to the brain and monitor balance; when falling, the cat learns to coordinate its body sufficiently to reach the ground landing on its feet. Cats can detect higher pitched sounds than the human ear, but deaf individuals will not respond to their kittens' calls. This condition affects Blue-eyed Whites in particular, which often congenitally lack the organ of Corti within the ear.

All the senses of the cat, as a true hunter, need to be highly developed, and vision is correspondingly acute. The eyes are effective over a wide range of light intensities. The

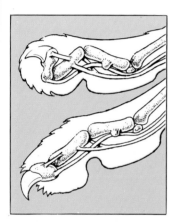

The domestic cat *(RIGHT)* shares many characteristics with its wild counterparts. The cheetah *(Acinonyx jubatus)*, however, is unique in lacking retracting claws. In all other cats, the claws are attached to the bones of the toe and can be retracted by means of ligaments, which are under muscular control *(ABOVE)*. The muscles exert their effect through tendons, attached to the bones. The cat's gait can be broken down into distinct stages, as shown in this sequence *(BELOW)* taken by the Victorian photographer Eadweard Muybridge (1830-1904). Muybridge was interested in the analysis of motion and published the results of his experiments in 1887 in *Animal Locomotion*. In the cat, the hindlimbs are especially powerful, providing the major thrust for running and enabling the cat to leap on prey.

pupils of the eyes adapt to the available light, narrowing to just a slit in bright light yet widening to their maximum diameter, to make best use of any light under conditions of almost complete darkness. Another adaptation for nocturnal vision is provided by the tapetum lucidum, located behind the retina in the posterior chamber of the eye. This serves to reflect light back to the retina so increasing the available intensity, and it is for this reason that a cat's eyes can appear to glow at night.

In order to catch prey, cats have developed binocular vision. The eyes pick up slightly different images by virtue of their differing positions, and these are fed back by each optic nerve to the brain. This overlapping field of vision enables prey to be located with pinpoint accuracy. The ability is not as pronounced in some breeds, such as Siamese, and these may not prove such successful hunters

The cat, as a hunter, needs to have acute senses for tracking and catching prey *(RIGHT)*. While hearing, taste, touch and smell all contribute to the cat's natural ability as a predator, vision is perhaps the cat's most important sense and the eyes are correspondingly the most noticeable feature. The cat can see over a very wide range of light conditions, although in dim light it cannot pick out much detail. At night, the tapetum lucidum, at the back of the eye, reflects light back onto the retina, enabling the cat to see in the dark.

THE ANATOMY OF SIGHT The eyes of the cat are set well forward in sockets in the skull, positioned to give efficient three-dimensional vision (1). The actual structure of the eye does not differ significantly from that of other mammals, except for the tapetum lucidum, a special feature designed to increase the intensity of light falling on the retina (2). The light-sensitive retina is the part of the eye where the image actually registers, and impulses from here are then conveyed along the optic nerve to the appropriate part of the brain. Because the eyes are set in slightly different positions, the cat's field of view is overlapping (3). This binocular vision enables the position of prey to be judged very accurately. Without such information, the cat would strike slightly off-target, allowing the prey to escape. By contrast, and befitting the cat's role as hunter rather than hunted, its peripheral vision is poor: the cat can only see in a fairly restricted field on either side of its head.

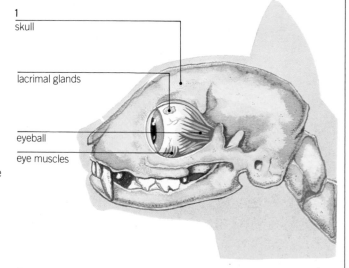

1

skull

lacrimal glands

eyeball

eye muscles

2

sclera

vitreous humour

cornea

iris

pupil

aqueous humour

lens

tapetum lucidum

retina

suspensory ligament

optic nerve

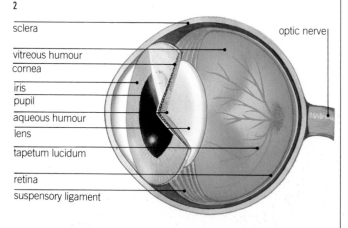

3

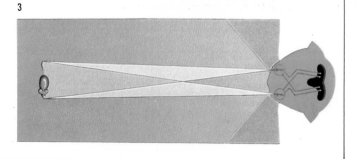

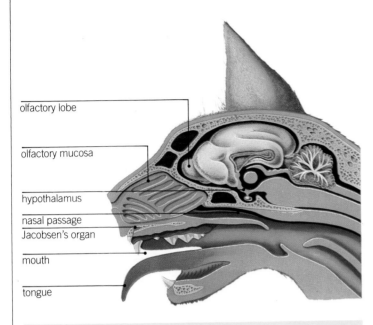

olfactory lobe

olfactory mucosa

hypothalamus

nasal passage

Jacobsen's organ

mouth

tongue

as a result. Kittens, being born blind, have to grow to understand the sense of vision and are unlikely to be able to use this faculty fully until they are at least 12 weeks old.

The hairs of a cat can be divided into various groups, with the longest being classified as 'guard' hairs; these form the outer coat. Beneath, the undercoat is comprised of shorter, softer fur. Certain hairs have become modified for sensory purposes, such as those behind the forelegs and the whiskers, which are sometimes referred to as vibrissae. Most breeds have about 12 whiskers below the nose on each side of the face, with additional ones above the eyes and on the sides of the head. Such whiskers have nerves at their base and will detect even a slight draught close by.

The cat's tongue is adapted for lapping fluids, forming a shape reminiscent of a ladle for this purpose. After several successive laps, the cat swallows the collected fluid in one gulp. The rough feel of the tongue results from the presence of papillae, which serve to hold prey in the mouth when necessary. There are various types of papillae distributed over the tongue, each of which have a distinct morphology. Taste-buds are also present on the tongue; unlike other mammals, cats do not appear to respond to sweet items, but actively recognize pure water. Smell is related to taste, which is particularly important in the case of the cat. It is likely to refuse all but the strongest smelling foods if this sense is impaired. This impairment is commonly due to a respiratory infection.

There is an addition organ of sense in the cat which does not exist in humans. This is known as Jacobsen's organ, and it is present in the upper surface of the mouth. Molecules of a scent are picked up from the air on the tongue, which is then pressed against Jacobsen's organ. A connection is made with the hypothalamic region of the brain, which triggers an appropriate response.

TASTE AND SMELL The senses of taste and smell are closely associated in the cat, since the nasal passage opens into the mouth, with impulses registering in the olfactory lobe of the brain *(TOP)*. Jacobsen's organ, located in the roof of the mouth, also demonstrates this link: molecules of scent are actually detected by the taste-buds, and the information is then passed on to the brain via this organ.
THE TONGUE The cat's tongue is an effective muscular ladle. When lapping fluid, the tongue becomes curled at its tip *(ABOVE)*. The surface of the tongue is rough, because of the presence of abrasive papillae, backward hooks which enable the cat to hold food, or prey, in its mouth. They also help the cat to remove loose fur during grooming. These rough papillae are located in the middle of the tongue, while other papillae around the perimeter and at the back carry the taste-buds. Wild cats, such as the leopard *(LEFT)* drink in a similar manner to their domestic relatives.

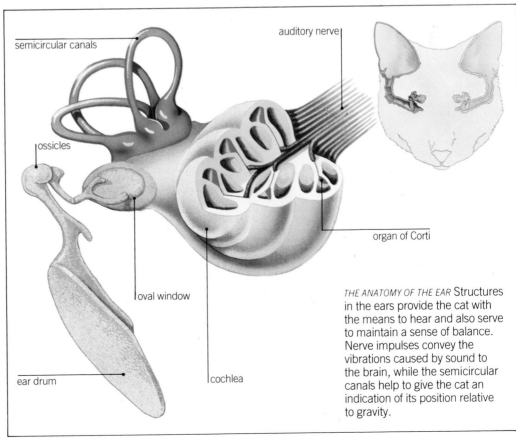

semicircular canals

auditory nerve

ossicles

organ of Corti

oval window

cochlea

ear drum

THE ANATOMY OF THE EAR Structures in the ears provide the cat with the means to hear and also serve to maintain a sense of balance. Nerve impulses convey the vibrations caused by sound to the brain, while the semicircular canals help to give the cat an indication of its position relative to gravity.

Behaviour
Vocalization and communication

Purring is the sound most closely associated with the domestic cat, and yet the actual means by which this noise is produced has never been fully elucidated. It is thought that the additional membranes close to the vocal cords are responsible, and purring results from their vibration. The sound is not audible in all members of the Felidae, however, but is typically confined to the smaller species. While purring is normally accepted as a sign of well-being and contentment, very sick cats will continue to purr and so the sound should not be taken as an indication of good health.

Cats are quieter than dogs, but they possess a distinctive range of vocal sounds, as well as purring. Their calls have been divided into three basic categories. Murmuring sounds, often made with the mouth closed, are reserved for times of intimate contact. The soft calls emitted while being stroked are typical of this group. The second set of vocalizations are by contrast more positive, and often described as 'vowel sounds'. These are specific calls, made with an open mouth, and with a closing of the mouth appearing to act as punctuation. Such calls are normally used to attract the owner's attention, whereas the third group of sounds provide a means of communicating with their fellow cats. This latter set of calls can be regarded as being more aggressive, with the teeth constantly visible. Facial characteristics alter, but the mouth itself remains open throughout the encounter.

There are two other types of call which do not fit into the above categories. Cats occasionally open their mouths as if to make a sound, but none is emitted. Such behaviour is normal and not indicative of ill health. This gesture is made especially when asking for food or milk, and can be interpreted as a sign of submission. Another call, actually uttered while hunting, is a quiet yet definite clicking sound, indicating to any other cats nearby that the individual is in pursuit of prey.

When badly frightened or angry, the cat may resort to spitting, as well as calling out loudly. Such behaviour is often linked to an arching of the back, and raising of the fur along the spine. Another indication of discontent will be signalled by the tail movements. Rapid waving of the tail is an expression of annoyance, whereas an upright tail which twitches only slightly is suggestive of an alert demeanour.

The eyes and ears are also utilized to communicate a cat's state of mind. When the ears are erect, the cat is expressing

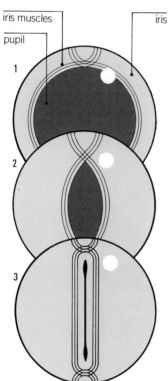

The diameter of the cat's pupils changes with its facial expression. When the cat is frightened, the pupils will be dilated (1), whereas they contract to a slit when the cat is angry (3). Changes in the available light also result in changes in the size and shape of the pupils. In dim light, the pupils are enlarged and circular (1); in moderate light, they are oval (2); in bright light, they contract (3).

EXPRESSION AND GESTURE Cats indicate moods using a variety of gestures and postures. Contentment will be shown by alert, upright ears, relaxed whiskers and a tranquil pose (1). Fear is demonstrated by a lowered head, with the ears and whiskers flattened (2). Anger is expressed by an arched back, raised fur along the spine, bristling whiskers and pricked ears pulled back (3). In an aggressive encounter, the dominant cat is the one in the higher position *(RIGHT* and *BELOW)*, and will deter an opponent by making an appropriate threat gesture.

SELF-GROOMING Cats are fastidious about grooming, spending long periods cleaning their coats each day. Licking serves many functions; it removes dead hair from the coat, it enables the cat to ingest Vitamin D which is produced on the fur by exposure to sunlight, and evaporation of saliva cools the cat down in hot weather, fulfilling the same function as sweat. The head is normally cleaned using the front paws. A degree of scratching is quite normal, but excessive scratching may mean fleas.

Compared to other animals, cats spend relatively long periods of their lives asleep *(LEFT)*. The usual pattern consists of many short 'catnaps' spaced throughout the day. Favoured spots will be soft, warm places such as beds.

Cats occasionally groom each other, especially if they have been reared together from kittenhood *(ABOVE)*. This is a sign of a close bond; such contact also gives the opportunity to groom inaccessible areas.

Grooming can also be a means of communication. Mutual grooming serves to reinforce a bond between two cats, whereas in some situations a cat will start to groom itself for no reason, perhaps when threatened or under stress.

Self-grooming

Under normal circumstances, a cat will groom to keep its coat clean. In so doing, it may ingest Vitamin D, produced on the fur by exposure to sunlight. In hot weather, saliva licked onto the fur fulfils the same function as sweat, helping to control body temperature by its evaporation. Sweat glands of the type widely distributed in humans are confined exclusively to the feet in cats, and are thus of little significance when it comes to losing excessive heat from the body. The cat has to rely on grooming and panting to cool itself.

Sleeping

Cats sleep, on average, twice as long as other mammals, and this behaviour is especially noticeable in both very young and very old animals. They may spend between two-thirds and three-quarters of the day asleep. The pattern of sleep is nevertheless variable, being influenced by external factors such as the companionship available. A cat left on its own tends to sleep more. It will choose from a wide range of localities for the purpose, but is usually particularly attracted by a soft, warm location such as a bed.

annoyance, and the pupils of the eyes are likely to be narrowed to a vertical slit. Flattened ears are suggestive of fear or submission, and are typically evident in the weaker of two cats disputing an area of territory. When actually hunting for prey, the ears are drawn back slightly, contributing to the cat's watchful appearance. A contented cat sits with its eyes semi-closed, while the ears are maintained in an upright position. There are known to be in excess of 20 different muscles controlling ear posture in the cat.

Close contact with another cat may result in the whole body being used to communicate. When ready to accept a mate, the female cat indicates this by crouching in a distinctive, recognized position described as lordosis.

The cat's method of sleeping has been extensively studied by attaching external electrodes to the head and monitoring the brain waves. The resulting trace on the machine is known as an electroencephalogram, often abbreviated to EEG. During the day in particular, light sleep prevails; the cat does not relax its muscles completely and wakes readily, giving rise to the description 'cat-naps' for brief periods of sleep. After a period of light sleep, however, extending up to about 30 minutes, the cat may enter a phase of deep sleep; this gives a characteristic change in the pattern of EEG. The eyes move rapidly in brief bursts during deep sleep, although the eyelids remain closed, and this has given rise to the alternative name of 'rapid eye movement' sleep, or REM sleep. There is usually an accompanying change of posture during REM sleep, and the body becomes more relaxed. Conversely, brain activity is actually increased during REM sleep, despite the way that the cat appears to be more soundly asleep. Periods of REM sleep alternate with light sleep once the cycle has started, until the cat wakes up.

Early lessons

A social structure begins to form in a litter of kittens almost immediately as each seeks out its own nipple, and a distinct pattern is formed by the third day after birth. A sense of smell is of particular importance at this early stage, to the extent that kittens will become confused if their dam's teats are washed. Sometimes they become side-tracked to the feet, where the odour of perspiration may be strong.

Kittens start playing with objects and each other from the age of three weeks. Studies show that in a litter comprised partly of males, female kittens tend to play more with objects than those in litters comprised solely of females. This habit of playing, developed during kittenhood, is vital to the cat's subsequent survival as a hunter. At first, kittens simply jump on their fellows and mother, but gradually a more sophisticated routine becomes evident. They start side-stepping and chasing each other more frequently, but do not actually bite at this stage. Under natural conditions, queens will teach their kittens to recognize prey from the age of six weeks onwards. They watch her kills, and are brought injured prey for killing.

One interesting study into the killing habit of cats, carried out during the 1930s, found that kittens reared with hunting mothers nearly all became killers in turn. It has also been found that prey taken during the formative stages of hunting remains favoured throughout the cat's life. On the other hand, only half of a litter reared by a dam who never preyed on mice would attack these creatures in later life. Kittens actually reared alongside mice hardly ever kill their early associates. All cats will play long after they have grown out of kittenhood.

Kittens are constantly learning, from their earliest encounters with their fellows onwards. As soon as the kittens have established themselves at their mother's teats, a rudimentary social structure will begin to develop *(RIGHT)*. Each kitten usually has its own nipple, with the liveliest often winning the best position and the weaker individuals relegated to the teats where the milk flow is not as plentiful. Kittens are born blind and need to learn how to use the sense of sight as it develops. About the third week after birth, once they have become proficient in this respect, they begin to show a degree of independence from their mother. Early games will simply consist of jumping on each other or on their mother, but as the kittens grow and become more mobile, their play routine becomes more complex. Although such behaviour is commonly referred to as 'play', it is in fact vital training. The inquisitiveness and playfulness of young cats are particularly appealing, but such traits are actually part of the process of learning to be a hunter *(FAR RIGHT)*. Kittens learn the routine of hunting from their mother, with prey often being presented to the litter for practising. This teaching by example normally only occurs if the mother is a hunter herself.

EARLY LESSONS Like any other young animal, a kitten learns by exploring and investigating the outside world, gradually honing its senses and reactions in readiness for a life as a hunter. The sense of smell is particularly important in encounters with strange, new objects – kittens will sniff cautiously before approaching closer *(FAR LEFT)*. Mock battles between kittens can become quite rough, but the infliction of real injuries is very rare *(ABOVE LEFT)*. Such behaviour has little to do with actual aggression, and is more often a way of practising hunting routines—stalking, pouncing and capturing. Kittens do not learn to bite until about six weeks old, and then only if taught by their mother. There is some evidence to suggest that while stalking and pouncing are instinctive procedures, triggered by the movement of prey, administering the final bite must be taught. Mothers who do not hunt themselves will not teach this skill to their kittens. Imitative and curious, the interest of one kitten in a particular scent will often serve to attract another to the same spot *(CENTRE LEFT)*. Kittens are fairly adept at climbing from an early age, but if this is not feasible, can support themselves on their hindlimbs in an attempt to investigate something out of reach which looks intriguing *(BELOW LEFT)*.

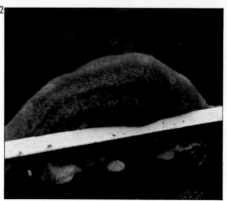

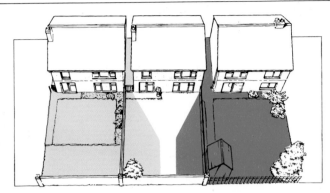

TERRITORIES Cats naturally establish distinct territories for themselves, centred on the home and extending outwards. In the country, or in the wild, these territories may cover a large area, but where space is more limited and the cat population is high, territories will be smaller. The area around a household where there is no cat will usually be divided among neighbouring cats who will adopt recognized routes to avoid conflict.

Territories

Each cat has its own clearly defined territory. The centre of this territory is known as the 'home base', from which the 'home range' extends. This is the region over which the cat normally roves, and can be as large as 60 acres (24 hectares), sometimes more. In colonies of feral cats, the availability of food appears to be the feature which determines the area of the home range. The hunting range may extend outside the home range, but is rarely established by domestic cats.

When a new cat is acquired it must establish itself, possibly at the expense of another. While tom cats may not object to the apparent intrusion of a female on their territory, neutered cats and queens will often actively resent a newcomer's presence. They will defend their relatively small territories vigorously, whereas toms tend to range over a much wider area which cannot be defended so easily. A new tom will be challenged by others in the area and will almost certainly have to fight rivals to gain a place in the social hierarchy. Queens will also attack others, without warning, if their kittens are threatened. Fighting only occurs in the last resort, however, as there exists a series of well-defined gestures which may be used to resolve the matter without bloodshed.

In a confrontation, ear and tail movements coupled with constriction of the pupils serve to indicate the aggressive demeanour of a potential combatant, forcing the other to adopt a defensive posture. The actual challenge follows an eye-to-eye meeting, and the weaker individual may then simply back off. If it cannot escape, or wishes to resist the challenge, then it moves into a position to resist the threat. It curls its tail and positions its body to emphasize its size, although the pupils remain dilated and the ears are down. The aggressor may then choose to advance on its crouched, hissing rival, who rolls over to meet the challenge with the claws of all four feet tensed and its sharp teeth ready. After a brief encounter of this nature, when one cat has had enough, it will escape, pursued by its opponent.

A subsequent challenge may have a different outcome. Domestic cats, partly because a high proportion are neutered, usually prove less aggressive towards a newcomer on their territory than their wild counterparts. They mark their territory by several means. Urine provides a pungent scent, while rubbing the head and tail on a favoured spot fulfils a similar role. Scratching provides both a visual and olfactory means of staking out a particular region. The high density of domestic cats in some areas has led them to evolve various methods for sharing a region without coming into conflict. They will have distinct recognized paths for crossing each other's territory, while a favoured spot may be shared, according to the time of day.

A newcomer in the neighbourhood will almost certainly be challenged by others in the area *(ABOVE LEFT)*. Toms do not appear to resent new females, but a new tom will probably have to establish his position. Although domestic cats are much less aggressive than wild cats, neutered cats and females will also defend their territories against a newcomer's intrusion. Many of these confrontations do not end in a fight but merely consist of ritual threat gestures, aggressive postures and vocalizations. To mark out their territories clearly, cats leave a variety of visual and olfactory signs. Spraying is just one such method *(ABOVE)*. Urine is a powerful and individual scent; toms will spray repeatedly around their territory to establish their boundaries. In the confines of the home, however, such activity is bound to be a problem, with the pungent smell lingering on furniture and surroundings. Many owners prefer to have their toms neutered in order to eliminate this habit as far as possible. Other territorial markers include scent, produced by glands on the cat's body *(LEFT)*. Rubbing the chin or head (1, 2) and tail (3) along fences and railings deposits scent from the glands located in these parts of the body. Scratching posts or tree trunks is another way of visibly marking out a particular area, and also leaves scent behind.

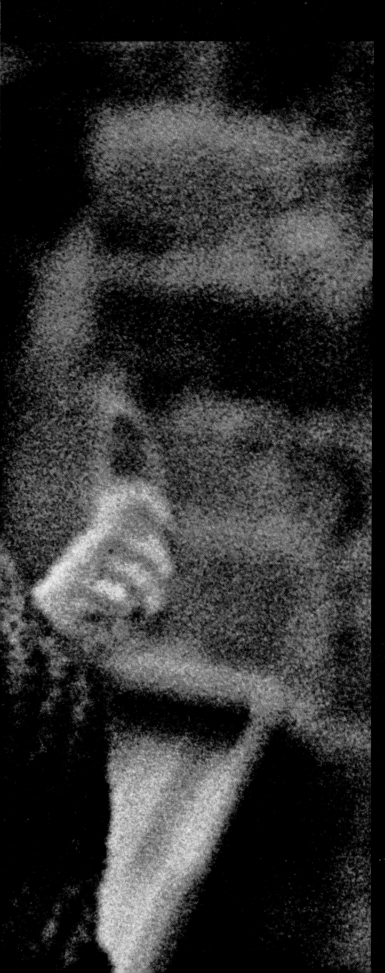

THE RITUAL OF FIGHTING An elaborate sequence of ritual displays, aimed at scaring the opponent, will be undertaken before a fight actually takes place. In most cases, the confrontation will end here, with the loser adopting a defensive posture and moving off. If the aggressor's challenge is met, however, fighting will occur. During a fight actual contact is kept to a minimum, with the loser breaking away, usually pursued by the victor over a relatively short distance. Fighting is always a last resort and is often of short duration. Reasons for fighting may include disputes over territory, or a mate; occasionally queens will attack to defend their kittens from intruders. Cat bites can be quite deep and there is considerable risk of abscesses forming in the puncture wound. Any such injury should receive prompt veterinary attention.

Breeds of the World

Cat breeds do not appear as easily distinguishable as dog breeds and classification varies from country to country. Points of difference centre on colour and markings, length and type of coat, and overall body type or conformation. In the United States, the term 'Persian' is synonomous with all longhaired breeds apart from the Angora, Balinese, Birman, Himalayan, Maine Coon and Turkish Van. This division no longer holds in Britain, where cats are divided into general categories based on coat-length — long or short — and origin. The British regard all breeds to be either British or Foreign in origin, whereas the Americans acknowledge some specific breeds to exist as separate categories.

Each breed has a breed number and a standard, which specifies the points on which the breed is judged. Classification is decided by the Governing Council of the Cat Fancy (GCCF) in Britain; in the United States, there are nine official associations, with the Cat Fanciers' Association (CFA) probably the most prominent.

Different colours within a breed are usually referred to as varieties; both varieties and breeds normally take capital letters to distinguish them from simple descriptions. For example, 'Black Longhair' refers to a particular breed; 'longhaired black cat' describes an individual. In this chapter the breeds are listed in alphabetical order, for easy reference. Alternative breed names are given in italics.

Basic Genetics

For the serious breeder, a sound knowledge of genetics is essential. All the features of the cat are controlled by genes, located on structures called chromosomes which occur in pairs. Genes exist in every living organism, and dictate every characteristic, including hair length, colour and type. If genes are identical, thus coding for the same characteristic, then the cat is described as being homozygous, but if they differ, then a heterozygous individual results. It is usually impossible to distinguish between such cats by sight, but their genetic make-up, or genotype, will become apparent when they breed, being reflected in their offspring.

Certain colours are said to be dominant over others. When pairing a black cat to a blue, all the resulting kittens will be black, yet because the kittens have genes from each parent, they are heterozygous with respect to blue. When such kittens are mated together, a proportion of *their* offspring will be blue when the appropriate combination of genes occurs. In some cases, however, neither gene will be dominant and the condition of incomplete dominance will result. An example is the pairing of Siamese and Burmese together, producing Tonkinese kittens which have an intermediate appearance showing characteristics of both parents. As well as Tonkinese kittens, there will also be Siamese and Burmese.

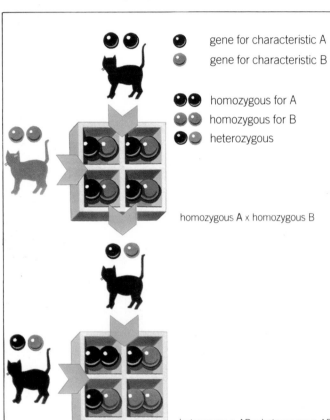

gene for characteristic A
gene for characteristic B

homozygous for A
homozygous for B
heterozygous

homozygous A x homozygous B

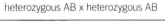

heterozygous AB x heterozygous AB

BASIC GENETICS Genes are the fundamental units of inheritance, a complete set acting as the blueprint for all the cells in the body. The cells have particular functions. Although the nucleus of each cell contains genes, located on pairs of chromosomes, only the ones contributing to these functions are used by the cell. Each bodily characteristic is governed by at least one pair of genes (coat length and colour, eye colour, and so on). One gene in each pair is inherited from each parent. If both genes in the pair are identical, the cat is said to be homozygous with respect to that characteristic; if both are different, it is said to be heterozygous. The result of the pairing of two homozygous genes is normally predictable; while only the average result of the pairings of heterozygous cats can be worked out.

EYE COLOUR Eye colour in the cat is not directly influenced by coat colour *(FAR LEFT)*. While the pupil is generally black, the outer ring, known as the iris, is the coloured component and this does vary. The irises may even vary in colour in a single individual — as in the case of the Odd-eyed White. Each breed and variety has a permitted eye colour, which is specified in the official breed standard. The Tonkinese *(LEFT)* results from the pairing of Siamese with Burmese, and shows the characteristics of both parents, due to the condition of incomplete dominance. When paired together, Tonkinese in turn produce Siamese, Tonkinese and Burmese in the ratio of one to two to one.

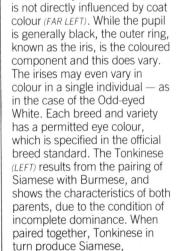

COLOURS, PATTERNS AND MARKINGS
Domestication and selective breeding has given rise to a vast number of coat colours, patterns and markings, in many different permutations. The original wild cats, from which our domestic cats are descended, were tabbies, striped in the mackerel pattern , rather than the classic or blotchy pattern which is more familiar today (1). The tabby pattern consists of dark bands of markings with 'agouti' markings in the light areas between the actual stripes. Together these form an effective camouflage, enabling the cat to blend with its background when hunting. Spotted cats are closely related to tabbies and have a similar pattern of markings to cats known in Ancient Egypt *(ABOVE)*. Self or solid-coloured (2) lack agouti markings (the yellow banding) so the stripes are not apparent, making a solid colour. A striking type of coat is the tipped or shaded variety, with the individual hairs tipped in a contrasting colour (3). The best-known 'pointed' breed is the Siamese (4). Tortoiseshells are just one example of multicoloured cats, where the patterning is not rigorous (5).

DOMINANT MUTATIONS One gene in each pair is inherited from each parent, one being termed dominant and the other recessive. The lack of a tail in the Manx breed *(ABOVE)* and the ear folding seen in the Scottish Fold *(RIGHT)* arise from dominant mutant genes. In these cases, when a cat showing such a mutant characteristic is paired to a normal cat, a proportion of the litter will also show the same feature. Manx cats can never be true-breeding; that is, they are all heterozygous, carrying only one Manx gene. This is because a pair of Manx genes would cause death in the womb; the 'lethal' factor.

Sex-linked pairings

In the case of the Tortoiseshell breeds, the genes for orange coloration are located on the pair of sex chromosomes, which are primarily responsible for determining the individual's gender. In males, one of the chromosomes, known as the Y chromosome, is shorter than the other member of the pair, identified as X. Tortoiseshell is the heterozygous form of orange; in this instance there is a visual (phenotype) distinction between the two genotypes. Since in the case of the male there is no opposing gene on the short Y chromosome to correspond to the gene on the X chromosome, then a heterozgote, and thus a Tortoiseshell, cannot result. Occasional Tortoiseshell toms are seen, and occur because the cat in question has two X chromosomes as well as the Y, making them XXY and hence heterozygous. Such cats are in effect masculinized females, and invariably prove sterile because of this chromosomal abnormality.

Dominant mutations

There are certain dominant mutations, such as ear-folding in Scottish Folds, and the absence of the tail in the Manx. This means that when a cat showing such a characteristic is paired to a normal cat, then a proportion of their offspring will also show this feature. One or both genes on the chromosomes concerned can be affected. All Manx cats are heterozygous, because in cases where both genes are mutated, the resulting kittens do not survive. This is then referred to as a lethal factor.

Showing Cats

The public showing of cats can be traced back to 1598, when a number were exhibited as part of the St Giles's Fair, held at Winchester in Hampshire, England. During subsequent years, occasional shows were held in association with such events, but only towards the end of the nineteenth century did serious competitions involving cats begin in earnest. Harrison Weir conceived the idea of selectively breeding and then exhibiting cats, and established the first standards, described as Points of Exhibition, to which

exhibits are still judged today. The first major show was staged at Crystal Palace on 13 July 1871, and attracted 160 entrants. Shorthairs were very much in evidence at these early shows, although at the 1875 exhibition there was a class for wild or wild hybrid cats, which was won by an ocelot. The trend towards exhibiting received a significant boost with the attendance of royalty at some of the major events during the latter years of the century.

It was inevitable that a body to oversee the development of both shows and breeds should come into existence and the National Cat Club was established in 1887. Harrison Weir was the first president, and a studbook and registry of breeds was begun. Cat shows in North America began in 1895, when a show was held at Madison Square Garden in New York. Cat breeders in other countries soon followed suit, and there are now a vast number of cat shows held throughout Europe, North America and elsewhere in the world. Standards have been modified over the intervening years, and cats are no longer classed predominantly on grounds of colour rather than breed, as happened at the first shows.

POINTS OF THE CAT To show a cat, it is important to study the standard laid down for the particular breed or variety. Although standards differ from country to country and between associations, a show cat must always display certain qualities: it must have good proportions overall and look healthy and alert. It must not be deformed in any way — polydactyl cats, for example (possessing extra digits usually on the front feet), are always disqualified. Aside from these general criteria, each breed standard specifies the body type, ideal head, colour of eyes and colour and length of coat. Marks are deducted if a cat fails to make the grade in any of these respects.

shape and size of tail

shape of head

eye colour

shape, size and position of ears

body type

condition of coat

coat length

colour, pattern or markings

length of leg

number of digits

Entering a Show

In Britain, shows are now held under the overall supervision of the GCCF, although the actual organization is undertaken by individual clubs. Pedigree cats must therefore be registered with the GCCF or the appropriate association in the United States. Registering a cat with several of these American organizations means that it can be shown at a larger number of events. It is also a good idea to join a local club, where experienced exhibitors will often help and advise the novice. All shows are publicized in the various cat magazines, and the first step is to obtain a show schedule listing all classes, and an entry form.

After careful study, the entry form should be completed and returned with the appropriate fees, well before the closing date. The structure of the show varies according to the country concerned. Exemption shows give the novice exhibitor a sound introduction. Championship shows provide the fiercest competition, with breeders seeking challenge certificates in the adult open classes. If the cat wins three times under three separate judges at different championship shows, it can then be called a Champion. This status allows entry to the Champion of Champion class at subsequent shows, and can lead to the description of Grand Champion if a further three wins result in this category. In the case of neutered cats a similar system operates, but winners are referred to as Premiers, rather than Champions.

Each exhibitor devises an individual system of preparation, but thorough grooming coupled with a bran bath or similar treatment will be essential. The cat must be in top condition with clean, sound teeth and claws which are not overgrown. Cats are benched in pens, which are usually lined with white blankets, and contain feeding bowls and a litter tray. Adequate training is necessary from an early age. A pedigree cat must be trained to be accustomed to being handled and confined in its pen.

At a British show, it is likely that the cat will first be inspected by a veterinarian, but elsewhere this formality does not always apply. Food is not given prior to judging, and after a final grooming of their cats, exhibitors leave the show hall so that judging can then take place in private. The judge examines all the entries, assisted by a steward who takes the cats out of their pens in sequence. Rosettes are given to all winners, although monetary rewards are small. The system differs somewhat in the United States, where public judging takes place. Irrespective of the regulations of the country concerned, one of the most enjoyable aspects of showing cats, whether they win or not, is meeting people with similar interests. This should never be overlooked in the pursuit of rosettes.

Cat shows are not only occasions for exhibiting and competing, they also provide an opportunity for old friendships to be renewed and new ones to be made. At larger shows, there are trade stands, displaying equipment relating to cats and their care, with the most up-to-date products much in evidence *(ABOVE)*. Cat magazines carry information on all such events.

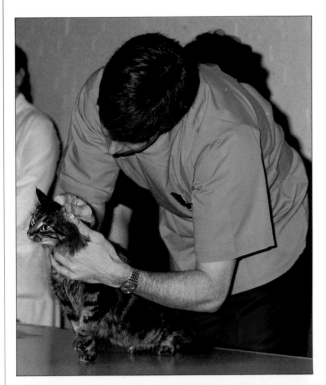

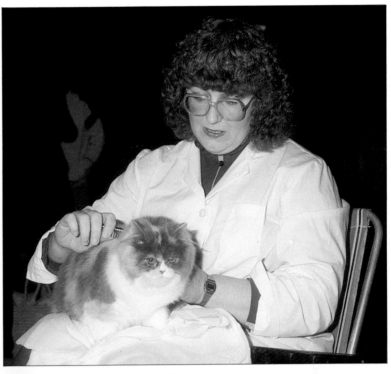

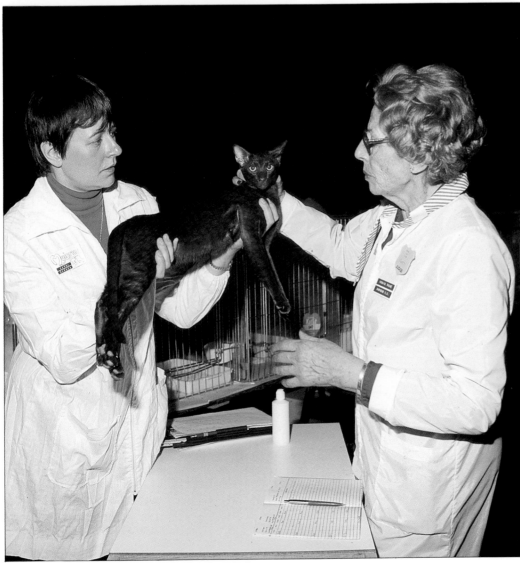

SHOWING A CAT At most shows, particularly large-scale events, a simple health check will be carried out by a veterinarian as soon as the cat arrives *(ABOVE LEFT)*. This is a sensible precaution, lessening the risk of diseases being contracted or transmitted, always a danger when many cats are brought together in one place. Owners usually like to make final preparations and adjustments to their cats prior to judging *(ABOVE RIGHT)*. Such last-minute grooming cannot disguise a cat in poor condition, but will add the finishing touch to cats in peak form. The coat should be entirely clean, tangle-free and shining with health. It is also important that cats which are exhibited regularly are not afraid of being handled by strange people *(LEFT)*. If a cat is nervous in its cage and tries to hide, or if it tries to escape while being touched or examined, then it is obviously not displayed to the best advantage. A cat's temperament is not unimportant in the show ring; proud, quiet cats are more likely to create favourable impressions than those that are wriggling or anxious. Methods of judging vary, depending on the country concerned. In general, both the overall condition of the cat and how close it comes to the ideal will be assessed. The important consideration is the impression the cat creates.

CLASSIFICATION OF BREEDS Britain was the first country where cat breeding became established on an official basis and where attempts were made to organize breeds into distinct groups for judging purposes. At that time, in the late nineteenth century, colour was seen as a important factor. Later, it was realized that breeds could more usefully be distinguished on the basis of type (the shape of the head and overall build), length of coat and on origin. Colours then distinguished varieties within individual breeds. As cats with a 'cobby' or stocky appearance were designated 'British' in type, all other body shapes were classed as 'foreign' or 'exotic' in origin. There is now one official organization in Britain controlling the official standards for each breed — the Governing Council of the Cat Fancy (GCCF). In the United States, by contrast, there are nine associations, with the Cat Fanciers' Association (CFA) the most prominent. These differ to a certain extent in recognition of breeds and in individual breed standards. Broadly speaking, in North America, the 'British' type is known as 'domestic' and the Angora, Balinese, Birman, Himalayan, Maine Coon and Turkish Van are classed as separate breeds from the other Longhairs, which are known as Persians. 'Foreign' or 'exotic' is also used to distinguish breeds originating outside the United States. Differences between both sides of the Atlantic extend further than nomenclature, however. Breed standards sometimes vary so much that the same cat could not win in Britain and the United States, although ostensibly it would be classed as the same 'breed'. Today, the GCCF organizes all breeds into four groups: Longhairs, Siamese, Shorthairs and Foreign Shorthairs. Each breed has a breed number: when new breeds and varieties are recognized, they are given new numbers.

BREED NUMBERS

Longhairs

1	Black	(4)	Lilac Colourpoint
2	White (Blue eyes)	(5)	Red Colourpoint
2a	White (Orange eyes)	(6)	Tortie Colourpoint
2b	White (Odd eyes)	(7)	Cream Colourpoint
3	Blue	(8)	Blue-Cream Colourpoint
4	Red Self	(9)	Chocolate-Cream Colourpoint
5	Cream	(10)	Lilac-Cream Colourpoint
6	Smoke	(11)	Tabby Colourpoint
6a	Blue Smoke	13c	Birman
7	Silver Tabby	13d	Turkish
8	Brown Tabby	50b	Self Chocolate
9	Red Tabby	50c	Self Lilac
10	Chinchilla	51 (1)	Red Shell Cameo
11	Tortoiseshell	(2)	Red Shaded Cameo
12	Tortoiseshell-and-White	(3)	Red Smoke Cameo
12a	Bi-coloured	(4)	Red Tortie Cameo
13	Blue Cream	52 (1)	Cream Shell Cameo
13a	Any Other Color	(2)	Cream Shaded Cameo
13b	(1) Seal Colourpoint	(3)	Cream Smoke Cameo
	(2) Blue Colourpoint	(4)	Blue-Cream Cameo
	(3) Chocolate Colourpoint	53	Pewter

Siamese

24	Seal Point Siamese	32a	Red Point Siamese
24a	Blue Point Siamese	32b	Tortie Point Siamese
24b	Chocolate Point Siamese	32c	Cream Point Siamese
24c	Lilac Point Siamese	32x	A.O.C. Siamese
32	Tabby Point Siamese		

Shorthairs

14	White (Blue eyes)	22	Tortoiseshell-and-White
14a	White (Orange eyes)	25	Manx
14b	White (Odd eyes)	25a	Stumpie Manx
15	Black	25b	Tailed Manx
16	British Blue	26	Any Other Variety
17	Cream	28	Blue-Cream
18	Silver Tabby	30	Spotted
19	Red Tabby	31	Bi-Coloured
20	Brown Tabby	36	Smoke
21	Tortoiseshell	39	British Shorthair Tipped

Foreign Shorthairs

16a	Russian Blue	29	Havana
23	Abyssinian	29c	Foreign Lilac
23a	Sorrel Abyssinian	33	Cornish Rex
23c	Blue Abyssinian	34	Devon Rex
27	Burmese (Brown)	35	Korat
27a	Blue Burmese	37	Foreign White
27b	Chocolate Burmese	37a	Foreign Black
27c	Lilac Burmese	38	Oriental Spotted Tabby
27d	Red Burmese	38a	Blue Oriental Spotted Tabby
27e	Tortie Burmese	38b	Chocolate Oriental Spotted Tabby
27f	Cream Burmese	38c	Lilac Oriental Spotted Tabby
27g	Blue Tortie Burmese	38d	Red Oriental Spotted Tabby
27h	Chocolate Tortie Burmese	38f	Cream Oriental Spotted Tabby
27j	Lilac Tortie Burmese		

Abyssinian

Cats of this type were probably kept for centuries in the Nile Valley before they were seen in Europe. A cat called Zula, brought to Britain by soldiers returning after the Abyssinian War ended in 1868, may have been the first to appear in the country. The unusual coat pattern of the Abyssinian cat gave rise to various early alternative names, such as Rabbit or Hare Cat. These cats are similar in appearance to the sacred cats portrayed in Egyptian culture and may share a common ancestry with the Egyptian Mau.

Recognition was given to the breed in 1882 in Britain and, although known in the United States by 1909, Abyssinians did not achieve much popularity until the 1930s. The bloodline here was developed from British stock, with a notable acquisition being a queen sent to Dr Ward Price by Mrs Menezes. While the First World War had badly affected the breed in Britain, it recovered well until hostilities broke out again in 1939. A more recent handicap has proved to be feline leukemia virus (FeLV), to which Abyssinians appear especially susceptible.

The Ruddy Abyssinian is the traditional form, possessing a coat which is a ruddy, golden brown, with black tips to the individual hairs. The underparts and the axillary region extending down the forelimbs must be orangish-brown, corresponding to the main colour. Any white coloration, except in the vicinity of the chin, is not permitted. Eye colour should be amber, hazel or green.

The appearance of these cats is both lithe and sleek, with the latter feature emphasized by their short, glossy coats. The prominent erect ears contribute to their alert demeanour, while the head itself is slightly rounded, especially in North American strains. The legs should be quite slim, ending in correspondingly small paws, while the tail is relatively long and thick at its base. Any trace of ring markings on the tail is prohibited.

A mutation of coat colour has given rise to the Red form of the Abyssinian. This variety was allegedly reported over a century ago, but only during the last two decades has the colour been appreciated, and was first recognized in 1963. Its body coloration is a rich copper-red, with the fur being ticked with two or three bands of black. The deepest coloured individuals are preferred and the contrasting colour on the lower parts should be apricot. In other respects, the Red resembles the Ruddy form. It has now been discovered that the red coloration results from a mutation of a light brown gene, and there has been a trend towards altering the description from Red. Both British and Canadian authorities refer to such cats as Sorrel Abyssinians, while other suggestions include Russet and Cinnamon.

Among other varieties of the Abyssinian, the Blue form has become more common over recent years, but it is not yet officially recognized. Ticking in this instance is blue, not black. A Silver mutant is currently being bred by a few British breeders, but is even more scarce than the Blue.

A longhaired variety of the Abyssinian, called the Somali, has now been successfully established. It was first developed in the 1960s from Abyssinian stock that possessed longhaired genes. Odd examples of this type had been bred before, but were generally overlooked by breeders. The longhaired characteristic may have been introduced at an early stage to the Abyssinian by crossing with Longhairs, prior to the 1930s. Although initially concentrated in North America, Somalis are now widely distributed both in Europe and in Australia, where the first individual was exhibited in 1965.

Ticking on the hairs of the Somali's coat is profuse, with up to 12 bands present; both ruddy and red colours are recognized. Certain strains have longer coats than others, but grooming does not present any special problems. The coat is slow to develop, however, only maturing fully when the cat is about a year and a half. Temperamentally, the Somali is very similar to the Abyssinian. Breeding the two forms together yields shorthaired offspring, all of which carry a longhaired gene. These, in spite of their appearance, have to be registered as Somalis under North American rules. Their coats are slightly more bushy than those of the pure Abyssinians.

The Abyssinian cats are generally not such prolific breeders as other cats, and there is often a preponderance of males in a litter. They are very popular as pets and their lively, affectionate personalities guarantee them attention. As a result of these factors, however, it may be difficult to acquire an Abyssinian kitten quickly.

American Shorthair

Early travellers across the Atlantic from Europe were responsible for the introduction of the domestic cat to the North American continent. It is likely that cats were carried on ships partly to reduce the rodent populations, and some were inevitably kept to fulfil the same function around the new settlements. This trait still remains with the contemporary American Shorthair, a noted hunter. It also has a deserved reputation for being hardy, intelligent and affectionate.

Only at the start of the present century was any attempt made to categorize and selectively breed from the various shorthairs then in existence in America. At first, these cats were mostly confined to Household Pet classes, while the longhaired Maine Coon flourished in New England area shows. First steps towards establishing the American Shorthair as a distinct breed were undertaken by a Miss Cathcart, who in 1900 registered an Orange, otherwise known as Red, Tabby tom which she had acquired in England. Belle as the cat was called, became the first Shorthair recognized by the CFA. Four years later, in 1904, a genuine American Shorthair, named Buster Brown, was acknowledged. Registrations confirm that only from the 1950s onwards did the Domestic Shorthair, as it was then known, really capture breeders' imaginations. The breed was renamed American Shorthair in 1966 and now nearly 30 colour varieties are recognized, often winning at major shows. Some associations have agreed to permit the registration of cats with no clear-cut pedigrees as American Shorthairs.

The type specified for the breed reveals the working nature of these cats, calling for an athletic appearance coupled with a muscular body. They are completely distinct from the Exotic Shorthairs, which, by virtue of their longhaired blood, have a cobby appearance. In terms of colour, white, black, blue, red, cream, chinchilla and shaded silver, shell and shaded cameos, and black, blue and

Abyssinian

The Abyssinian breed is characterized by a ticked coat, with each hair showing three distinct bands of dark markings. The traditional form is the Ruddy Abyssinian, which has a golden brown coat with black tips on each hair (1). Variations include the Sorrel, which first appeared during the 1950s (2) and the Blue, which is not yet recognized. Ticking on the Blue is blue, not black (4). The Somali is a longhaired form of the Abyssinian, first developed in the 1960s, but still relatively rare in Britain, where the first Somalis were imported from North America as recently as 1980 (3). The Sorrel variety of the Somali (5) is one of the two colours recognized.

American Shorthair

The American Shorthair is essentially regarded as a working breed. The coats of these cats are thick, particularly during the winter, reflecting their hardy, outdoor natures. They are bred in a very wide range of colours, but their overall body type is always judged to the same standard. Eyes, nose and paw pads differ in colour according to the variety. Six different colours of tabby are recognized, including the Blue (1) and the Silver (4), the latter being perhaps the best-known variety of the breed as a whole. Other colours include the Blue-cream (2) and Shaded Silver (3).

cameo smokes are all acceptable. Tabbies in six colours are recognized, these being silver, cream, blue, brown, cameo and cream, in both classic and mackerel forms. Tortoiseshell and calico varieties, as well as bicolours and blue-creams can also be registered. Faults which can be common to all colours include fluffy coats, abnormal tail structure and significant abrupt changes in nose profile.

American Wirehair

The American Wirehair is so-named because of the characteristic texture of its coat, which has a crimped appearance. The fur feels rough and springs back into place after being touched. Wirehair cats came into existence as a breed completely by chance, following a mutation which occurred in Vernon, New York. A litter of kittens bred during 1966 included a single individual with a thin wiry coat. This was brought to the attention of a serious cat breeder, who took the kitten and a littermate with a view to fixing the coat characteristic over several generations. Study of the hair of the mutant revealed that its structure was unlike that of other similar cats, such as Rexes.

The pairing of the littermates led to the production of two further wiry-coated kittens, and the emerging breed was named after the wirehaired terrier. Great interest has subsequently been aroused by these cats, fostered by the American Wirehair Cat Society. Breeders decided to establish the Wirehair on the same lines as the American Shorthair and the list of colours given in the description of that breed also applies in this case. The breeders' quest has been helped by the fact that wiry hair is a dominant feature, so cats with such coats can be bred in the first generation following the mating of a Wirehair to a Shorthair of good conformation. The use of longhaired breeds has been avoided in order to maintain the distinctive appearance of the coat. This must not be patchy, although on some parts of the body, typically the underparts, it is not quite so wiry. The Wirehair has a similar temperament to the American Shorthair.

Every Wirehair in the United States is descended from the original tom which was called Adam, but this mutation has also occurred spontaneously in Britain. Following the bombing of London during the Second World War, large colonies of feral cats established themselves on the resulting waste grounds, often in the heart of the capital itself. The Wirehairs, which appear to have corresponded to the American form, were taken from such a locality and exhibited at the National Cat Club Show approximately two years before Adam was born. The characteristic was not fixed in this instance.

Angora
Turkish Angora; Turkish

This breed originated in Turkey and was named after the capital city, Angora (now known as Ankara). The early development of the breed is shrouded in mystery, but it was first seen in Europe as long ago as the sixteenth century. Some believe that the Angora may have been bred from the Pallas's cat (*Felis manul*), but it is generally accepted that the longhaired characteristic of the breed arose directly, and

was established in cats which otherwise showed the typical 'foreign' body type.

Like other longhaired breeds, the Angora was initially described as a 'Persian', which is in fact much more stocky in appearance. By the middle of the nineteenth century, the various Eastern breeds were being recognized as having separate origins and characteristics, and the Angora itself lost favour when compared with the true Persian. It virtually disappeared from outside its native land and interest in the breed was only rekindled after the Second World War. During the 1950s Angoras were again seen in Britain, while others were sent to North America and Sweden; they have become increasingly popular.

Although bred in other colours, the Odd-eyed White, referred to by Turks as *Ankara kedi*, is regarded by many as the natural type. Unfortunately, as with other white cats, a significant proportion are deaf; this handicap can be a distinct disadvantage, especially for potential owners living near busy roads. Among the other recognized colours are the two tabby forms, the *teku* (silver) and *sarman* (red).

The status of these cats at championship shows has altered as their popularity has grown. In the United States, the white form only was recognized by the CFA until 1978, but now various other colours are acceptable, ranging from tabby to tortoiseshell-and-white, known as calico in the United States, and black to smoke. The British standard only recognizes the red and white form, known as the Turkish cat, developed initially in the area around Lake Van, which gives rise to its American name of Turkish Van.

The Angora breed in Britain, officially acknowledged in 1977, is actually an artificial recreation of the Turkish form, bred using oriental shorthaired cats possessing longhaired genes, which are related to the Balinese. Although resembling the original breed in all respects, these Angoras have voices more reminiscent of Siamese, and they have been bred in a much wider range of colours, including chocolate (known as chestnut in the United States). Like the original Angora, these cats have a distinctive coat which is fine and silky, lacking the woolly undercoat of the Persian, and so always remains sleek.

Angora cats are lively and very playful by nature, yet gentle. They do need adequate space for exercise however, being less happy in a fairly confined environment than the Persian. The true Angora has on average four kittens per litter, but the new British strain is more fecund. They will moult heavily during the warmer months, losing their winter coats and need adequate grooming especially at this time. The absence of a thick undercoat makes this easier.

Balinese

This breed was developed in the United States, using Siamese discarded for their longhaired characteristics, and became officially recognized in 1968. The origins of the Balinese — named for their elegant shape and movement after the native dancers on the island of Bali — go back to the 1940s, when breeders on opposite coasts, in California and New York, decided to establish these longhaired Siamese as a distinct breed. Since the longhaired characteristic is inherited in a recessive manner, all such cats are homozygous, and thus when paired together can only produce offspring with similar coats.

Siamese of that period were somewhat heavier and had smaller heads than those being bred today, and these features have been retained in the Balinese. In order to bring the type of the Balinese into line with the present-day Siamese, some breeders in North America have used the latter variety in matings with Balinese, and then paired the resulting progeny together. The kittens of the first generation are heterozygous, possessing one gene of the longhaired characteristic, and their coats differ slightly in texture from a pure Siamese. They cannot be registered as Siamese, however, and some Siamese breeders are opposed to the use of their cats in this way, being concerned to prevent a subsequent deterioration in quality.

Balinese remain scarce in Britain, where Angoras are preferred to Siamese to improve the type of the new breed, so eliminating the introduction of shorthaired blood. The breed is not recognized at present in Britain, although individuals can be shown in assessment classes. Since matings to Siamese only are allowed by the CFA in the United States, this means that just the colours accepted for

American Wirehair

The characteristic coat of the American Wirehair is the most significant feature of this breed for exhibition purposes. The fur is rough, wiry and should spring back into place after being touched. Many colour varieties are now established including the Silver Tabby (1) and the White (2).

Angora
Turkish Angora Turkish

The Angora was bred in Turkey for centuries, long before it was seen elsewhere in the world. Whites are accepted as the traditional form of the breed, although their eye colour can vary. Unfortunately, as with other white cats, Blue-eyed Whites are usually completely deaf, whereas in Odd-eyed Whites deafness is normally confined to the blue-eyed side.

Balinese

The Balinese is closely related to the Siamese — and is essentially a longhaired form of that breed. Balinese are bred in similar colours to the Siamese and possess the same characteristic 'point' markings, shown in these kittens in the Chocolate form. Other recognized colours include blue, lilac and seal. They do require more grooming than Siamese, but not as much as other longhaired breeds.

Bicolour Longhair
Bicolour Persian

The Bicolour Longhair has been bred in a variety of colour combinations, set against white. The original form was black and white but blue, cream or red are now acceptable. For exhibition purposes, the areas of colour must be clearly delineated and a good contrast between the coloured areas and the white is significant. The long coats of these cats need regular grooming to keep them in the best possible condition.

Birman
Sacred Cat of Burma

The Birman is said to have had an illustrious history and its alternative name, the Sacred Cat of Burma, makes reference to this. Many breeders believe, however, that the breed has simply descended from Siamese crossed with Longhairs. The typical areas of white on the paws are referred to as gloves, whereas the white areas extending up the hindlegs are known as gauntlets, terminating at points called the laces.

Siamese are permitted for Balinese. Blue, chocolate, lilac and seal forms are therefore exhibited. Other cats, including those with points of tortie, red and lynx (known as tabby in Britain), have been produced, using Colourpoint Shorthairs. These are now classified by the CFA as Javanese.

With their close ancestral links to the Siamese, Balinese possess many of the characteristics of this breed. They enjoy climbing and are quite athletic. Their voice can be persistent, but the call itself is generally lower in pitch. Balinese are affectionate cats, but can also prove rather aloof, like true Siamese. Compared to other longhaired breeds, they do not require as much grooming, and their coat is less likely to become tangled. Balinese usually make good parents, and are often exceptionally playful with their offspring.

Bicolour British Shorthair

These cats are bred in various colour combinations like their longhaired counterparts. The standards again call for the colour to be clear and evenly distributed. It must not constitute more than two-thirds of the total coat area, whereas white markings should be restricted to a maximum of half of the coat. Traces of white in the coloured fur is a serious flaw, as are tabby markings and any sign of brindling. The eyes must be pure orange or copper without any sign of green rims. Colour should be present on the face and a white blaze is popular.

The coat needs sufficient grooming to emphasize the contrasting colour, while white areas must be clean. As with related shorthairs, the coat should be thick, yet short and fine. The overall conformation ought to appear balanced, with legs in proportion to the body, and a reasonably short tail. Although the body should be muscular, it does not have the stocky appearance characteristic of the Bicolour Longhair. As pets, Bicolours are hardy, affectionate cats and suit domestic life.

Bicolour Longhair
Bicolour Persian

The Bicolour, as its name suggests, has a coat comprised of a solid colour broken by white. Its type resembles that of other longhaired breeds. These cats were initially much more popular in the United States than Britain, where they were first shown in Any Other Colour classes. Lady Alexander tried to encourage their development, with special classes at Crystal Palace shows early in this century, but these were not well supported. Black-and-white Bicolours, known as 'Magpies', were regarded as the correct combination of colours. It was then planned to reproduce in Bicoloured cats the markings seen in Dutch rabbits, right down to equal distribution of white and black on the head, but in practice this proved too difficult to achieve and affected their popularity.

New standards have since been devised and other colour combinations, such as blue, cream or red, (otherwise known as orange), all set against white, are now acceptable. Most official bodies now demand that, at maximum, half of the coat should be white while up to two-thirds can be coloured. Contrast is significant and the areas of colour must be clearly delineated. Both coloured and white patches should be present on the face. Bicolours are usually robust cats and breed well, although their long coats require regular grooming. They have also contributed to the production of the Tortoiseshell-and-White breed, known as the Calico in the United States.

Birman
Sacred Cat of Burma

The history of this longhair is obscure, although its alternative name, Sacred Cat of Burma, suggests that it originated in the East. These cats, according to legend, were kept at the Temple of Lao-Tsun, which housed an image of a golden goddess, Tsuyn-Kyan-Kse. One of the cats there, called Sinh, formed a close attachment to the head priest, Mun-Ha. During a raid on the temple centuries ago, Mun-Ha was killed while praying and as he lay dying, he was touched by Sinh who was suddenly transformed. The cat's yellow eyes changed to blue, like those of the goddess, and the fur of the body became golden. His face, tail and legs took on a brown hue, but where his paws were in contact with the priest, the fur was pure white, which symbolized goodness.

Sinh himself died shortly afterwards, but the dramatic change in his appearance encouraged the remaining priests to fight off the attack. When they met to choose a successor to Mun-Ha, the priests were amazed to observe that all the temple cats had changed like Sinh. When the cats surrounded one of the priests, called Lioa, this was taken as a sign of divine choice, and Lioa became the new head priest.

During the early years of the twentieth century, the temple was again attacked, but this time the attack was repulsed with the help of two Europeans, Monsieur Paire and Major Russell. As a gesture of their gratitude, the priests sent two of their sacred cats to France as gifts for the men. Although the tom died on the journey, his mate survived and produced kittens and these are said to have heralded the start of the Birmanese line in Europe.

The breed was first recognized officially in France in 1925, but supposedly only two European individuals survived the Second World War. Afterwards Birmans soon attracted the attention of British visitors to French cat shows, and some were subsequently imported. Meanwhile, two Tibetan Temple kittens were acquired in 1960 by an American enthusiast, Mrs Griswold, and the close relationship between the two breeds was immediately apparent. Shortly afterwards, Birmans from France were brought to the United States, where the breed was recognized in 1967. The British GCCF had granted recognition to the Birman during the previous year and the breed is now common and popular on both sides of the Atlantic.

Birmans are not usually temperamental cats and as a result have proved popular both as pets and on the show bench. Their coat is long and silky, responding well to daily grooming. A variety of colours have been produced; in the United States, chocolate, lilac and blue with the appropriate points are all recognized, whereas the British standard is currently confined to the latter two varieties. The so-called white gloves on the paws form an important

Black British Shorthair

The Black British Shorthair is recognized as a distinct breed. Individuals must possess a jet black coat. Any trace of brown is a definite fault in adults, although kittens may have a brownish tinge in their fur. Superstitions and legends about pure black cats are still common in many parts of the world, usually to do with luck (good or bad) and witchcraft.

feature of a good exhibition Birman of any colour. Those on the back feet are referred to as 'gauntlets', and extend up the back of each hindleg to end in points known as 'laces'. Some breeders feel that, in spite of its supposed illustrious origins, the Birman was in fact created simply from selected Longhairs crossed with Siamese. There is, however, no link between the Birman and the Burmese, which is a shorthaired breed.

Black British Shorthair

The Black British Shorthair was first recognized as a dintinct breed at the end of the last century. The coat must be jet black to its roots, showing no trace of brown coloration. Kittens, however, may have a rusty tinge to their coat. The eyes should be orange or copper, free from any hint of green. The head is relatively large, but not out of proportion to the rest of the body, which should resemble that of the Bicolour in type.

Black Longhair
Black Persian

Black Longhairs or Persians have a long history and were represented at the first cat show held in Britain in 1871. At the time they were unusual for their orangish eyes, in contrast to the large number of green-eyed breeds. Only a few Black Longhairs were exhibited and only 17 were registered when the GCCF took over the tasks of the National Cat Club in 1910. During the next year, however, the fortunes of the breed took a turn for the better, with the birth of Dirty Dick, who went on to win 14 championships and had a major influence on successive bloodlines. Indeed, the interwar period saw a revival in the popularity of the Black Longhair as a breed, led by the breeder Cyril Yeates, who later became chairman of the Governing Council.

Black Longhairs have always maintained a strong following in the United States where King Max achieved the distinction of three successive wins at the Boston Cat Show, beginning in 1877. While European cat breeding was

Blue-cream British Shorthair

The standard, and therefore the appearance, of the Blue-cream differs significantly on opposite sides of the Atlantic. In the United States separate areas of blue and cream in the fur are required, whereas British breeders aim to produce cats with mixed, even coloration. The cream hairs tend to be finer than the blue; the breed has contributed to the development of the Blue and Cream forms of the British Shorthair.

Black Longhair
Black Persian

The Black Longhair is a striking cat, which was represented at the very first British show, held in 1871. The colour takes some time to develop, however, and is likely to be fairly poor until the cat is about six months old. Individuals who seem unpromising at an early age may well develop into the best adults, with jet black coats.

Blue Longhair
Blue Persian

Blue Longhairs were once very fashionable cats to own, their popularity increasing dramatically when Queen Victoria acquired one. The exact shade of blue is not an important consideration but any sign of white is a serious fault. Eye colour should be orange, with no green showing around the rims.

dramatically affected by the Second World War, the development of the Black Longhair continued virtually uninterrupted in the States. Grand Champion Pied Piper of Barbe Bleue kept the breed in the limelight by becoming Cat of the Year in 1951. Eight years later, his great-grandson, Grand Champion Vel-vene Voo Doo of Silva Wyte, was to take the same honour.

The persistent pairing of Black Longhairs together is not recommended, because the coat quality will soon deteriorate. Blues have been commonly mated to Blacks to overcome this problem. Various other colours, typically Tortoiseshells and Orange-eyed Whites, have sometimes been used in place of Blues. The colour of young kittens' coats should not be taken as being indicative of their subsequent appearance. Kittens may be greyish rather than black; even experienced breeders can encounter problems in distinguishing between Blacks and Smokes in a crossbred litter. At the time of birth, however, Smoke kittens have grey markings on their head and feet.

Blue Longhair
Blue Persian

The early Blues often showed tabby features as well as white markings, and were first exhibited in Any Other Variety classes. At the Crystal Palace show of 1889, a class was first established for self-coloured Blues and the breed became very fashionable, especially when Queen Victoria acquired one. Classes for kittens were soon arranged; in 1901, the Blue Persian Society was founded, to promote and improve the breed. This society produced the first official standard and organized specialist shows. The Blue was also used to upgrade the type and appearance of other Longhairs, or Persians, typically the Black, as well as contributing to the development of the Himalayan Longhaired Colourpoint.

Blues can be bred in various shades. At first only the darker-coloured individuals possessed the desired orange eye colour, which was much in demand. A common fault

which still emerges occasionally is the presence of green rims around the eyes themselves, but now selective breeding has produced light Blues with good eye colour. For exhibition purposes, any shade of blue is acceptable, providing the coat is free from white hairs, which are considered a serious fault. Tabby markings are also not permitted, but some self-Blue kittens may appear tabby when first born. These lines disappear as the cat matures. Males in particular are very large, stocky cats, possessing a fine, thick coat, which is soft to the touch. In some individuals, the tail appears kinked, and this flaw can be transmitted to the offspring of such cats.

Blue-cream British Shorthair

The Blue-cream was bred in Britain during the 1950s and contributed to the development of both Blue and Cream forms of the British Shorthair. The colour standard is similar to that for the corresponding longhaired form, with the same difference between British and American regulations over distribution of colour. Pairing Blue-creams together often yields the best coloured offspring. The cream hairs of the coat tend to be finer than the blue, and regular brushing will be necessary to remove these when the cat is moulting.

Blue-cream Longhair
Blue-cream Persian

Blue-creams were only officially recognized in Britain in 1930, although their origins extend back into the nineteenth century when they aroused little interest among breeders. They arose from matings between Blues and Fawns (now called Creams). One fancier who did appreciate their significance, however, was Mrs D'Arcy Hilyard, who produced prize-winning Creams in 1901 from her Blue-cream queen Sanga, paired to D'Arcy, who was a

Bombay

These sleek black cats were derived from Burmese crossed with black American Shorthairs. The coat should resemble satin in texture and should lie close to the body. The body is reminiscent of the Burmese; a strong, intense copper is the preferred eye colour. The breed was given a standard in the United States in 1976, but has not yet received one in Britain.

Cream tom. Some confusion obviously existed over the usage of Blue-creams in the breeding of Creams; only later was it confirmed that because of the genetics involved, male Blue-creams were exceptionally rare and invariably sterile. In addition, the choice of the tom had a direct influence on the offspring's colour.

Although Blue-creams were recognized in conjunction with Creams, they were never thought of as separate variety. Their type was good overall, however, although their coloration was patchy, and some breeders therefore decided to concentrate on improvements in this area. Unfortunately, their early efforts gave rise to Blue-creams which were often tinged with red, and led others to describe such cats as 'Blue Tortoiseshells', an unpopular term with the breeders themselves.

The standard laid down in Britain differs from its American counterpart to such an extent that the same cat could not win on both sides of the Atlantic. Such a discrepancy has arisen because the early Blue-creams sent to North America had coats with clearly delineated colours and this became the accepted pattern of markings. In Britain, both colours should be intermingled in the coat, while a cream blaze extending from the nose to the forehead is favoured.

Pale Cream toms are preferable for producing good Blue-creams, although it is not always possible to pick these out at birth, because kittens which appear pale blue may develop into Blue-creams. Like the Blue, these cats are affectionate and loyal, often seeking out the company of their owner. They enjoy being petted and are naturally active.

Bombay

This striking breed is of fairly recent origin, being developed from sable brown Burmese crossed with black American Shorthairs. The breeding programme began during 1958, but it was only in 1976 that the CFA gave a standard for Bombay cats. They are named after the black form of the leopard which exists in parts of India. The coat is a prominent feature of the Bombay, being short and possessing a characteristic patent leather appearance. It should be jet black in colour, although paler in kittens. The fur becomes more sleek in adult cats. Acceptable eye colour ranges from gold to copper, but the tendency is to prefer cats with the darker coloration, if two individuals are equal in all other respects.

The body of the Bombay should show its Burmese ancestry, being lithe yet muscular. The head must be quite broad, and the eyes well spaced. The ears should not end in pronounced tips, but need to be rounded, while the neck is narrow. Any kink in the relatively long tail will be penalized at a show.

The Bombay remains largely confined to its North American homeland, but will probably become more widely seen over the course of the next few years. The breed is perhaps not ideal for the purposes of those seeking a pet, since it is active and occasionally rather temperamental, as well as having a large appetite relative to its size. Males can become quite large when they mature, and yet they retain their elegant appearance. There is no official standard in Britain at present for the Bombay.

British Blue Shorthair
Exotic Shorthair Blue; Chartreuse

The history of the Chartreuse extends back to at least 1558, with records showing that this shorthaired breed was being bred in France by monks at the monastery of La Grande Chartreuse. It was said that they only sold neutered animals so that the breed remained based exclusively at the monastery. During the eighteenth century, Linnaeus, who did much to establish a system of classifying creatures and plants, regarded the Chartreuse as a distinct species and as recently as 1930, it was given the scientific name of *Felis catus cartusinorum* by a French veterinarian.

The breed has now been amalgamated with the British Blue, known in the United States as the Exotic Shorthair Blue. These two varieties are judged to the same standard. At some American shows there are separate classes, with the Chartreuse having slightly more silver coloration.

The standard specifies a pure coat colour between medium and light blue, showing no dark markings or white hairs. The eyes must be orange or copper, not green. Best breeding results are generally obtained by using Blacks as an occasional out-cross, which serves to darken the colour of the resulting Blues and also keeps their solid bone structure.

Blues make ideal pets for those seeking a truly companionable cat, as they are phlegmatic by nature and generally content to stay in the same place for relatively long periods. Unlike some shorthairs, Blues are not noisy cats.

Burmese

Burmese first attracted attention in North America, where Dr Thompson was instrumental in establishing the breed using the queen Wong Mau, which he imported from Burma in 1930. When first exhibited at a San Franciscan show, however, other cat fanciers were not greatly impressed with these cats, regarding them as poorly coloured Siamese. There were records of brown Siamese dating back to the nineteenth century. Undeterred by this reaction, Dr Thompson began a programme of selective breeding, which had to involve Siamese, since no other Burmese was available to pair with Wong Mau.

It is likely that Burmese originated as artificially produced hybrids, with Siamese contributing to their bloodline. Burmese possess a similar gene which restricts the distribution of colour in the coat, although its effect is not as pronounced as in the Siamese, where the points are a prominent feature. A proportion of the original Siamese-Burmese hybrids bred in America were a richer brown, with little contrast between body coloration and points, and from these, the breed was gradually evolved. Further cats were obtained later from Burma, but never more than a few individuals, so Siamese still continued to be used as out-crosses. The imported Burmese also proved difficult to acclimatize successfully, readily succumbing to some respiratory diseases.

The CFA recognized the Burmese during 1936, and then in 1954 the Burmese Cat Club was founded in Britain. The first members of this breed had been seen here after the

Blue-cream Longhair
Blue-cream Persian

Blue and Cream Longhairs have both contributed to the development of the Blue-cream. Pairing either colour to a Blue-cream will yield offspring of each colour, as well as Blue-creams. These kittens come from the litter of a Blue-cream dam.

British Blue Shorthair
Exotic Shorthair Blue; Chartreuse

The British Blue Shorthair is now considered to be indistinguishable from the Chartreuse, which originated at the monastery of La Grande Chartreuse in France during the Middle Ages. Once thought to be a distinct species, the breed is now amalgamated with the British Blue. Coat colour must be pure blue; eye colour must be orange. Quiet, calm and affectionate by nature, Blues make excellent pets.

Burmese

One of the most popular pedigree breeds, the Burmese was established in the United States in the 1930s, first appearing in Britain in the 1940s. Up until 1963 the original Brown was the only colour available and many breeders today still maintain that this is the only acceptable form of the breed (1). Various other colours are now established, but few are recognized universally. These include the Brown Tortie (2), Cream (3), Red (4), Lilac Tortie (5), Blue Tortie (6), Chocolate Tortie (7), Lilac (Platinum) (8), Blue (9) and Chocolate (Champagne) (10). Tortie forms are not officially recognized in the United States. Irrespective of colour, however, the Burmese are deservedly popular as pets, being sociable, hardy and affectionate. Because of their habit of retrieving, they earned the nickname of 'dog-cat' when they first appeared.

Second World War, and passed into the care of Mr and Mrs France. The subsequent acquisition of champion Laos Chili Wat and Cas Gatos de Foong then gave the British bloodline a major boost. The breed is now well established throughout much of Europe and has a strong following in both Australia and New Zealand.

The standard still differs in North America and the rest of the world, since American breeders aim for a head of rounder proportions and a slightly stockier body. Round eyes are preferred by American judges, whereas a flatter, more elongated shape is selected elsewhere. There are no significant discrepancies with regard to type, however, with a medium length, muscular body being required. The fine, glossy short coat conveys a deceptive indication of the cat's weight, since Burmese should be heavier than their appearance suggests. The coat must be a rich seal-brown in colour, slightly paler on the underparts, but with virtually no contrast on the points. Tabby markings are only permitted in kittens, while their eyes should be golden in colour and as rich as possible. Green or blue eye coloration is a significant fault, as are any areas of white fur in the coat.

Apart from the traditional Brown, other colour forms of the Burmese are now being bred. In the same way that the Blue-point Siamese was produced as a dilution of the Seal-point, so a Blue variety of the Burmese has been established. It was first recognized in the United States in 1960, but has not gained universal acceptance. The CFA view it as a Blue Malayan, while the Burmese Cat Club only accept the Brown as being Burmese. The Blue form is in reality a relatively pale blue, really a silver-grey. These cats are not as sleek as their brown counterparts, since their fur is not so fine at present. The gene responsible for this coloration was probably transferred across from Siamese in the early days when Browns were being developed.

Various other colours are also known, and the majority are recognized by the GCCF in Britain, but not by American associations. The Chocolate, known as Champagne among North American fanciers, and its paler form, referred to as Lilac, or Platinum in the United States, were largely developed during the 1970s. The chocolate coloration is in fact creamy brown, becoming darker on the legs, tail and head, whereas the lilac is greyish with a pinkish tinge. It is not always easy to distinguish between these varieties in the same litter, until the kittens are several weeks old, since at birth both are whitish in colour.

British breeders were largely responsible for developing the red strains of the Burmese which now include Creams, Reds and Tortoiseshells. Actual red coloration in such cats is more tangerine than red, although the ears of the Red are of a significantly deeper shade. In spite of opposition from some quarters, British breeders decided to cross these new varieties of the Burmese with the idea of improving their overall type, as well as creating additional colours. Both Chocolate and Lilac Tortoiseshells have been produced as a result. A longhaired form of the Burmese, bred from crossings with Longhairs, is known in the United States, where such cats are described as Tiffanies. In common with the majority of the new colours though, Tiffanies have yet to be officially recognized.

Burmese, irrespective of their colour, are active and adaptable by nature. They are friendly, self-confident cats and, although like Siamese in some respects, they do not prove so demanding. Burmese generally live longer than other breeds, often surviving well into their middle teens.

Cameo Longhair
Cameo Persian

Cameos were developed quite recently, first bred in the United States by Dr Rachel Salisbury in 1954. These were derived originally from Smoke and Tortoiseshell pairings, although other colours have also been used since, not always to the benefit of the breed. The introduction of Chinchilla blood, for example, contributed green eye colour, which has subsequently proved very difficult to eradicate completely. Copper eyes are favoured.

The breed has grown rapidly in popularity in the United States, where five basic colours are recognized, although the overall aim is to produce cats with a red coat and silver underfur. The Red Shaded or Shaded Cameo has a white-cream belly with red or cream on the sides, according to the American standard. The Smoke Cameo or Red Smoke possesses this feature, with red bands on the body, referred to as 'tecking'. The two other variants are the Shaded and Shell Tortoiseshell varieties, which are exclusively female. In addition, Cameos with cream tipping to their fur have been bred, but are excluded under current standards.

Cameos are currently on the increase in Britain, and are no longer being shown in assessment classes. Kittens are virtually white at birth, and only later develop their characteristic colouring. They are cobby like other Longhairs and the coat requires similar care.

Chinchilla Longhair
Chinchilla Persian

There are several versions of how the first Chinchilla Longhair was bred. It may have appeared in a litter resulting from a Tortoiseshell mated to a Blue or a Silver Tabby. Alternatively, it has been suggested that the breed developed from the offspring of a Silver Tabby which lacked the characteristic markings. The original kitten was owned by an Englishwoman, Mrs Vallence, who obtained it from a Miss Grace Hurt in the late nineteenth century. Known as Chinnie, this kitten was eventually mated with a tom called Fluffy and yielded another kitten called Beauty. When paired with a light Smoke, Champion Perso, Beauty produced the tom acknowledged as the 'pillar of the Chinchilla studbrook', Silver Lambkin.

The naming of the new breed led to great controversy: a wide variety of terms, such as Silver Grey, Chinchilla Tabby and Silver Chinchilla were in popular usage at the time. The decision to adopt the term 'Chinchilla' was thought by some breeders to be ill advised, because the chinchilla (a rodent kept as a pet or for its fur) has a coat coloration which is opposite to that of the cat. In the latter case, the undercoat is white, with black or silver tipping to the fur itself. The correct eye colour was another area of dispute, as cats were being bred with yellow, amber and green eyes. Indeed, at one early show, a green-eyed individual was disqualified, but, later, blue-green or emerald eyes were specified in the standard.

Further problems arose over the depth of coat coloration. At first, the majority of Chinchillas were quite dark, even lavender in some cases, although littermates could vary in this respect. Those which were lighter in colour became classed as Chinchillas proper, whereas darker individuals were included in the Shaded Silver category. This rather vague classification eventually had to be clarified when a cat was entered in, and won, both Chinchilla and Shaded Silver classes at the same show. For this reason, the Shaded Silver was amalgamated with the Chinchilla during 1902. Outside Britain, the distinction remained, however, and today the Shaded Silver is re-emerging as a breed in assessment classes at British shows.

There is now a clear distinction between the two forms. Although both have the same eye colour, the Chinchilla is significantly lighter and has a tipped coat. Although both forms can still occur in the same litter when it is difficult to distinguish between them, once a kitten is registered it is not possible to transfer it to the other category. Good quality Shaded Silvers remain hard to produce, requiring the characteristic shadings on the face, forming a mantle, which extends down the sides to the tail.

In the pursuit of paler coloration at the turn of the century, Chinchilla breeders tended to ignore the type of the cats they were producing, so that smaller, less hardy animals were being bred. This failing has now been rectified and, although Chinchillas are often not as cobby as other Longhairs, no trace of weakness remains today. Several new colour forms have been created recently in the United States, such as the Golden, which is being bred in both the Chinchilla and Shaded Silver forms. These cats have cream undercoats, with brown rather than black tips to the individual hairs. Irrespective of colour, considerable preparation is necessary to show these varieties to best effect, but as house pets they are no more demanding than similar breeds. They are not prolific breeders.

Colourpoint Longhair

Himalayan Longhair; Khmer

This breed was artificially created, both for the purpose of genetic study and also to transmit the characteristics of the Siamese to a longhaired variety. The quest began in the 1920s, when a Swede, Dr Tjebbes, paired White Longhairs with Siamese, but no data emerged from this work. Similar attempts followed in the United States. The first-generation kittens were all shorthaired, but carried the longhaired characteristic in their genotype. By pairing these together, a longhaired Black queen was produced. Having been mated back to her father, this cat, appropriately called Debutante, gave birth to a pointed Longhair in 1935.

In Britain during the same year, Mrs Barton-Wright established the Experimental Breeders Club, to follow on the work undertaken at Harvard. The aim in this case was primarily to produce Siamese markings and a longhaired body type. Debutante, although longhaired, retained the lithe appearance of her Siamese ancestors. The feasibility of such a project was reinforced by chance in 1947; a longhaired queen with Siamese markings but otherwise resembling a Persian, was given to Mr Stirling Webb, who was already attempting to breed such cats. Finally, eight years later, the Colourpoint was recognized by the GCCF.

American fanciers had also embarked on a selective breeding programme, but first concerned themselves with improving the body type, rather than concentrating on exhibiting them. The development of the breed passed largely unnoticed until 1957 when two individuals were entered in a show at San Diego. Here they aroused great interest and, almost simultaneously, the ACFA became the first association to acknowledge the breed, followed by the CFA in the next year, with all the other associations following suit by 1961.

In the United States the breed is known as the Himalayan because the coat patterning is similar to that of the Himalayan rabbit. Further confusion over nomenclature arose when the description 'Khmer' was used on mainland Europe for a brief period. These cats are also classified differently within the longhaired category on opposing sides of the Atlantic. British breeders recognize the Colourpoint as a colour variant of the Persian, whereas it is classed as a distinct breed in the United States. Crossbreeding using Persians has been permitted in the United States for over two decades now, to upgrade the Himalayan's type. Cats such as Lilacs bred from these pairings are then described as self-coloured Himalayans. Accepted colours are generally as for the Siamese.

Recognition of colours		
UK only	US only	UK and USA
Cream varieties	Chocolate (solid)	Seal-point
	Lilac (solid)	Blue-point
	Tabby (Lynx)-point	Chocolate point
	Blue-cream-point	Flame (Red)-point
		Lilac-point
		Tortie-point

Deep points are favoured in exhibition cats, but the depth of coloration can never be as intense as in the Siamese itself. This feature is affected by the local environmental temperature. The long hair of the breed has more of an insulating effect than the short coat of the Siamese, causing lighter coloration. Nevertheless, by way of compensation it is less difficult to produce a pale fur on the body of the Colourpoint, compared to the Siamese. Eye colour under the CFA official standard is as important as both body and point coloration, and must be deep blue.

Siamese ancestry reveals itself not only in the appearance, but also the character of Colourpoints. Queens can breed earlier than other Longhairs, even as young as eight months, although it is preferable to wait until they are at least one year old. Males are, however, slower to mature, and may not be sexually competent for a further six months. This is normal, and should not give cause for concern. Litters are generally rather small, with often fewer than four kittens being produced at one time. They are creamy in colour at birth, with their points only beginning to appear after a few days. It may take up to 18 months or so for this feature to develop to its full extent. The coat also grows with age, and should reach a length of about 5in (12cm). The colour may darken slightly in cats which have naturally dark points, such as the Seal-Point. These cats prove very affectionate and can become quite devoted to their owners. They will often seek attention.

Cream British Shorthair

The shorthaired Cream has not achieved the popularity of its longhaired counterpart, probably because of a genetic quirk. Females are scarce and crossbreeding with other

Cameo Longhair
Cameo Persian

The Cameo is a breed typified by contrasting colours. The undercoat should always be white; the tips of the hairs coloured. The actual intensity of the colour varies, but should be deepest around the head, on the feet and legs and along the back. Varieties include the Cream Shaded (1), Red Tortie (2) and Red Shaded Cameo (3).

Chinchilla Longhair
Chinchilla Persian

The Chinchilla and the Shaded Silver are somewhat similar in appearance; at one time the breeds were amalgamated in Britain, although outside the country the distinction has always remained. In Britain today, the Shaded Silver is re-emerging as a breed in its own right. The Chinchilla (1) is lighter in colour than the Shaded Silver (2).

Colourpoint Longhair

Himalayan Longhair; Khmer

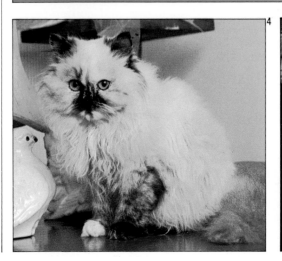

The Colourpoint Longhair combines the point markings of the Siamese with the body type and coat length of the Longhair. Today these cats are being bred in a wide variety of colours, which include Blue-point (1), Seal-point (2), Tortie Tabby (3), and the Tortie-point (4). Recognition of colours varies somewhat between British and American associations, with the Americans accepting solid-coloured cats as well. In the United States the breed is known as the Himalayan. In all cases kittens are born relatively pale in colour, with point markings only becoming fully apparent at the age of 18 months or even later (5).

Cream Longhair
Cream Persian

The Cream Longhair must have a pure coloured coat, free from any markings. A serious fault is reddish fur, usually seen along the back and known as a 'hot' coloration. Creams are now deservedly popular on both sides of the Atlantic, but the breed took some time to win acceptance with breeders in Britain.

colours has proved necessary, yet the percentage of Creams produced is not high. Serious interest in the breed began during the 1950s, although a standard had been produced nearly three decades previously.

The coat of these cats must be a true, even cream colour, with no markings or paler fur, although lighter shades are given preference. Any signs of red at all along the back or elsewhere are penalized, while eye colour must be either copper or orange, as hazel is not now considered acceptable. The texture of the coat is as for other British Shorthairs, and must be dense, yet fine.

gave rise to the Blue-cream. Recognized exhibition flaws in contemporary Creams include 'hot' reddish fur, seen typically along the back, and uneven coloration caused by a pale undercoat. Young kittens should lose any signs of barring by about 10 weeks of age. Those with the broadest heads even at this stage are likely to develop into the most promising exhibition cats. Eye colour is not a constant feature, since Creams are born with blue eyes which should soon turn to the desired colour of deep copper. Temperamentally, Creams do not differ significantly from other Longhairs.

Cream Longhair
Cream Persian

The origins of the Cream can be traced back to the Fawn variety of the Angora, although the coloration is now noticeably different. Such cats did not prove very popular in Britain at first, and many early Creams were ignored in breeding, but Americans took to the colour immediately. British fanciers may have been deterred by the shortage of good breeding queens, which proved a major handicap at first. Contemporary records show that the first noted Cream was a tom, bred in 1890 and named Cupid Bassinio by his owner Mrs Kinchant. He had tabby markings.

The increase in popularity of Creams was discernible at the turn of the century; by 1920, the breed was well established. At first they were shown in company with Fawns and then it was ruled that their colour should be equivalent to that of Devonshire cream. The standard has now again been modified, perhaps clarified, to stipulate a shade classed as 'pale to medium' under British rules, whereas American breeders aim to produce Creams with an even coat colour of buff cream.

The original Creams had different facial features from those seen today, possessing bigger ears and noses. Faults could arise with successive Cream to Cream matings, and so Blue Longhairs were used as out-crosses, which in turn

Egyptian Mau

This breed has been kept in its homeland for many generations, but was first seen in the United States during the 1950s. Princess Troubetskoy obtained a pair in the early 1950s, christened Gepa and Ludol, which had originated in Egypt. Their coat pattern, resembling that of a spotted tabby, can be traced back in Egyptian art to 1400 BC. There were close links between such cats and contemporary deities. The sun god Ra, who battled and destroyed the serpent Apepi, took the guise of a spotted tabby.

As might be expected, the markings of the Egyptian Mau (*mau* meaning 'cat') are considered very significant under the CFA standard. The forehead should show a characteristic 'M' pattern, with frown marks extending back and separating into individual spots along the spine. These coalesce again over the hips, to form a solid line. The tail is banded with thick stripes and ends in a dark tip. Two 'mascara' lines are recognized around each of the eyes, extending to the sides of the face. Barring is seen on the legs, with distinct matching spots being preferred on the body itself. On the underparts, spotting should contrast against the relatively light coat colour.

Three body colours are permitted, and all are shown in the same class. The Bronze form has a bronze-coloured body, becoming creamy on the underparts with brown markings. The Silver has a similar distribution of colour, set against charcoal black markings. In the case of the Smoke, the charcoal grey body has a jet black patterning superimposed upon it. The eyes in every case should ideally be gooseberry green, although this feature is not well developed in young Egyptian Maus.

The type of these cats resembles that of the Abyssinian. It is a blend between the oriental appearance of the Siamese and the cobby conformation of the Longhair. Musculature is an obvious feature, and Maus are powerful cats. The coat should be short and glossy, contributing to a sleek demeanour. They prove to be active, relatively quiet cats and, although affectionate, do not readily take to strangers.

In Britain, the Egyptian Mau has a very recent history, being only imported for the first time in 1978. Prior to this the description was used for another breed, now referred to as the Oriental Spotted Tabby. There is a distinct difference in body type between these two breeds, with the Spotted Tabby having a more extreme foreign appearance, probably introduced from Siamese crossings. Like the Mau, the scarab markings on the forehead, taken to be a symbol of holiness by the Egyptians, are pronounced in the Oriental Spotted Tabby. A wider range of colours have bred, including Blue, Chocolate and Lilac, where the eyes should be green. In the case of the Red and Cream Oriental Spotted Tabbies, acceptable eye coloration can range from copper to green. The spots themselves, which must not develop into extended or broken lines, should again be darker than the basic ground colour of the coat.

Exotic Shorthair

The Exotic Shorthair is a composite variety bred from Longhairs crossed with American Shorthairs. The aim was to produce cats with a relatively cobby appearance and medium-length coats which did not need as much grooming as true Longhairs. For a period, Burmese were used to contribute to the pedigree of the emerging breed, but this was frowned upon in the United States, and input of new blood was restricted to Shorthairs and Longhairs.

While the Exotic Shorthair is not recognized in Britain, it has flourished in the United States, being bred in the same wide range of colours as the genuine Longhair. The coat remains a prominent feature, and needs to be medium in length, yet plush and soft. It must not lie flat to the body, nor appear to flow, being of an intermediate nature. Exotic Shorthairs make ideal pets, possessing the characteristics of both main ancestors, but with the advantage of not needing such regular grooming as a genuine Longhair.

Foreign Colours
Oriental Shorthairs

Although the pointed forms of the Siamese were favoured outside Asia, similar type cats with a single coat colour and no points were also being bred in the East. The ruling of the Siamese Cat Club that only blue-eyed forms of the breed would be encouraged meant that these self-coloured cats with yellow or green eyes could not be exhibited as Siamese. Their popularity declined initially but now they form a distinct breed on their own, known as Oriental Shorthairs in North America. The description 'Oriental' in British cat circles is confined to cats with a mixed or patterned coat, and selfs are classified 'Foreign', followed by the appropriate colour.

Two varieties are currently recognized for championship purposes in Britain. The Foreign Lilac arose from the quest to establish the Havana Brown. The first example of this latter breed had a Lilac-pointed Siamese parent, and during its development, which entailed further usage of such Siamese, the solid-coloured Lilacs were produced. The coat colour of the Foreign Lilac is frosty grey, with a pinkish tinge. Significantly, no points are present and any markings on the coat are penalized, although these may be present for a period in young cats. The eyes must be oval-shaped, and green in colour. Type closely resembles the Siamese.

The Foreign White is a distinctive, blue-eyed, pure white coat. Attempts to produce a breed of this appearance not afflicted with deafness began in earnest during 1962. Some bred by Miss Turner and exhibited at York during 1965 were greeted with great enthusiasm by fellow cat fanciers. Foreign Whites were recognized in 1977, with the standard stipulating a body type similar to the Siamese, which they also resemble in temperament.

The GCCF in Britain has only granted provisional status for the Foreign Black at present. As kittens, these Blacks often show white hairs and other markings in their coats, which should disappear as they mature. Their sleek appearance resembles that of the previous varieties. Any sign of a squint, revealing their Siamese ancestry, is a definite fault.

Oriental Shorthairs are recognized in a wider range of colours than their Foreign counterparts. The Oriental black form is known as the Ebony, with the equivalent of the Foreign Lilac being the Lavender in the United States. Oriental Blues, which need to be of a lighter rather than a darker shade, Chestnuts, rich Reds and buff-coloured Creams, as well as Whites, can also be entered in the Solid Colours classes. The Shaded Colours class features both Silvers and Cameos. The Smoke equivalent of this latter variety, and those of all the solid colours apart from Red and Cream, are eligible for the Smoke Colours class. There are also Tabby classes, where ticked, spotted, mackerel and classic patterned coats are all permissible. The American Parti-colours class, as its name suggests, exists for combinations such as Tortoiseshell Oriental Shorthairs and Lavender-creams. Two recent developments are the breeding of both Caramel and Cinnamon forms of the Oriental Shorthair. The latter type is a mutant derived from American strains of the Havana.

Havana
Havana Brown; Chestnut Brown

The Havana, with its rich brown coat and green eyes, has a very distinctive appearance. Although chocolate cats had been reported during the nineteenth century, it was only during the 1950s that a serious attempt was made to fix this colour, based on Siamese type and distinct from the paler coloration of the Burmese. The first kitten fulfilling these criteria was bred using a Seal-point Siamese paired with a shorthaired Black of Seal-point Siamese ancestry. The emerging breed was first exhibited a year later, during 1953,

Egyptian Mau

The Egyptian Mau, with its characteristic pattern of dark markings, may be the only cat breed to be naturally spotted. These markings are far more important in exhibition terms than the body colour. Three colours are recognized: Bronze (with brown markings), Silver (with charcoal markings) and Smoke (with pure black markings). Green eyes are preferred, but amber is also permitted. Eye colour changes slowly in young cats.

Exotic Shorthair

The Exotic Shorthair is a breed which shows characteristics of the Longhair and the American Shorthair, displaying a cobby body with an even, full coat, not quite as short as a Shorthair's. These cats are popular in the United States, and have been bred in a wide variety of colours, including the tabby forms shown here.

Foreign Colours
Oriental Shorthairs

The Foreign Black (Ebony Oriental Shorthair) has a long body, giving it a svelte and elegant appearance. Its close relationship with the Siamese is further emphasized by the occasional presence of two faults — a squint and a kinked tail — to which Siamese are also prone. In Britain the Foreign Black is not recognized as a separate breed; only Lilacs (Lavenders) and Whites are accepted. In the United States, a much wider range of colours are recognized, ranging from Solid Colours, Shaded Colours, Smoke Colours and Tabby to Parti-colours.

having been named after the Havana rabbit which has a similar coat colour. The search for recognition began during 1956, but it took two years for the GCCF to finally accept the breed as the Chestnut Brown Foreign. Anxiety was expressed over the similarities between the Havana, as it subsequently became known, and the Burmese, which was becoming established in Britain at the same time.

Havanas did not encounter such opposition in the United States, being recognized by the CFA in 1959. The breed does appear to have become isolated from its British counterpart during subsequent years, to the extent that a different type of cat has evolved under the same name on both sides of the Atlantic. This has resulted from British breeders preferring to develop the breed on the lines of the Siamese, which has given it a more foreign appearance than its American counterpart. The head profile of the American Havana does not extend down evenly but has a distinct and pronounced curve from the forehead to the nose.

In the United States, the Havana is judged to the same standard as the Russian Blue, apart from the obvious difference in coloration. The Oriental Self Brown, is in fact a closer counterpart to the British Havana than the American breed bearing the same name. Green eye coloration only is allowed under the GCCF standard, but American judges will accept a colour range extending from chartreuse to green. Eye shape in the American Havana must be oval, not oriental as is specified under British rules. There is also a corresponding difference in temperament, with British Havanas resembling the Siamese in character, whereas North American breeding has produced quieter, although equally affectionate and intelligent cats.

Japanese Bobtail

Domestic cats have been kept in Japan for over a millennium, and the Bobtail is the breed traditionally associated with the Japanese. Such cats are popularly regarded as providing good fortune for their owners. The variety most in demand is the *Mi-ke* or three-furred type, which corresponds to the tortoiseshell-and-white form of other breeds. The coat is comprised of a combination of red, white and black fur.

For centuries, the Japanese Bobtail remained in Japan, but during the 1960s it was introduced to North America. A breeder who had lived in Japan for a number of years after the Second World War dispatched the original group of three Bobtails, before returning to the United States with a further 38 cats which she had carefully bred there. A standard for the Japanese Bobtail was then established in 1970.

Emphasis was placed on colours which correspond to the original Japanese form. Tricolours are therefore favoured, along with composite colours such as Whites, Blacks and Reds. Bicolours, being black or red and white are also recognized, along with a tortoiseshell form. The development of the breed in the United States has given rise to other colours as well, so that now only Siamese markings and the agouti appearance of the Abyssinian are expressly forbidden. When there is more than one colour present in the coat, then good contrast and bold markings are sought in Japanese Bobtails.

The distinctive tail is significant for judging purposes. Its natural appearance is deceptive because it looks much shorter than it is until the fur is combed out. The tail may prove to be as long as 5in (12.5cm) at its maximum length, but only appears to be about half this size under normal conditions when it is held in an upright position. As a result of its similarity to a rabbit's tail, it is known as a bobtail, which gave rise to the breed's name.

The charm of these cats has yet to be encountered by the majority of British cat fanciers. It appears that only one example has been imported, and this was a pet brought back from Japan which died in 1977. An unusual characteristic of the Japanese Bobtail is its highly developed sociable nature. Separating a mother from her kittens proves difficult, and it is preferable to keep at least two of these cats in the same household. They make affectionate pets.

Korat

The Korat is named after the province in Thailand where the breed is thought to have originated many centuries ago. In their native land, such cats are known as *Si-Saurat*, a term which refers to the fact that their colour is believed to bring good fortune. Korats have always been highly prized for this reason. They were not confined exclusively to the province of Korat however, being portrayed in the culture of other areas of Thailand as long ago as the fourteenth century.

The breed appears to have altered little through the centuries, still possessing a distinct, intermediate body type which is more cobby and less foreign than that of the Siamese. By contrast, other Eastern breeds have been selectively altered and no longer resemble their original form. The Korat was first shown in England in the same class as the Siamese during the 1896 National Cat Club Show, but was disqualified much to its owner's indignation. There is virtually no trace of Korats again outside Thailand until 1959 when two were sent to the United States from Bangkok. By 1965, the breed had been developed sufficiently for a specialist club to be founded, and all North American associations recognized the Korat.

Some Korats were transferred to Britain in 1972 and became officially recognized by the GCCF three years later, although championship status was not granted. Korats remain rare and cannot be recommended as being hardy cats: they are prone to respiratory infections and seem susceptible to cold. This latter characteristic is probably caused by the virtual absence of an undercoat in the Korat, whose coats lie sleek and close to the body. Keeping this breed in relatively cool conditions causes the fur to grow longer, ruining it for exhibition purposes. Korats can be reasonably prolific when breeding, producing up to nine offspring on rare occasions, although four is normal. Kittens have the silvery blue appearance of adults while still young, but are unlikely to show their full potential for several years. The eyes of the mature Korat have a luminous, intense quality.

Maine Coon
Maine Cat

The Maine Coon is a North American longhair, developed during the 1850s using Angoras brought back to the State of

Korat

The Korat is relatively rare in Britain, although more popular in North America. It is highly prized in its native Thailand, where it is regarded as a symbol of good fortune. Over the centuries, the breed has changed little. The coat should be a definite blue-grey all over, with a silvery sheen; due to the absence of an undercoat, however, Korats are not very hardy and can suffer from chills and respiratory infections in cooler climates.

Maine by sailors. These cats were then crossed with local shorthairs, and their offspring had coats which were reminiscent of that of the indigenous common racoon (*Procyon lotor*). Although hybridization between cats and racoons is impossible, the breed took the popular abbreviation used for these creatures — 'coon' — as part of its name.

Maine Coons have evolved into a hardy, thick-coated breed well able to survive in the harsh winter conditions prevailing in New England. They were especially popular as farm cats for catching vermin, and have proved to be one of the largest breeds, a feature emphasized by their long legs and bodies. Toms can naturally weight as much as 15½ lb (7 kg). The earliest record of the breed comes from the writing of Mr F. Piece who, in 1861, described his attractive, predominantly black Maine Coon, which enjoyed the name of Captain Jenks of the Horse Marines. The breed obviously attracted much attention in the region of New England, and was commonly exhibited at cat shows during the 1860s, even winning at the large Madison Square Garden Show of 1895.

When faced with the arrival of Longhairs from England however, the Maine Coon began to lose its popularity among cat fanciers, although it remained a valued household pet. The breed did not start to attract interest from an exhibition viewpoint again until the 1950s. The Central Maine Cat Club was established during 1953 and staged an annual show to find the Maine State Champion Cat of the Year. The Maine Coon Breeders and Fanciers Association came into existence 15 years later; in 1976, the CFA finally recognized the breed. It remains virtually unknown in Europe, however, although some Maine Coons have been sent to West Germany during recent years.

Colour is a relatively insignificant feature of this breed, with much more emphasis being placed on type, but tabbies remain the most popular of the varieties. A range of eye colours, from green and gold to copper, are acceptable and there is no direct specified relationship between eye and coat coloration. Both these features only count for a maximum 15 percent of the available points under the CFA official standard. The head, body and coat are scored highly, however. The head itself should be relatively long compared to other breeds while the conspicuous ears must appear to taper to a point at their tips. The body needs to appear muscular, and the legs and tail long. A heavy, shaggy coat is also stipulated, yet this must have a silky texture which belies its appearance.

Maine Coons make very attractive pets and are companionable and quiet by nature. In spite of their predatory habits, they are not aggressive. A European breed which is similar to the Maine Coon, having evolved in similar natural surroundings, is the Norwegian Forest Cat, although the two are not related.

Japanese Bobtail

The characteristic tail of the Japanese Bobtail resembles that of a rabbit. The breed has been introduced to the United States from Japan, but remains scarce elsewhere. Colours include tabby (1), black and white (2) and red tabby -and- white (3).

Maine Coon
Maine Cat

The Maine Coon is a hardy American breed, somewhat similar to the Norwegian Forest Cat. It was developed in New England during the latter part of the nineteenth century and has enjoyed a revival of popularity over the past few decades. The best-known variety is the original brown tabby form, whose patterning resembles the coat of the racoon, a similarity which gave rise to the name of the breed. Originally a working cat, the Maine Coon retains a rugged, tough nature and is capable of withstanding harsh winter conditions.

Manx

The Manx is often considered to be a tailless cat, but the remnants of a tail are often present and these cats are described accordingly, depending on the actual tail length. The origins of the breed remain obscure, although its development was initially centred on the Isle of Man, off the west coast of England. Manx are bred in a variety of colours and markings, including white (1) and black-and-white patterns (2, 3).

Manx

These cats are closely associated with the Isle of Man, an island located off the west coast of England opposite Ireland, but how they arrived there will always be a mystery. Various legends have grown up over the years to explain their origins, presence and tailless appearance. The Manx may have been introduced from Japan where the Bobtail has flourished for centuries, but there is no doubt that a different mutation gave rise to the former breed. The relative absence of a tail in the Manx results from a dominant genetic mutation, whereas this is a recessive condition in the Bobtail. An alternative theory suggests that a Spanish ship wrecked off the coast of the Isle of Man after the Armada may have been carrying cats acquired in the Middle East, a few of which reached the shore and started breeding. Some stories say the tails of the cats were cut off by Irish invaders of the island as trophies, while others maintain the queens always bit the tails off their offspring.

As a genetic mutation, there is a lethal factor associated with the reduction in the length of the Manx tail and so such cats must be paired to individuals with normal tails and not to each other. The length of the Manx tail is variable. The ideal is to have no sign of a tail but just a spot at the end of the vertebral column. When a few vertebrae remain, forming the remnant of a tail, such cats are referred to as 'rumpy-risers'. In cases where the stump of the tail can actually be moved, the cats are described as 'stubbies' or 'stumpies'. 'Longies' have a tail only slightly shorter than a full-tailed cat.

The Manx is a self-contained breed, and rather than using American or British Shorthairs for out-crosses, breeders usually opt for the normal-tailed individuals of Manx litters. The contours of the breed are noticeably rounded from the head to the rump. The vertebrae down the length of the spine are often shorter than usual and reduced in number, contributing to the Manx's arched appearance. There is a significant level of spina bifida associated with the Manx, and it may be worth supplementing the diet of breeding queens with folic acid. Preliminary tests suggest that raising the level of Vitamin B in pregnant mothers decreases the incidence of spina bifida in their babies. Another defect sometimes seen in Manx is an abnormally small anus, which leads to constipation.

In spite of these problems, Manx cats are intelligent, and live well alongside dogs. At the end of the last century, for example, a Manx which was a great companion of a bulldog was actually exhibited with the dog, and together they attracted much attention at the South London Bulldog Show. Manx cats often live to a good age; one famous American Manx, Grand Champion Nila-Blite Pola won a Best in Show award at the age of 13.

This champion was a White with copper-coloured eyes, but any colour is acceptable under the GCCF standards established for the breed, providing the eye colour corresponds. The coat of the Manx is unusual, resembling rabbit's fur in its structure. The undercoat is both soft and dense while the topcoat is thick and long, a combination which gives these cats a large appearance. Their characteristic gait results from a combination of a shortened spine and long hindlegs, and they appear to hop like rabbits instead of walking like other breeds.

The CFA standard for the Manx differs slightly from its British counterpart, since any sign of a hybrid ancestry, reflected by chocolate, lavender (known as lilac in the United States) or Himalayan coloration is outlawed. Head shape in this case should be more rounded. A longhaired form of the Manx, christened Cymric after the original name for Wales, first appeared in North America towards the end of the 1960s. This feature was almost certainly introduced by using normal shorthairs which carried the longhaired gene.

Various sections of the Cat Fancy are opposed to the breeding of any Manx because of their skeletal defects. It must be stated that if the breed was presented for recognition today, its development would almost certainly not be encouraged. Nevertheless, Manx have been in existence for nearly 500 years, possibly longer, and have gained a special place in cat folklore. Apart from the Siamese, they form the most instantly recognizable breed, and have featured on the coinage of their native island.

Norwegian Forest Cat
Norsk Skaukatt

These longhaired cats originated in Norway, where they were bred from a combination of both farm and feral stock. As may be expected, the breed has a well-developed coat, comprised of thick underfur and a fairly long, water-resistant outer coat. Norwegian Forest Cats are intelligent, proving agile climbers, with affectionate natures.

There is no restriction on their coloration, as with the Maine Coon, but the forelegs of the Forest Cats must be slightly shorter than their hindlimbs. They are equally easy to groom, in spite of the dense undercoat. The majority are still found in Scandinavia.

Peke-face

The Peke-face is a type variant of the Red and Red Tabby Longhairs, in which facial appearance has been developed to resemble that of a Pekingese dog. As a result, the nose appears abnormally compressed into the face, and there are excessive skin folds in the facial area. The Peke-face is not recognized in Britain.

Given their reduced and distorted facial characteristics, it is not surprising that these cats can suffer from respiratory difficulties, as well as overcrowding of teeth in the mouth. Tear-staining of the fur, because of deviation and constriction of the ducts draining the eyes, has also been reported. In order to try to maintain some normality of function in the facial region, breeders typically pair Peke-faces with the appropriate form of the Red Longhair, rather than to each other. The eyes are considered an important feature of the Peke-face.

Red Self Longhair
Red Self Persian

This is certainly one of the hardest varieties to breed successfully for exhibition purposes, because the standard

Peke-face

The Peke-face resembles the Red forms of the Longhair in all respects except its face, which is compressed in the manner of the Pekingese dog. The cat has been selectively bred for this feature. This characteristic may, in fact, give rise to certain health problems, especially respiratory difficulties and overcrowding of the teeth in the mouth. While popular in some areas of the United States, the breed is not recognized in Britain.

Red Self Longhair
Red Self Persian

The Red Self Longhair is one of the most difficult varieties to breed successfully for exhibition. The standard stipulates that the coat should be a uniform red but, in practice, it is often marred by tabby markings. Because it is genetically impossible to produce uniformly red coats, breeders have concentrated instead on reducing the tabby markings as far as possible, but they often remain on the face, legs and tail. The long coat helps to make the markings less noticeable elsewhere.

Norwegian Forest Cat

Norsk Skaukatt

The Norwegian Forest Cat is a very hardy breed, somewhat reminiscent of the Maine Coon in appearance, although the two breeds are totally unrelated. The Norwegian Forest Cat has a long, weather-proof coat in two layers, the woolly undercoat providing warmth, the glossy outer coat keeping out rain and snow. Despite the length of the coat, these cats are not difficult to groom and the coat does not mat or tangle easily. The hindlegs are longer than the forelegs, making the rump higher than the shoulders. Still rare outside Scandinavia—only 16 were registered in the United States in 1982—Norwegian Forest Cats are particularly noted for their disposition. They have a reputation for making affectionate and intelligent pets.

Rexes
Cornish and Devon

Two distinct forms of Rexes are recognized; these differ not only in appearance, but also genetically. Called the Cornish Rex and the Devon Rex, the two forms are named after the English counties where they first appeared. These cats are very affectionate and are sometimes described as 'poodle cats' because of their curly coats. Devon Rexes have much wider ears and shorter noses than their Cornish counterparts. Both Rexes are now bred in a wide variety of colours. Varieties include the Cornish Tabby (1), Cornish Red (2), Cornish Red-point (3), Devon Grey Tabby (4). Devon Smoke (5), Devon Tortie (6) and Devon Blue Tabby (7).

calls for a cat free from all markings. The most common fault is the presence of tabby markings, especially on the head. At first these cats were classed as orange, rather than red, and could be either marked or unmarked. Orange females were scarce, and toms proved popular to improve other varieties. They are still often used to breed tortoiseshells, and the Tortie-and-White Longhair.

Attempts to selectively remove tabby markings using Creams were only partially successful, since the body coloration itself was diluted. As the darker cats were preferred, the description 'orange' was ultimately dropped in favour of 'red'. During the 1940s, the Red Self virtually disappeared from Britain, although the colour is being bred again, it remains scarce. One of the best postwar examples was Champion Pathfinders Golden Dawn, but the majority still possess some markings to a variable degree. Indeed, both Red Selfs and Red Tabbies can occur in the same litter.

Rexes
Cornish and Devon

The Cornish form of the Rex was first bred in 1950, when a kitten with a curly coat was born on a farm in Cornwall. Prior to this, a similar cat had appeared in East Berlin at the end of the Second World War, although the development of the German Rex did not start in earnest until 1951. Further Cornish Rexes were produced by pairing the original kitten, called Kallibunker, back to his shorthaired dam, who was tortoiseshell-and-white in colour. The breeder, Mrs Ennismore, then crossed a son of Kallibunker, known as Poldhu, to shorthaired queens to prevent excessive inbreeding. All the smooth-coated offspring carried the Rex gene and so the breed was developed. The name for the breed was derived from a variety of rabbit called the Rex.

In 1960 in the neighbouring county of Devon, another form of the curly-coated Rex appeared. It was shown to be a separate mutation when the two strains were crossed. Only kittens with short, not curled, coats were born and repeated matings led to the same outcome. If the new form had been the same mutation as the Cornish Rex, then only curly-coated Rexes would have been bred and normal shorthaired cats would have been impossible because the Rex characteristic is recessive.

There was a slight difference in the appearance of these two forms of the Rex, as the Devon type had a curlier, but thinner coat than its Cornish counterpart. Head shape is now quite distinct. The Devon Rex has a head with large, wide ears and a small face. The nose is short, whereas that of a Cornish Rex is much longer. A wide range of colours are acceptable for show purposes, although the Bicolour is not recognized by the GCCF for the Devon Rex. The CFA do not allow lavender (known as lilac in the United States) or chocolate forms of either breed. In addition, the Siamese form of the Rex, known as Si-Rex, is currently outlawed, despite enjoying considerable popularity. In this case, the curled hair of the Rex is superimposed on the Siamese.

The original German form of the Rex has proved to result from the same mutation as that which gave rise to the Cornish Rex. Cats of both types were bred together in North America and yielded curly-coated offspring. Continental breeders having developed the German form while following the British standard, still refer to it as the German Rex. The distinction between Cornish and Devon Rexes

was acknowledged in Britain in 1967, but these breeds were not separated in America until 1979.

Rexes make good pets and do not shed their hairs with the same regularity as other breeds. The coat, especially in the Devon, is thin and does not provide much insulation, so these cats should be kept in relatively warm surroundings. Any hairless patches are considered a serious fault in adult cats of either breed, as is white fur, except in the case of the Tortoiseshell-and-White. Their large, open ears can get dirty and should be checked and cleaned regularly.

Russian Blue
Maltese; Spanish Blue

The Russian Blue is said to have been introduced to Europe by sailors from the port of Archangel on Russia's northern seaboard, although where the breed actually originated is unknown. These Blues were exhibited at the Crystal Palace shows from the mid-nineteenth century onwards, and were immediately distinguishable from the British Shorthaired Blue by virtue of their foreign body type, although they were shown in the same classes. Judges tended to favour the British cats, and only from 1912 onwards were Russian Blues allowed to compete separately.

While the breed remained popular until the Second World War, it was then virtually lost in Britain. Only one breeder, Mrs Rochford, managed to maintain a bloodline during this period and from her cats the postwar strain was developed. Unfortunately, as a result of the shortage of genuine Russian Blue stock, hybridization involving both British Blue Shorthairs and well as Blue-point Siamese became rife and seriously damaged the formerly distinct breed. The standard had to be altered to accommodate these hybrids which had an exaggerated foreign type. In 1966, however, this trend was reversed as breeders endeavoured to recreate the Russian Blue in its original form.

The coat of these cats needs to be both short and dense, which causes it to stand out from the skin. Careful grooming is necessary to emphasize this feature before a show. Although delicate to the touch, the fur provides an effective insulation against the cold. It must be blue and even in colour throughout, with no trace of any markings. A silver tinge to the coat is normally apparent as a result of the guard hairs which are tipped with silver. The eyes must be bright green in colour, while the British standard also requires these cats to have pronounced whisker pads, with ears set right on the top of the head.

Russian Blues were known in the United States by 1900 and called Maltese, but they did not make any significant impact until the early 1970s. Interest in the breed was rekindled by the importation of Swedish and British cats, which contributed a recognizable type to the various bloodlines. A Russian White form has also been bred, but has never attained the popularity of the Blue, although it is quite well known in Australia. Both types are similar in temperament, and prove affectionate as well as quiet.

Scottish Fold

The shorthaired Scottish Fold arose as a spontaneous mutation. On a farm in Scotland in 1961, William Ross, a farm worker, spotted a kitten whose ears were folded down. Eventually this queen produced a further two kittens, one of which Ross acquired. He registered the white female and set out to establish a new breed. It became apparent that the ear folding was a dominant trait, so that at least one of the parents had to possess this feature for it to appear in their offspring. Scottish Folds can be either homozygous or heterozygous for the characteristic, as there is no lethal factor involved which would make the homozygous form non-viable. The extent of folding is quite variable between individuals and appears unrelated to their genotype.

Some Scottish Folds also had thicker tails and these were preferred at first, but in such cases there was also a corresponding thickening of the hindlegs, which interfered with the cat's normal gait. The incidence of this fault is low, but affected cats are disqualified from shows. Breeders have avoided using such cats, and have out-crossed stock using British or American Shorthairs as an additional precaution. The mode of inheritance of the disability remains unclear and it can affect both homozygous and heterozygous individuals, but not all kittens in a litter will be afflicted.

The floppy ears of the breed are also classed as a deformity by some cat fanciers, with a body of opinion suggesting that Scottish Folds are especially susceptible to ear infections. Such opposition led the GCCF in Britain to cease to recognize the breed, and it disappeared from shows about a

Russian Blue
Maltese; Spanish Blue

Russian Blues have very soft, short fur, a medium blue in colour with a silvery tinge. Eyes should be a vivid green, set wide apart. Early examples of the breed tended to vary in type and did not differ enough in this respect from other shorthaired breeds. Today stricter breeding controls have strengthened the breed. Russian Blues are very quiet cats, rarely using their voices, and prove very affectionate. They can become very devoted to their owners.

Scottish Fold

The Scottish Fold is instantly recognized by its folded, flat ears. Now banned from exhibition in Britain, because of fears that the unusual ears might give rise to infections or deafness, the breed is nevertheless popular in North America, where it has been bred in a wide range of colours. Folded- and normal-eared kittens are identical at birth, folding beginning to show at four weeks.

Siamese

The elegant and graceful Siamese has long been one of the most popular pedigree breeds. Its origins are obscure, but it was certainly known for a considerable time in its native land, Siam (Thailand), before first appearing in the West some time in the late nineteenth century. Siamese quickly established a following, despite initial reactions that they were unnatural looking. In the 1920s, the blue-eyed 'pointed' Siamese were recognized as the only true forms of the breed. The original Siamese is the Seal-point variety, which possesses the characteristic intense blue eyes and coloured mask, ears, legs and tail. The body is lighter in colour, and muscular (1). Other traditional varieties include the Chocolate-point (2), with a darker brown body, the Lilac-point (3), a combination of Blue- and Chocolate-points, and the Blue-point (4), first recognized officially in the 1930s.

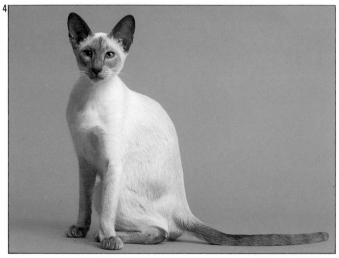

Some controversy has arisen over the more recent forms of the Siamese. These new varieties are still described as Siamese under British rules, although they are given a different breed number to the traditional forms. In the United States, however, these cats are referred to as Colourpoint Shorthairs, not Siamese. The Red-point (6) and Tortie-point (7) were the first new colours to be established; the Cream-point (5) and the Tabby (Lynx)-point (8) soon after. Other varieties continue to be developed. Siamese by nature are extremely demanding cats; in return they can be among the most rewarding and responsive. Highly intelligent, they can even be trained to walk with a harness and leash. They are also highly sexed, with the females maturing early, calling raucously when on heat. As they grow older, their body coloration darkens.

decade ago. Scottish Folds sent to America rapidly became very popular and were given a standard by the CFA in 1978. Acceptable colours are as for the American Shorthair, with smaller, flatter ears being preferred to those having a larger, more floppy appearance. It is important that the overall type is not neglected in development of ear folds, because such cats are penalized.

Scottish Folds are not recognized by European bodies, such as the *Fédération Internationale Féline d'Europe*, but individuals are still kept and bred, and have also appeared in Australia. These cats are quite hardy and make good pets. Their ears should be inspected regularly and cleaned carefully as necessary. Scottish Folds cannot be picked out from their normal-eared counterparts in a litter until they are about a month old, although those with thicker tails are soon evident.

Siamese

The evolution of Siamese is shrouded in mystery. Some authorities suggest the breed originated from temple cats kept in Burma. Another theory is that Siamese are descended from the sacred cats of Egypt. Some support for this idea comes from the resemblance of the Siamese to the cat goddess, variously called Bast, Bubastis and Past. What is known for certain is that the breed was kept for centuries in Siam (Thailand) before it was brought to Britain. Ownership of the Siamese in its native land was a privilege confined to the royal family; only after protracted discussions lasting years was a Miss Walker permitted to take one pair plus a single queen to England. Siamese cats were first exhibited at a British show in 1871, where reaction to them was less than favourable. One contemporary report described them as 'unnatural'.

These early Siamese proved extremely delicate. Long before the era of antibiotics or vaccinations, they frequently succumbed to enteritis and respiratory diseases. Nevertheless, the breed was established in Britain and by 1880, Siamese were also seen in the United States. Many individuals suffered from squints and kinked tails. Such deformities were accepted by breeders at first. Early winners such as Wankee, who was the first champion recognized in Britain, would never achieve such status today. Elaborate tales were told to justify the continued presence of these faults in the breed. According to one story, Siamese were left to guard a highly prized temple vase and such was their devotion to the task that they never took their eyes away from the vase, which caused them to develop a squint. Their kinked tails supposedly resulted from holding the precious vessel. In fact both these defects have a genetic origin. Cats affected with a squint appear to be staring intently at their noses. These traits still remain with the breed, although to a much lesser degree than previously, and merit disqualification when such cats are exhibited in shows.

A prominent feature of current Siamese is the relatively long head, especially encouraged by the American standard. The skull itself must be flat and the jaws should meet correctly. Malocclusion can occur because the lower mandible is relatively short. The ears need to be large, while the body has a characteristic lithe, relatively long appearance offset by firm musculature.

Although various colours had been recognized during the early years of this century, from the 1920s on the Siamese Cat Club of Britain decided to restrict recognition to blue-eyed pointed forms only. The current position is that the GCCF treats the traditional breed colours, which are Blue-, Chocolate-, Lilac- and Seal-point as one variety, while more recent colours such as Red are listed under a separate grouping, but still classified as Siamese. Americans make a more significant distinction between these two categories, classing the latter colours as Colourpoint Shorthairs.

The original Siamese seen in Europe were Seal-points, with the points being defined as the ears, paws, mask of the face, tail and lower parts of the legs. The seal-brown colour of these points is darkened in the case of the Chocolate-point Siamese. It is unclear when this form was first bred, because of confusion arising over the description 'chocolate', which was also used for solid colour cats. Chocolate-points may have appeared as long ago as 1900 but were certainly known by 1931, although at first they were initially shunned as poorly coloured Seal-points. This new variety was finally accepted by the CFA in 1950 and a year later it had been acknowledged by other American associations. The body colour should be ivory, rather than the creamy shade of the Seal-point. Both varieties have distinctive bright blue eyes. The coat may fade in colour during the summer months when the weather is warmer. Kittens also have pale points, which develop as the cat matures.

The Blue-point Siamese could have been bred as early as 1896 and was certainly known before 1900. It was first recognized in America in 1932, four years before a standard was established by the GCCF in Britain. This variety may have been produced previously in Siam because, apart from Seal-points, a solid blue form was known and crossing these two types together would have yielded Blue-points. Such cats have a frosty, glacial white body colour, blending into blue along the back. The points should be somewhat darker in colour. At the beginning of this century Major and Mrs Rendall were largely responsible for establishing and developing this form of the Siamese in Britain. Early examples had heads which were considered to be too rounded in shape; Blue-points have subsequently been improved by crossing with Seal-points. Some breeders think there might be a link between head shape and ideal coloration, because this latter feature has deteriorated at the expense of type.

The Lilac-point encompasses both blue and chocolate coloration and is hard to produce. The points are often unbalanced, showing too much blue on the nose and excessive chocolate on the tail. The points need to be a delicate shade of pinkish-grey, with faded lilac pads and nose offset against a milky body coloration. First attempts to produce Lilac-points were made over 80 years ago, but only since 1955 has there been a concerted effort to breed them. In North America the cats were first known as Frost-points and this name is still in use today.

Since the Second World War, various 'new' colours of Siamese have been created, although such developments are not favoured by all breeders. This is because it proved necessary to use other breeds, such as the Abyssinian, to introduce the desired modifications to the points; Siamese then had to be used to 'purify' the resulting hybrids, with the resulting cats being virtually indistinguishable from Siamese.

Smoke Longhair
Smoke Persian

The Smoke Longhair is a difficult breed to exhibit in the peak of condition; both rainy weather and excessive sunlight will spoil the coat. The fur should be contrasting, with a white undercoat set off by coloured tips on the individual hairs. This breed has always been relatively rare and is bred in a range of colours, the Black and Blue currently being recognized in both Britain and the United States.

Sphynx
Hairless Cat

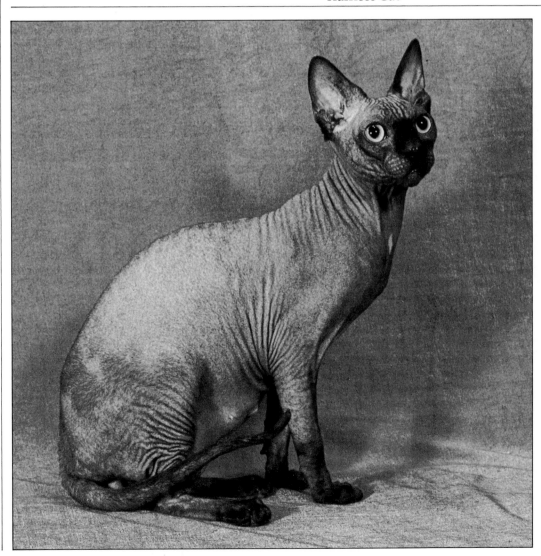

The Sphynx is sometimes referred to as the Hairless Cat, although this breed does possess a thin covering of hair, notably on the extremities of the body. The first hairless cat appeared in Canada in 1966 and the breed was subsequently established using American Shorthairs as out-crosses. Refused recognition by most official associations, the Sphynx remains a controversial breed.

Spotted Cat

The Spotted Cat is reputed to be an old breed—cats showing a similar pattern of markings were known in Ancient Egypt. The British standard is more specific over the precise pattern of markings than its American counterpart. Colours include the Silver Spotted (shown here), Red Spotted and Brown Spotted.

Tabby Shorthair

The Silver (shown here) is one of the three shorthaired Tabby varieties, the others being Red and Brown. In the Silver form the coat must be silver, with black tabby markings on top. As a general rule, all Tabbies have affectionate natures and make good pets, but the Silver Tabby is considered especially friendly. Classic Tabby markings include the 'butterfly' pattern on the shoulders, evenly spaced dark rings on the tail and spots on the abdomen. A variation of this pattern is seen in the Mackerel Tabbies, where the markings—a dark line running along the back with bands descending on either side of the body—resemble a fish skeleton.

Tabby Longhair
Tabby Persian

The Brown Tabby Longhair (1) is the oldest variety of this breed; although very popular during the last century, it is now relatively obscure. Silver Tabbies (2) are also quite scarce, since it is quite difficult to achieve a good contrast between the ground colour and the markings. Other colours include the Red Tabby (3); the Brown Tabby-and-White (4) and the Blue Tabby-and-White (5) are not yet recognized.

The Red-point and Tortie-point were among the first of the new colours to be bred. Red-points were exhibited in England in 1934, when they were known as Orange-points, but today's bloodlines have a more recent origin, and are derived from breeding programmes undertaken during the late 1940s on both sides of the Atlantic. The use of longhaired Red Tabbies introduced the desired colour into the Siamese but type suffered because of the cobby nature of the out-cross. Considerable argument over recognition followed. The CFA classified them as Colourpoint Shorthairs in 1964 and two years later the GCCF in Britain finally gave the Red-point status as a Siamese, but under a new breed number from the four traditional varieties. The Red-point should have deep red points, offset against a clear white body.

Tortie-points are female, as with other tortoiseshell varieties, and have been produced in the original range of Siamese points, with a corresponding body colour. The characteristic tortoiseshell markings consist of red, cream or a combination of both, superimposed on the normal points. A tabby form of the Siamese was recorded as long ago as 1902, with a number being created deliberately by a Swedish geneticist. They were then bred in Britain in 1940 but remained scarce until the 1960s. This variety has become known as the Lynx-point in North America. Although at first most of these tabbies were of Seal-point origin, other colours have also been produced, so that the four traditional forms, along with Red and Cream are recognized by the GCCF. The Cream-point Siamese has a white body colour with cream points.

Developments of these new forms led to various difficulties over identification. It proved impossible to distinguish between Red-points and Red Tabby-points by sight, although there is a significant genetic difference for breeders. A similar problem arose in the case of the Tortoiseshell- and Tortoiseshell Tabby-points, and it was therefore resolved to list them under the tabby heading, unless it could be shown that they were in fact genuine Tortoiseshell-points.

Among the scarcer new colours is the Silver form, which is only currently recognized in New Zealand. Elsewhere, it is generally classified with other Tabby-points. Body coloration in this instance is paler than normal. Shadow-points are now being bred in increasing numbers and are still sometimes referred to as Smoke-points. They appeared in Britain during the late 1960s but have yet to be officially recognized. Cinnamon-points are also known, as well as Lavender-points, but perhaps the most striking of this group of new colours is the Albino form. Albinos are, however, blue-eyed and not red-eyed, so the British description of Recessive White is preferable. American breeders classify such cats as Oriental Shorthairs. One hybrid breed with a Siamese ancestry which is now becoming more widely recognized is the Tonkinese, first bred in Canada from crosses involving Burmese. The points in this case are still recognizable, with body coloration being a paler form of the Burmese.

Siamese, irrespective of their colour, are probably the most demanding of all breeds and yet in return must rate among the most responsive. Their lively nature and acrobatic disposition can prove overwhelming on occasions, especially if they are housed permanently indoors; many owners find that the solution is to take them out for walks using a harness and leash. Their intelligent, adaptable personalities will respond to this stimulus. They can also be extremely affectionate but, if roused, Siamese are likely to be very difficult to handle and are not always so tolerant with children as some more phlegmatic breeds.

The sexual side of their nature is highly developed and neutering is essential if the cat is not being kept for breeding purposes. Intact toms will spray monotonously, while queens call repeatedly and loudly when on heat. Siamese are a forward breed, maturing early and producing large litters. Their kittens in turn develop rapidly and can be walking on their own when only a month old. They may then start calling just four months later. Siamese do not have a long show career. Their body coloration often darkens so that they no longer meet exhibition requirements, sometimes by only three years old.

Smoke Longhair
Smoke Persian

The Smoke has always been a rare breed, although it was first shown in its own class in 1893, rather than as a member of the Any Other Variety classes. The subsequent decline in the fortunes of the Smoke can then be seen through official studbook records. There were 30 registered in 1900, a number which had fallen to 18 by 1912. At the end of the Second World War, the breed was almost extinct in Britain.

Two colour variants of the Smoke are currently recognized in both Britain and the United States. In the Blue variety, the dark markings of the Black are merely replaced by blue. One of the most prominent features is the silvery ruff around the neck, contrasting with the black head. The undercoat is white and the topcoat coloured, so that when the cat moves the contrast of colour is most pronounced, although considerable grooming is necessary to show this feature to best advantage. The feet must be black, while the eyes should be orangish, never green. Like the Chinchilla, the Smoke tends to be of a lighter type than other Longhairs, and it is necessary for breeders to strike a balance between colour and type, without compromising either feature.

Various other Smokes have been bred in the United States where the breed has always been popular. These colours are not recognized in Britain at present and are exhibited in assessment classes. The Cameo Smoke, with its red top coat, shows a contrasting white undercoat when moving. This form, like the Blue Smoke, is difficult to breed without tabby markings. The Tortoiseshell Smoke is also being bred, with females only being produced in this case. They have the characteristic tortie markings, and the white undercoat in this case is tipped with black.

Smokes can be paired together, but their features generally deteriorate over the course of several generations unless good Blue or Black Longhairs are used as out-crosses. It is often difficult though to divide a litter into Smokes and Blacks. The young Smokes may show a small amount of white around the eyes and perhaps a greyish tinge around the belly. Colour counts for 40 percent of the available points. To show a Smoke in the peak of condition requires considerable preparation; indeed, the coat may only be in really top condition for about two months every year. Both wet weather and excessive sunlight will spoil its appearance, and so exhibition Smokes have to lead somewhat restricted lives prior to a show to keep their coats in peak condition.

Sphynx
Hairless Cat

The hairless condition, which is also seen in other creatures such as mice, first occurred in the cat in Ontario, Canada in 1966. The kitten born was ultimately paired back to its mother, giving rise to both hairless and normal offspring. In spite of its name however, the Hairless Cat does possess a thin, down-like coat. There is considerable opposition to the breeding of such cats, and neither the CFA nor the GCCF recognize the Sphynx, although some smaller American associations accept them. Their standards do not place any restrictions on coloration, although bicolours must be symmetrical, with white confined to the chest and abdominal regions. It is possible to distinguish coloration in both the sparse coat and the skin, which must appear tight on the body. The eyes must be golden, with no trace of green. Despite their rather grotesque appearance, if these cats are kept warm, they do not appear to present any significant problems with regard to care.

Spotted Cat

The Spotted Cat is an old shorthaired breed, portrayed in Egyptian mythology as the killer of the serpent which represented evil. It was first shown in Britain over a century ago, and became classified as the Spotted Tabby. Tabby markings have since been outlawed, although stripes are still permitted on the head and face under current standards. It is vital that the spots are clearly defined, and do not overlap, but their actual shape is not specified, nor is colour. The only stipulation in this respect is that the spots should correspond to the coat colour, as must eye coloration.

The British standard is more rigorous than the American, requiring head markings to match those of a tabby, and either a pattern of broken rings or spots on the tail. The presence of white in the coat is a definite fault. In the case of a Silver Spotted, eyes should be green or hazel, while for a Red Spotted they must be bright copper in colour. Orange, hazel or rich yellow eyes are permitted in the Brown Spotted. The coat resembles that of other British Shorthairs in texture. Although not perhaps as common as other varieties, Spotted Shorthairs have become increasingly popular again since the 1960s. They show no significant differences in temperament from other shorthairs and make good pets.

Tabby Longhair
Tabby Persian

There are currently five forms of the Tabby Longhair, with the Brown being considered the original type. This colour has lapsed into relative obscurity over recent years, although it was extremely popular during the last century. A Brown Tabby christened Birkdale Raffles won a signed photograph of the then Prince of Wales, later King Edward VII, at the Crystal Palace show of 1896. Prior to this, Birkdale's owner, a Miss Southam, had refused to show him for a period because lesser-marked cats had been beating him at other venues. Previous judges had chosen to ignore his fine sable colour, coupled with the contrasting black bands on his coat.

Interest in Brown Tabbies in North America then reached such a pitch that one cat, imported from Britain, attracted a bid of 1,000 dollars, which was over 20 times the average price of the time. While American fanciers continued with this colour, its popularity declined in Britain. The problem of finding suitable out-crosses may have contributed to the Brown Tabby's demise, and pairing these cats together over several generations results in a loss of type. It is also not easy to produce the desired sable coloration. The American standard differs from its British counterpart in permitting both the usual whorls and the so-called 'mackerel' pattern of vertical striping on the sides.

The Red Tabby was first known as the Orange Tabby, and its colour was required to match that of the fruit. The tabby markings had to be darker than the body coloration itself. The eye colour proved an area of controversy among early breeders. Some favoured a shade of yellow-bronze while others attempted to fix the blue coloration, seen only in kittens, as a permanent characteristic. This proved impossible; the standard today calls for copper-coloured eyes.

There was an initial trend towards eliminating the white markings often seen around the lips, rather than to improve the tabby markings. As with the Red Self, there was a shortage of female Red Tabbies which was overcome when it was realized that to produce queens, both parents had to be of this colour. Although the type of the Red Tabby today is generally good, problems over obtaining the correct markings still exist. The pattern can however be ascertained in young kittens, and changes little as the cats mature.

Silver Tabbies, like the Brown, are now rare, although at the end of the last century they were frequently seen at shows. In those days, as contemporary photographs confirm, the tabby markings featured prominently, at the expense of type. Such cats had relatively long noses and lacked the broad head called for in the current standard. Attempts to improve these features using both Black and Blue Longhairs simply led to a deterioration of the markings. Faced with the rise of the Chinchilla, the Silver Tabby began to fade into obscurity. Persistent arguments broke out over the correct eye colour, and served to divide the remaining breeders. The standard now required either green or hazel eye colour. By the 1930s, classes for Silver Tabbies were attracting such little support that it was not unusual only to have two entries, and some had none.

The difficulty of achieving a basically silver coat with black tabby markings still presents a challenge for determined breeders. The search for good Silver Tabbies is further complicated by the fact that often the darker kitten in a litter proves to be the best-marked adult, whereas those which appeared most promising as kittens lose their markings. The use of Brown Tabbies as out-crosses has given some Silvers brown markings in their coats, while Black Longhairs often lead to Silvers with orange eyes.

There are two other forms of the Tabby Longhair which are not currently recognized in Britain. The Cream Tabby has a pale cream body, with the characteristic tabby markings. The Blue has a pale bluish-white coat with a slightly darker pattern of markings. Both have copper-coloured eyes.

Tortoiseshell

The Tortoiseshell, commonly known as the 'Tortie', has been bred in both shorthaired (1) and longhaired (3) forms. Tortoiseshell-and-White cats (2) –black, cream and red set on a white ground—are also established in both shorthaired and longhaired forms. Such cats are known as Calico Shorthairs and Calico Persians in North America.

Turkish Van
Turkish Cat

This breed is closely related to the Angora and originated from the area around Lake Van in Turkey. An unusual breed, one of the most striking peculiarities of these cats is the fact that they appear to enjoy water and will even choose to bathe. They have white coats with auburn markings on the face and tail. Like Angoras, they do not have a thick undercoat.

White

White coats are bred in both shorthaired (2) and longhaired (1, 3, 4) forms. Eye colour also varies—the Orange-eyed (4), Odd-eyed (1) and Blue-eyed (3) Whites being recognized as distinct forms of the breed. Blue-eyed Whites, however, may well be handicapped by deafness; Odd-eyed Whites are likely to be deaf on the side of the head that corresponds to the blue eye. This is a congenital disorder and there is no treatment for it. In the past, Whites were often considered stupid, before this defect was discovered.

Tabby Shorthair

There are three recognized forms of the shorthaired Tabby, and it is important for exhibition purposes that the tabby markings are clearly discernible. The Brown Tabby remains quite scarce, although it has undergone a slight revival in popularity over the last decade. The basic colour must be coppery brown in these cats, set against black tabby markings. Permitted eye colours are hazel, deep yellow or orange, while green is also acceptable under the CFA ruling. Any trace of white fur is a serious flaw, and brindling is also penalized.

Red Tabbies are red in colour, with a darker pattern of markings on their coat. Eye colour must be copper and, as with the Brown Tabby, any deviation from the standardized colour results in certificates being withheld. Silver Tabbies have a silver coat, with the typical tabby markings superimposed in black. Their eyes should be either green or hazel. The tail, as in the case of all tabbies, needs to be evenly ringed with the darker colour, and the abdominal regions must be spotted.

A modification of the classical tabby pattern is seen in the so-called Mackerel Tabbies. The markings in this case are reminiscent of a fish skeleton. A dark line runs along the back from head to tail, and bands run off from this down either side of the body. These need to be thin, yet complete and numerous. Tabbies resemble other British Shorthairs in type with relatively short legs and powerful, muscular bodies. They make ideal pets, with the Silver form often considered the most affectionate.

Tortoiseshell Longhair
Tortoiseshell Persian

The Tortoiseshell has a coat of three colours — cream, black and red. The origins of the Tortoiseshell are completely unknown, but it is thought that crossings between shorthaired cats of this type and Black Longhairs gave rise to the longhaired variety.

The Tortoiseshell is only bred in the female form; males are extremely rare, and invariably sterile. The mystery associated with the breed is further compounded by the fact that tortie kittens cannot be guaranteed to appear in any given litter. Pairings to Cream or Black toms are preferred because using Tabbies is likely to give rise to unwanted markings in the kittens. The current standard calls for distinct, bright tortoiseshell markings. It is not unusual for a good individual to be spoilt by the presence of excessive black in the coat. The CFA insists on a patch of colour, usually cream and referred to as a 'blaze', extending from the head down to the nose. This characteristic is also favoured by British breeders. Tortoiseshells are lively and intelligent, and can be relied on to care well for their colourful mixture of kittens.

Tortoiseshell Shorthair

As in the case of other Tortoiseshells, the shorthaired form is virtually a female-only breed. Its origins are obscure, and

breeding for well-marked individuals is often a frustrating process. The standards require three colours — black, light red and dark red — to be present on the body, and also on all paws. These colours must be distinct, and the eyes need to be either bright copper or orange. Green rims around the eyes, as well as any evidence of tabby markings or white fur will be penalized. A red blaze on the head is preferred according to both the CFA and GCCF standards. Tortoiseshells have long been popular as pets, and are typically mated to either Red, Black or Cream Shorthairs.

Tortoiseshell-and-White Longhair
Calico Persian

The Tortoiseshell-and-White Longhair, sometimes known in Britain by its old name of Chintz, has proved difficult to breed on a regular basis. Females in this case often produce Bicolours, rather than producing further Tortoiseshell-and-Whites. Faults in this variety include dilution of coloured regions with white hairs, technically called 'brindling', and any signs of tabby markings. Type should be similar to that of other Longhairs, but the frill is slightly longer.

Tortoiseshell-and-White Shorthair
Calico Shorthair

Females also predominate in this shorthaired breed. The tricoloured arrangement of black, cream and dark red should be set clearly against the white ground, and needs to appear balanced. A white blaze on the head is favoured. Eye colour is as for the Tortoiseshell, with hazel again being acceptable under the CFA standard, while green rims to the eyes are outlawed. White should not appear to dominate the coat, with predominantly coloured individuals being preferred. Tortie-and-White Shorthairs do not differ significantly in temperament from the pure Tortoiseshell, being affectionate and gentle by nature. Bicoloured males are used for breeding.

Turkish Van
Turkish Cat

The Turkish Van is believed to be a form of the Angora, which was developed in the area around Lake Van in southeast Turkey. It was first brought to the attention of British cat fanciers by chance. Two travellers saw a pair of these longhairs in Turkey in 1955 and were immediately struck by their resemblance to the Angora.

Having enquired about the breed, they were allowed to bring a pair back to Britain. These cats bred true, producing kittens which had chalky white coats, with auburn markings on both tail and face which were noticeable from birth. It soon became apparent that they moult extensively during the summer, assuming a virtually shorthaired appearance. This is almost certainly a natural climatic adaptation, because the region of Turkey where they occur can be extremely cold in winter and hot in summer. Another rather unusual characteristic of the Turkish Van is its penchant for water. They will actively choose to bathe and even swim, unlike many cats.

The breed was officially recognized in Britain in 1969, but has yet to achieve a matching level of popularity in North America. Turkish Vans, like Angoras, lack a thick undercoat and therefore can be groomed easily. They possess hearty appetites and although some have nervous natures, these cats will make good pets if handled regularly from an early age.

White Longhair
White Persian

The White is considered to be one of the oldest longhaired breeds and was originally introduced to Europe from Asia. When first seen in Britain, they were called French cats, since they were brought over from Paris. The Blue-eyed form was bred from the Angora and deafness proved a common defect. At first this was not appreciated and such cats were regarded as being merely stupid. The problem of deafness is only very rarely noticed in the Orange-eyed White, which was descended from Persian stock. The coat of the Orange-eyed Whites cats is not as soft as that of the Blue-eyed forms.

Considerable controversy was generated at the early shows, with the Orange-eyed form constantly preferred, because of its Persian type, over Blue-eyed Whites. This led to a separation of the two varieties in 1930, but left the Odd-eyed Whites being shown in the Any Other Variety classes for a period, until separate classes for the two varieties were established again.

Whites were much in demand during the early years of the present century, and well represented in the leading catteries of the period. Some were imported, presumably from the East, at about the same time, and were discovered to be aggressive. In the United States, Whites enjoyed continuing popularity over the years, but faded in Britain until the 1960s. Inspired perhaps by the use of white cats in television advertisements, breeders again turned to this breed. Orange-eyed Whites became dominant, partly because the Blue-eyed form deteriorated in type without the use of out-crosses such as Blacks, but this then introduced orange eyes to the breed. In addition, some potential owners were deterred by the disability of deafness present in many Blue-eyed Whites. Deafness may be the result of a congenital lack of the organ of Corti.

At birth, White kittens appear pinkish and all have blue eyes. A colour change may become evident from the age of five weeks onwards, affecting one or both eyes. If the eyes have remained blue by the time the kitten is about two months old, they are unlikely to alter in colour. The deepest colour is preferred, while the coat itself should be pure white. There must be a prominent frill around the neck.

In spite of their appearance, Whites do not need a lot of extra attention to keep their coats clean — most are very fastidious, spending long periods licking and cleaning their fur. Regular grooming, as with all Longhairs, is, however, essential. Whites are not delicate by nature either. They prove affectionate, although perhaps remaining aloof with strangers. This breed has contributed to the development of the Tortoiseshell-and-White, as well as the Bicolour.

White Shorthair

The White Shorthair has the same eye colours as its longhaired counterpart, with deafness again associated with the Blue-eyed form. In the case of Odd-eyed Whites, this disability is likely to be confined only to the ear on the blue-eyed side of the face. Orange-eyed Whites generally do not have any impairment of hearing, but eye coloration cannot be guaranteed until the kitten is at least eight weeks old. Green rims will be penalized in all cases.

Coat colour must be pure white, and free from any hint of yellow. The coat should be short and dense, and may require rather more care than in the case of other shorthairs, to keep it in top condition. Whites are often paired together to preserve their appearance, but can be out-crossed to Tortoiseshell or Tortoiseshell-and-Whites.

Other Longhairs
Other Persians

Various other longhaired breeds are currently being developed. The Pewter is typical of this group, being reminiscent of the Shaded Silver at first glance. It was bred from Blue and Chinchilla stock, with the addition of Black Longhair blood as well, and is sometimes known as the Blue Chinchilla. Its eye colour differs from the latter variety, however, since it is not green, but either orange or copper. Pewter describes the colour of the mantle in this breed of cat.

The Chocolate Longhair is another new breed, with similarly coloured eyes to the Pewter, while its fur has a solid, even depth of coloration. The Lilac, by contrast, is pale grey, with a pinkish tinge to the coat. A tortoiseshell form of the Chocolate is also known.

Other Shorthairs

Shorthaired forms of the Smoke are recognized by the GCCF. Colour in these cats must be either blue or black, with a pale silver undercoat. Yellow or orange eyes are permissible, but an excessively long coat, signs of white hairs or tabby markings are all penalized. The CFA regard such cats simply as colour varieties of other breeds (the Manx, Rex, Exotic and American Shorthair).

Another less common variety in the shorthaired classes is the British Tipped. The type of these cats should closely resemble that of other British Shorthairs. The undercoat must be white with tipping largely confined to the upperparts, although it can extend lightly to the legs. Any colour acceptable for the British Shorthair can be present in a British Tipped. Chocolate or lilac tips to the hairs are also permitted, with the colour itself giving a sparkling appearance to the fur. Acceptable eye colour must be green in the case of cats with black tipping, and ranges from orange to copper for other colors.

Aside from new colour varities, other new shorthaired breeds have also been developed. The Tonkinese is the result of Siamese crossed with Burmese; the Burmese has also contributed to the development of the Burmilla.

Other Longhairs
Other Persians

The Lilac (1) and Chocolate (2) Longhairs are two of the more recent additions to the Longhaired group of cats. The Ragdoll (3), although not universally recognized, is now being bred in a variety of colours. All such cats are said to have descended from a White Longhair queen, which was once involved in an accident. As a result, they are supposed to be relatively insensitive to pain, but there is no evidence to support this claim.

Other Shorthairs

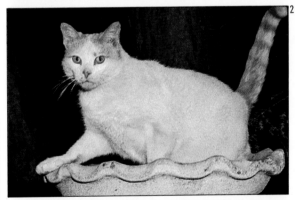

New Shorthairs are always being developed. The Tonkinese (3) arose in Canada, a result of hybridization between Siamese and Burmese. The latter breed also contributed to the ancestry of the Burmilla (1). In the United States a shorthaired form of the Turkish Van is now being bred (2), while in Britain, both Colourpoint (4) and Chocolate (5) Shorthairs are being developed. Recognition of new breeds and varieties depends on the organization and country concerned. As numbers increase, such cats will become more common at shows.

Obtaining a Cat

Owning a cat is a long-term responsibility which can extend over a period of two decades or more. Deciding to acquire a cat — or any living creature — as a household pet should not be undertaken hastily or casually, and before proceeding it is important to consider carefully all the advantages and disadvantages that will be involved.

During its lifetime, the cat will have to be fed daily and is likely to need some veterinary care, if only for annual vaccinations. If the cat is not to be bred, it will also need to be neutered. Some reorganization will be needed in the home to prevent accidental damage; there will also be the expense of providing bedding and litter. Holiday periods may mean boarding the cat in a kennel while its owners are away. Added to these considerations is the slight but nevertheless real risk of infection and disease: this applies in particular to pregnant women and to households where there are young children.

Offset against such negative factors are the enjoyment and companionship cats bring to many people. Despite their reputation for being aloof, cats often seek out their owners and respond well to affection and attention. Unlike dogs, they can also be kept indoors on a permanent basis: this will be essential, in fact, in areas where the traffic is an ever-present hazard, or in the case of a valuable stud animal. Cats are reasonably clean and straightforward to care for; their graceful beauty, mystique and playfulness can make them ideal pets for considerate owners.

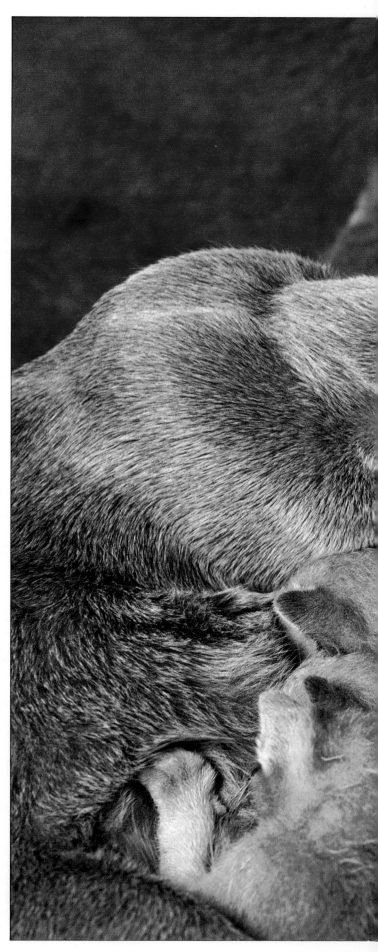

Kittens need more care than older cats, but are probably a better choice for first-time pet owners. Inquisitive by nature, they should not be allowed outside without supervision; otherwise, they may wander away *(TOP)*. Inside, it is a good idea to confine the kitten to one room until it becomes accustomed to its new surroundings *(ABOVE)*. Cats make good mothers, but tend to lose interest in their kittens once they start to grow older: this is a natural part of weaning *(RIGHT)*.

Choosing a Cat
Basic considerations

AGE Kittens, although initially more demanding, will generally settle better in a new environment than older cats. They are often more responsive to their new owners and are less likely to wander or get lost although, by way of compensation, an adult cat will probably be housetrained already. The age and history of a kitten will be familiar, whereas with an older cat, details such as its past vaccination record, if any, may not be known. This may not necessarily be important, but it will be virtually impossible to age the cat with any degree of certainty.

BREED Many people do not opt for a pedigree cat, being quite content to choose mongrel individuals whose parentage over the past generations has never been tightly controlled. Such cats are often affectionately termed 'moggies' or 'alley cats'. At the same time, breeds of domestic cat are less distinctive, if only in terms of size, than their canine counterparts. There is likely to be a very significant financial difference, however, between a cat with a pedigree and an ordinary cat, the high cost of a pedigree reflecting the work entailed in building up a bloodline. It may be possible to acquire a pedigree animal at a relatively cheap price if it has a fault which prevents it from being shown but such bargain offers must be viewed with slight scepticism, until the cat in question is seen. While incorrect coat or eye coloration will not affect the cat as a pet, the squint seen in certain Siamese, for example, can be a real handicap.

Some breeders will also allow responsible owners to have their kittens on breeding terms. This generally means that once the cats are mature, they can be mated as the breeder wishes, with the resulting offspring being divided as agreed beforehand. With such an arrangement it is sensible to have the terms set out clearly on paper from the outset so that both parties know their obligations and responsibilities, thus lessening the risk of a dispute arising at a later date. A breeding agreement of this type helps the breeder to maintain more cats than would be possible otherwise, for either financial or spatial reasons.

When deciding on a pedigree kitten or cat for a pet, the breed chosen is in the end a matter of preference. Apart from variations in appearance, there are, however, noticeable differences in temperament from breed to breed. These are discussed elsewhere in the book under the individual breed headings. At the same time, it should be remembered that all cats are individual and respond to their environment accordingly.

To summarize, longhaired (Persian) cats require more grooming than shorthaired varieties, and tend to leave more hair around the home. Both Blue and Blue-cream Longhairs generally make good pets, while Tabbies also respond quite well to affection. Colourpoint Longhairs (Himalayans) can show great devotion to their owners and have become very popular. Turkish Cats will need less attention paid to their coats than other Longhairs, but shed their fur quite profusely when moulting.

British and American Shorthairs are hardy breeds and affectionate by nature, and have much to recommend them to a potential owner. More delicate breeds, such as the Rexes, need fairly warm surroundings, which could be a drawback in cold climates. Abyssinians make delightful pets, but have been seriously affected as a breed by feline leukemia virus. The tailless Manx, with its unusual

Choosing a cat is not only a matter of deciding on age, gender and breed; your own circumstances must also be taken into account. Like any other pet, a cat will need care and attention. Whether or not there are other pets or children in the household should also be considered. Make sure to keep caged birds out of the cat's reach (ABOVE). Teach young children how to handle their new pet (RIGHT). A new kitten will probably settle in more readily with other animals than an older cat (FAR RIGHT).

CHOOSING AN INDIVIDUAL Kittens vary in temperament, even within the same litter, but, in general, litters vary more than kittens do in any one litter. It is important to pick a kitten from a good home, where the entire litter should be healthy and alert. Aside from basic health considerations, colour and overall conformation will be factors for those seeking a pedigree cat, while those looking for a pet will probably be interested in general behavioural traits. Most people, however, will find that they respond more to one kitten than to the others: this type of appeal is, more often than not, purely subjective. The best advice is to spend as much time as possible observing the litter in order to make the right decision. While a few guidelines can be suggested, it is important to bear in mind that on another occasion, the kittens may behave quite differently.

THE AGGRESSIVE KITTEN A kitten that bullies its littermates, scratches, hisses or snarls unnecessarily when handled gently may be overly aggressive. Such reactions may just be a reflection of the circumstances but a kitten that displays persistent bad temper will not make a good pet and may even be suffering from illness.

THE OUTSIDER Typically the 'runt' or the smallest of the litter, a kitten that hangs back or seems shy may not have received the same amount of attention from its dam as its littermates. Such kittens do not necessarily make poor pets; size is only a crucial factor for those seeking a good example of a pedigree breed. In any large litter, one or two kittens will always be smaller than the rest.

THE LIVELY KITTEN Kittens who seem more lively and curious than the others may be more alert naturally, but equally their temperament may simply be the result of more frequent handling. In either case, a forward disposition is a good indication of intelligence and adaptability.

THE NERVOUS KITTEN Improperly handled kittens are likely to be excessively started at loud noises or sudden movements. This is a question of degree, however, and if one kitten in a litter shows these faults, some of the others are likely to be similarly afflicted, since it is to a large extent a reflection of their environment.

SIGNS OF HEALTH Eyes should be clear of any discharge and the nose and ears should be clean. The coat should be free from dirt and glossy, with no signs of fleas. When the kitten walks, there should be no lameness or lack of coordination; when it is picked up, its abdomen should not feel too swollen—a sign of roundworms.

appearance, will appeal to those who want a cat which has a distinctive characteristics. Some breeds tend to be more remote and aloof, with Siamese, for example, retaining a strong and independent streak, yet proving extremely affectionate as well.

While it is easier to predict what the temperament of pedigree cats is likely to be, crossbreds are certainly not lacking in either colour or character. They can become just as devoted to their owners and, contrary to some stories, are no more susceptible to illness than pedigree cats. The amount of grooming which they require is obviously dependent on the appearance of their coats; those with relatively long fur will need to be combed and brushed more regularly.

GENDER The choice between a male (tom) or female (queen) cat will largely depend on whether the cat is to be kept as a pet or bred. For breeding purposes a queen is preferable if only one cat is to be kept, as she can be mated to a tom without difficulty, on payment of a stud fee. There are real problems in keeping an intact male cat, once it has reached the age of about seven months and is sexually mature. They tend to wander and fight; in the home, carpets and other furnishings will be soiled with their pungent urine. Intact females are easier to control, but they may cycle every three weeks and pregnancy is very likely to result unless they are kept indoors on a permanent basis. Their calling during this time can be disturbing; some will also urinate around their environment.

Neutering should be considered from the outset if you do not want the cat to breed. This surgery costs more for females since the operation is more complex. In either case, however, neutering is relatively safe; subsequently, there is no real difference in personality between the sexes. Nevertheless, some people prefer neutered females, claiming that they are more affectionate.

Sources

When obtaining pedigree cats, direct contact with a breeder is recommended. Addresses can usually be obtained through the various cat magazines or by visiting shows. There are also other ways of finding breeders locally, either by studying advertisements in local papers or through a veterinarian.

Most breeders will give every assistance to a customer and, if possible, it is well worth travelling to their premises, even if they live some distance away. It is important to choose the cat in person. Some kittens may be more forward and friendly than the others in a litter, or their colour might simply be more striking. The surroundings in which they are living can also be noted. As a rule, kittens reared in a home where they have received a lot of human attention from an early age are likely to settle better as pets. Those which have lived in a cattery since birth are often shyer when transferred to a domestic environment, and older individuals will generally take longer to adapt to such a move.

Pedigree kittens are occasionally sold in pet stores, but crossbred litters are much more often seen in these establishments. There are strict rules governing the sale of pets from such premises; kittens must be weaned, eating independently of their mother. Under British law — The Pet Animals Act — kittens need to be at least eight weeks old before they can be sold; 12 weeks, for pedigrees.

Equal care should be taken when obtaining a non-pedigree cat from a friend. Seeing the litter at first-hand gives an opportunity to observe the kittens all together and establish which individual has the best temperament or is simply the most appealing.

Animal welfare organizations often have a number of kittens and cats which need permanent, caring homes. The work of such groups in the vast majority of cases is entirely voluntary; whenever adopting a pet from such an organization, a donation should be made to their funds, so the work can continue and other animals benefit. In cases of genuine hardship, many of these charities will assist with the cost of neutering, but if possible, this sum should be paid back over a period of time.

Picking an individual

Aside from more personal preferences, the two most important considerations when selecting a particular cat or kitten are its disposition and general health. Before beginning a specific health check, it is a good idea to simply observe the litter to establish differences in temperament. Avoid kittens which are over-aggressive as well as those who hang back or do not seem particularly lively — passivity may indicate a cowed nature or be a sign of ill health. Kittens should be gregarious, playful and inquisitive; older cats will be less playful, but should not be timid or aggressive at the approach of strangers.

Once you have established which kitten you would like, spend some time checking its overall appearance for any sign of illness. The eyes must be free from any signs of discharge, and not obscured by the 'third eyelid', more correctly known as the nictitating membrane. When the pad of fat behind the eyes shrinks due to illness or poor condition, the eyes sink back into their sockets, causing the nictitating membrane or 'haws' to become prominent. It will be evident at the corner of the ear, nearest the nose. The nose itself should be clean, with the nostrils unblocked, while the ears must not show any excessive accumulation of wax, or appear dirty.

Stroking the cat will give an indication of its overall condition. Note any trace of flea dirt, scurf or soreness in the coat. The anal region should not show signs of staining, which could be an indication of diarrhoea. Deposits resembling rice grains around the anus itself indicate a tapeworm infection. The cat then must be encouraged to walk a short distance, so that any signs of lameness or lack of coordination will become evident. If such disabilities are noticed, the whole litter should be viewed with suspicion, as they may be infected with feline panleucopaenia or suffering from a dietary deficiency.

Next, ask the owner's permission to carry out a closer examination. It may be necessary to have assistance to look in the mouth. With one person restraining the cat by grasping round its shoulders at the top of the forelegs, the task will be relatively simple. The left hand should be placed around the upper jaw, over the nasal region, while the lower mandible can be gently prised down with the other hand. Lefthanded people may find it easier to do this the other way round.

A final check on the cat can be made by picking it up. An arm should be gently placed round the chest just behind the front legs, while the other arm is used to support the rear. If there is no support given to its hindquarters, the cat will be very likely to struggle and may scratch, for fear of falling.

HEALTH INSPECTION It is essential to inspect a cat or kitten thoroughly for any signs of illness. Ask the owner's permission to carry out these routine checks. Open the mouth to examine the gums and teeth, looking out for any indication of soreness or bleeding (1). Inspect the eyes to make sure they are free from discharge and are not obscured by the 'third eyelid' or nictitating membrane – a sign of poor condition (2). Stroke the cat to judge overall condition and note any traces of fleas (3). The ears must appear clean (4). Feel the abdomen to make sure it is not swollen: this may indicate the presence of roundworms (5). Inspect the anal region for signs of tapeworm (6). To carry out a close examination, it will be necessary to pick up the cat or kitten. It should always be supported firmly, with one hand under its hindquarters *(BELOW)*. Picking a cat up by the scruff of the neck is only advisable in the case of feral cats.

Stray or feral cats are much harder to handle, resenting all attempts to lift them up. Under these circumstances, a slightly different approach is necessary, which entails holding the cat firmly by the loose area of skin over its shoulders, known as the scruff, while again supporting the hindquarters. This will restrain the cat more effectively, preventing it from biting and scratching.

Lifting the cat up will give an indication of its weight. The underside of the abdomen should be felt gently; if this is very rounded in a kitten, it is a likely sign of roundworms. Moving forward in the direction of the chest, a small swelling may be felt. This is likely to indicate a hernia of the umbilicus (or 'belly-button'), with tissue protruding through a small hole in the body wall. It is not a serious problem and can be corrected surgically if necessary, but will detract from the cat's value. Some breeders believe hernias of this type may be inherited.

SEXING Sexing a kitten is harder than sexing an adult cat; although an experienced breeder is unlikely to make an error in this respect, a staff member in a pet store may not be so competent. It is worth checking to be quite sure. The distinction between the sexes is made largely on the basis of the relative distances between the openings below the base of the tail. In female kittens, the two openings — the anus with the vulva beneath — are virtually in contact with each other and the vulva appears as a distinct slit. The slit opening of the vulva of the mature female cat is more distant from the anus than in a kitten, but it is impossible to distinguish between neutered and intact females by this means. Male kittens do not have an external penis. The organ is contained in a circular opening, spaced a short distance below the anus. This gap is filled by the scrotum, although the testicles will not be prominent in a young kitten. Intact males have a distinct swelling in this region.

BACKGROUND INFORMATION Having chosen a particular cat, there are certain questions which should be asked of the vendor. It is important to know the vaccination history of the individual concerned and whether it has been wormed recently so that this information can be passed on to the veterinarian. For a kitten, a diet sheet setting out the feeding regimen should be obtained and closely followed for the first week or so. This will lessen the risk of any digestive upsets following the move. In the case of pedigree animals, the registration documents will need to be filled in correctly and the official body concerned notified of the change of ownership. Failure to do this may result in subsequent disqualification if the cat in question is later shown.

Preparation
Equipment

A vast array of products for cats is now marketed through pet stores but only certain items should be regarded as essential, and purchased before the cat itself is obtained. A dirt box and litter, three bowls and a bed will be required from the outset. Other items, such as scratching posts, heating pads and toys can be acquired later.

If necessary, various items around the house can be adapted for use in an emergency. A cardboard box of suitable size with its top removed and one of the sides cut away to form an entrance will suffice as a bed. An old seed tray or vegetable box with low sides and a solid base should prove adequate as a dirt box; plastic is preferable, because the wood will soon start to smell, even if used in conjunction with a deodorant cat litter. Saucers make very adequate feeding receptables in an emergency, but it is inadvisable to use them again for domestic purposes once the cat has licked them. The bacterial flora present in a cat's mouth is generally unpleasant.

Dirt boxes are produced in various sizes; those made of sturdy plastic are relatively cheap and easy to disinfect. They can also be obtained with a partial lid fitting around the perimeter, which acts as a shield to prevent litter being scratched all over the floor. The sides of the box for a kitten should not be more than 3in (7.5cm) in height, although deeper designs may be preferable for older cats.

The litter itself is sold in both pet stores and many supermarkets; a variety of brands are now on the market. Those containing fuller's earth are often preferred, since this absorbs well and also acts as a deodorant. Cat litter also comes in a range of colours. Fuller's earth brands are grey, whereas there are white 'lightweight' litters and a pink type which is claimed to be both absorbent and dust-free. There should be sufficient litter to give a reasonable pile on the bottom of the dirt box. To facilitate cleaning, it is a good idea to line the tray with a plastic sack held in place with the lid. The litter is poured onto the plastic and once soiled can be lifted out on the the sack for disposal.

Cat litter is relatively expensive and heavy to carry in any quantity. As alternatives, garden soil or even peat can be used but these tend to spoil the coats of paler longhaired breeds in particular. Sand may prove abrasive; sawdust may contain toxic chemicals used for wood preservation and could prove poisonous if consumed by a kitten. Fine particles may also enter the eyes, causing severe irritation. To economize on litter, a special scoop can be bought to remove faeces along with soiled litter from the dirt tray. This is not a pleasant task, however, and should not be undertaken by pregnant women because of the slight risk of contracting toxoplasmosis.

The scoop and dirt tray should be washed with a suitable disinfectant after use. Many of the disinfectants regularly used around the home are, however, potentially toxic to

A playpen is a useful investment for new kittens. They can be confined safely in the pen, away from other pets, until they become accustomed to their new surroundings (ABOVE). It is a good idea to introduce the cat to its basket at a very early age so it is not frightened of moving (RIGHT).

cats. These include such well-known brands as TCP and Dettol, as well as Jeyes Fluid. One of the quaternary ammonium group of disinfectants, such as cetrimide, should be obtained specifically for attending to the cat's needs. A reliable pharmacist will know the type of disinfectant required, if it is not clear from the container. Bleach can also be used under certain circumstances, for example for washing out cat pens or catteries, but can whiten surfaces, which may prove a disadvantage.

All such products must be used as indicated on the container, and made up using hot water. Soiled objects should always be washed with a detergent and rinsed to remove as much organic matter as possible, because this will otherwise handicap the action of the disinfectant. Maximum benefit will be obtained from a disinfectant if the object concerned can be immersed in the solution for several minutes. Another thorough rinse will then be necessary to remove any remaining traces of the disinfectant.

BASKETS Sleeping baskets for cats range from the traditional circular wicker designs to plastic beds and even 'bean bags'. Plastic baskets are much easier to keep clean. They can be lined with newspaper and bedding placed on top. Cats do, however, enjoy bean bags, which contain polystyrene foam in the form of granules rather than real beans. Such bags must have removable, washable covers. If they are thought

to be harbouring fleas, regular spraying with a suitable preparation coupled with repeated washing of the covers should keep these parasites at bay. Depending on the environment, it may be worth considering the purchase of either a fibreglass bed with a fitted electrical heater or a removable heating pad.

BOWLS Food and drinking bowls will also be necessary and must be sturdy enough not to tip over easily. This can be a disadvantage of stainless steel containers, although they are easy to keep scrupulously clean. Plastic feeding bowls can be scratched or chewed and may harbour germs. Glazed bowls are probably the best choice, as they are both heavy and simple to wash thoroughly, although they break readily if dropped. Three bowls will be needed — one each for food, water and milk. These should be cleaned separately from other household dishes.

TOYS Toys do not need to be elaborate or expensive to appeal to a kitten or even an older cat. It is important to ensure, however, that pieces cannot be accidentally ingested by the cat. Simple discarded household items, such as old cotton reels or lengths of string will fascinate a cat for ages. Table tennis balls, which can be pawed and then pounced on, are another popular toy, while various rubber mice and similar items can be bought in pet stores. Special catnip toys are also available.

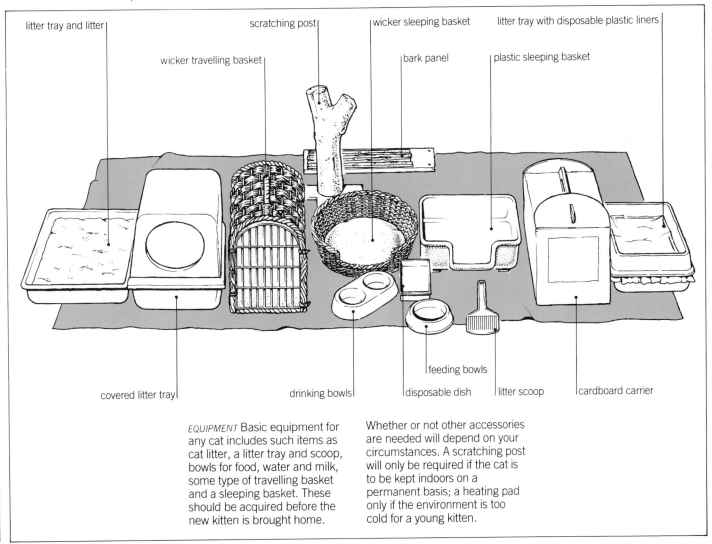

EQUIPMENT Basic equipment for any cat includes such items as cat litter, a litter tray and scoop, bowls for food, water and milk, some type of travelling basket and a sleeping basket. These should be acquired before the new kitten is brought home.

Whether or not other accessories are needed will depend on your circumstances. A scratching post will only be required if the cat is to be kept indoors on a permanent basis; a heating pad only if the environment is too cold for a young kitten.

HAZARDS IN THE HOME Cats are naturally inquisitive; this characteristic, together with their proficiency at climbing, exposes them to many dangers in the home. A certain amount of forethought and rearrangement will be necessary to maintain a safe environment for both you and your pet. Common hazards include: pans of boiling water or fat which the cat may spill (1), open oven doors (2), accessible rubbish bins containing small bones which may lodge in the cat's throat (3), boiling kettles (4), sharp utensils left out (5), household detergents and cleansers (6), open fridges (7), open dryers or washing machines (8), sockets and electrical cables which the cat may chew (9), open doors leading onto high balconies (10), objects resting precariously on table edges (11), precious ornaments on shelves (12), fires with no fireguards (13), various houseplants which may prove poisonous (14), drawers left open where the cat may become trapped (15), young children or babies left alone in a room with a cat (16). Cats should be discouraged from stealing food (FAR LEFT).

Cats should be trained not to walk over kitchen surfaces, where they may be exposed to danger from sharp kitchen utensils or may ingest common household detergents and cleansers, which may prove poisonous (ABOVE). Cats will investigate all secluded places. These include the interiors of washing machines and driers, where they may be attracted by the warmth (RIGHT).

If allowed outside, a cat will readily eat grass, although the reason for such behaviour is not known. If confined indoors, the cat may turn its attention to houseplants. Some common varieties are poisonous if consumed, including rhododendrons, azaleas, poinsettias and oleander. To discourage cats from eating plants, provide grass *(LEFT)*. Although they are graceful creatures, cats may accidentally knock over ornaments; their curiosity will lead them to investigate all intriguing nooks and crannies in the home *(RIGHT)*.

Settling In
The new kitten

There are a number of potential dangers facing the kitten in a new home, and it is advisable to restrict its domain at first. A kitten should only be obtained when there is someone who will be in close attendance for much of the day. Left alone to its own devices, the young cat may become tangled up in curtains, start to scratch a cherished piece of furniture or knock ornaments over. The kitten cannot be let out safely until its course of vaccinations is completed, and if allowed total freedom in the home, there is always a risk that it will slip outside undetected should a door or window be left open accidentally.

The necessary preparations should have been made for the newcomer in advance. A quiet corner of a room, out of direct sunlight, makes an ideal location for the kitten's sleeping basket and dirt tray, and it will soon come to recognize this area as its own territory. It is sensible to place a thick sheet of clean polythene over the floor in this area to avoid unnecessary soiling. Although cats are not really messy eaters, a certain amount of food or drink may be spilt on occasions, and the polythene will make it much easier to clear up. The feeding surface should always be wiped over daily, in any case, to ensure that it remains clean. Apart from presenting a direct health hazard to the kitten, meat residues attract flies in hot weather. A further advantage of the polythene is that any accidents close to the dirt tray can

also be cleaned up and disposed of more thoroughly.

When the new kitten first arrives home, open the travelling box as soon as the room is prepared and all doors and windows are shut. Other cats or dogs should be excluded at this stage. The kitten is likely to be upset after its journey and will need to be left quietly to settle down without unnecessary interference. Some kittens will venture out from their basket immediately, whereas others will be reluctant to leave and should be lifted out firmly.

The kitten will investigate the room cautiously, stopping to sniff around at intervals. After perhaps 15 minutes, if it has ignored the dirt box, it should be gently placed on the tray. Scooping the litter in front of the kitten for a brief period and using a restraining hand should encourage the animal to remain and use the box when it is freed. Cats are naturally clean animals. Once the kitten has adopted the tray, it should return of its own accord to perform its natural functions. After feeding and waking are usually the times for such activity; the tray must then be emptied as soon as possible after use because some kittens will ignore a soiled box.

After a drink of tepid milk and some food, the kitten can be placed in its basket and stroked to encourage it to sleep. Bedding must be provided in the basket; an old thick blanket is ideal for the purpose. It will help to keep the kitten snug, and cannot be ripped apart or accidentally consumed. Bedding must be washed regularly, particularly

during the warmer months, because it will also prove a secure refuge for fleas.

In cold conditions, especially for the thinner-coated breeds, it is a good idea to put a heater right in the basket. There are heaters specially designed for this function, which operate on a low wattage and can therefore be run around the clock, if necessary, at very low cost. Such heaters are made in the form of a metal pad, generally about 10 x 6in (25 x 15cm), although certain manufacturers will make larger sizes to order if required, with the element underneath. Heat spreads evenly over the plate when weight is applied to its surface. These units are extremely durable and safe, and can be easily wiped clean if soiled. It is also possible to protect the pad by enclosing it in a plastic bag, although more mischievous kittens may get their heads inside, unless it is adequately sealed.

In a home where children and other pets are present, it can be useful to construct an enclosed wire pen where the kitten may be safely confined for periods. The cage should be large enough to house the sleeping basket, dirt tray and feeding bowls, with enough space for the kitten to move around. Various collapsible models are now on the market, which will store flat when not in use.

A major advantage of such a pen is that it enables the kitten to be fed separately from other cats or dogs. Fights are especially likely to break out over food, and in such instances a small kitten could be easily killed by a dog. In a household where cats are coming in and out, it is also possible to supervise the food intake of the kitten, without fear of the others consuming its meal.

Cats will either remain wary of each other for a considerable period of time, or settle in quickly together without difficulties. They should not be forced into acquaintance but introduced carefully, preferably after having been fed, with someone present to keep a discreet eye on them. There is much less physical contact between two cats meeting for the first time than is the case with dogs. Intact toms are an exception and will have to be kept apart in pens at first or serious fighting will be inevitable.

Children will also need to be supervised with a cat, especially if they have had little prior experience of animals. They may otherwise injure their new pet unintentionally. Perhaps the most common problem in this category occurs when rubber bands are wound tightly around the kitten's tail by playful young fingers. These will not necessarily be obvious against the fur at first, but if allowed to remain in place, the circulation is likely to be interrupted, and the tail will ultimately drop off.

The older cat
The reactions of an older cat to a new environment are similar to those of a kitten, but under no circumstances should it be let out of the house for at least two weeks, unless it is used to walking on a harness. This applies especially to intact (unneutered) animals, which may stray off immediately, and not return to their new home. By keeping the cat indoors for a period, it will come to accept this region as part of its territory, where it can retire for food and warmth.

If by any chance a cat does not return after being let out, then the first step must be to carry out a thorough search in the immediate vicinity. By following their owners too closely, cats can find themselves locked in outbuildings, garages or sheds, and it is always worth checking such

Cats soon establish themselves as members of the family, even if other pets are present. New friendships will have to be monitored at first and introductions made gradually. Kittens should be kept in a safe place, such as an enclosed wire pen, for a little while after their arrival to ensure they do not get injured by other animals in the household. Squabbling is especially likely to break out over food (BELOW). Older cats settle into a new home almost as readily as kittens, but they should be confined indoors for the first few weeks to prevent them from straying. Once they are used to their new environment, they can be allowed to wander out into the garden (RIGHT).

localities. Adult cats are quite hardy creatures, and, if they are in good condition, they can survive at least several days without food, although water is a more critical necessity.

Having contacted neighbours, an advertisement in a local shop or newspaper, giving a brief description of the cat and any distinguishing features, may lead to information. Other sources of help to consider are animal welfare groups operating in the area, neighbourhood radio stations, some of which broadcast details of lost and found pets, and possibly the police.

Given the rather fickle nature of many felines, it may simply be that a kind person had adopted the cat by chance, without realizing that it already had an owner. For this reason, some cats are fitted with special elasticated collars, which have an address or telephone number attached, often inside a small waterproof plastic capsule. The major drawback of such collars is that they may catch on something and prevent the cat from struggling free, although the elastication is provided to prevent accidents of this nature. A collar may also slightly damage the fur of a prize pedigree.

Daily Care

Like all pets, cats need a properly balanced diet, an organized routine of feeding and basic care, and regular grooming. With a minimum of training cats adapt readily to most households; only slight adjustments will be needed to avoid any potential damage or disruption that certain activities, such as hunting or scratching, may cause. Aside from these practical aspects of care, cats do need and enjoy attention and affection. Play is important for kittens; comfort and company for older cats. Cats are, to a certain extent, naturally independent creatures, but individuals vary considerably and there is no excuse for neglect.

Feeding

Nutritional requirements

As with all creatures, the nutritional requirements of the cat vary during the course of its life. Kittens, for example, need a high input of food, especially protein, to support their fast rate of growth: at the age of seven weeks, they may consume one-fifth of their total body weight in food each day. A similar increase in the intake of food is needed by breeding and lactating queens. In old age, cats may eat less, and their diets should be adjusted to ensure they receive a balanced intake of essential elements.

Cats are not as adaptable as dogs in terms of the type of food they require and need to be fed a higher level of protein throughout their lives. For this reason, prepared foods for cats are generally more expensive than those marketed for dogs. In addition, the cat does not take readily to carbohydrate, which features prominently in many cheaper brands of dog food. The energy requirements of cats are therefore met partly from protein, and not carbohydrate as in many other mammals, including man.

The protein supplied to cats must also be largely of animal origin, because protein derived from plant sources does not contain the necessary balance of essential amino acids. Proteins are comprised of various amino acids, fused together in chains, and their sequence gives the protein its characteristic nature. Some of these amino acid residues are essential. Because they cannot be manufactured in the body they must be present in the diet if a deficiency is not to occur. Taurine is typical of this group, and is particularly important to cats because it maintains good vision. The recommended average level of protein in cat diets is between 30 and 40 percent.

Fat metabolism in the cat also differs significantly from that of the dog. As with protein, certain fatty acids are essential. Vegetable fats cannot be converted successfully by cats to meet their essential fatty acid requirement, so fats of animal origin must again be included in their diets. The level of fat will have a direct influence on the palatability of the foodstuff to the cat, and they can consume relatively high levels of fatty foods with no adverse effects. On a regular basis, however, excessive intake of fat — of the order of 40 percent of the total diet — will lead to obesity.

Fat provides a very concentrated source of energy, liberating twice as many calories as the equivalent amounts of either protein or cabohydrate. In the form of lipids, fats are vital for the correct functioning of cell membranes throughout the body. Fat can also act as an insulator, protecting against heat loss and trauma to vital organs.

Carbohydrates, sometimes referred to as 'starch' (in reality just one form of carbohydrate), are of relatively little significance to the cat as a true carnivore and are not present in significant quantities in their natural prey. Mice, for example, are basically comprised of protein and fat, as well as vitamins and minerals. In mammals, any excess carbohydrate is liable to be converted for storage as fat, rather than to starch, as in the case of plants. Carbohydrate, in the form of cereals, can nevertheless be fed to cats and does feature in many prepared foods, but such items should be cooked first to improve their digestibility. Cats rarely accept more than one percent carbohydrate in their diet, unless it is well disguised by fatty food. Carbohydrate in other forms, such as the disaccharide lactose which is present in milk, may prove indigestible to some cats and could result in diarrhoea.

Although only relatively small amounts of vitamins are required, they perform a variety of vital functions within the body. There are two types of vitamin: fat-soluble, which can be stored in the body; and water-soluble which cannot. Deficiencies, as well as excesses in some circumstances, can have serious consequences. The cat is known to require at least 13 vitamins, out of which Vitamin A is probably most significant. Cats need relatively high levels of this vitamin, which assists in promoting healthy eyesight and maintaining the integrity of body surfaces against infective agents. Whereas other animals can convert the precursor, carotene, present in plant matter, to Vitamin A, cats must have the actual vitamin present in their food. A deficiency is liable to lead to blindness especially at night, poor skin condition and reproductive failure.

Liver is a particularly rich source of this vitamin. However, it can in fact be harmful for this reason, when it is fed on a regular daily basis causing an excess which results in a condition called hypervitaminosis A. Cats thus affected are likely to show signs of lameness in the forelimbs, which results from changes in the cervical vertebrae of the neck, or even in the limbs themselves. Abnormal bone development occurs and ultimately joints may become fused together, restricting normal movement accordingly. The actual development of the disease is not clearly understood at present, but the characteristic changes can be identified by radiology, showing up clearly on the resulting X-rays. It is also possible to measure the Vitamin A level present in blood plasma.

Vitamin D3 is another significant member of the group of fat-soluble vitamins which are stored in the body, and is found typically in the liver. It is responsible for controlling the levels of calcium and phosphorus, which are especially vital for bone development. A deficiency of Vitamin D3 gives rise to the condition known as rickets, where the limbs appear bowed because the long bones have become distorted during their development. It is most apparent in young animals; in skeletally mature individuals, inadequate Vitamin D3 causes the bones to become fragile and fracture easily. This disease is referred to as osteomalacia.

The vitamin itself can be manufactured naturally in the skin, from a precursor substance which is known as 7-dehydrocholesterol, under the influence of the ultraviolet component of sunlight, but fish oils are also a valuable direct source of D3. The correct ratio of Vitamin A to Vitamin D3 in a cat's diet should be 10 to one. Problems over the vitamin content of the diet are, however, only likely to arise if the cat is being fed on fresh foods.

Vitamin E is the other member of the fat-soluble group and, contrary to popular belief, does not appear to improve fertility in the feline. It does, however, have an important role in muscle function, and can be inactivated by the presence of fish liver oils.

The water-soluble vitamins include the Vitamin B group, particularly important in metabolic reactions and often acting in association with enzymes. Thiamin, also known as Vitamin B1, is present in large quantities in yeast, and supplementary tablets can be offered directly to cats, or sprinkled over their food. This is often recommended when feeding fresh items such as raw fish, since a deficiency can arise under these circumstances. The other vitamin of particular significance is Vitamin K, which is closely involved in the blood-clotting process. Prolonged antibiotic therapy can destroy the bacteria present in the gut which produce this vitamin, predisposing the animal to haemorrhages. Supplementation of Vitamin K given intravenously at first, will also be necessary in cases of Warfarin poisoning. Cats, unlike humans and guinea pigs, can manufacture their own Vitamin C, and so are not at risk from scurvy.

The minerals of main importance to the cat are calcium and phosphorus, which should be present in a ratio of about one to one: any imbalance is harmful. In some fresh foods, typically offal, this ratio can widen dramatically, to perhaps one to 50 in liver. Kittens, with their developing skeletal structures, are most at risk from a deficiency of calcium. Initial signs may simply be lethargy and mild lameness, which progress to gross bone abnormalities over a relatively short period unless treated. The condition, referred to as osteodystrophia fibrosa, can still occur in kittens given milk, since the relative imbalance of the two minerals may not be corrected. It is most likely to occur in kittens fed on meat alone, but can be simply prevented by adding calcium carbonate to their food, at a level of 8 grains per 3½ oz (0.5g per 100g) of meat.

Magnesium assumes greater significance for the older cat, especially neutered toms. High levels may indirectly predispose the animal to the serious condition of urolithasis, particularly when fluid intake is reduced. Iodine deficiency can occur in cats fed exclusively on meat, while too much manganese can result in a darker fur in the case of partial albinos like Siamese. Such problems, however, are extremely unlikely to arise when the cat is fed a well-balanced diet.

GRASS AND CATMINT Most cats will consume grass from time to time given the opportunity, although the reason for this behaviour is obscure. It has been suggested either that the grass acts as a purgative, assisting the passage of fur balls through the digestive tract, or that it simply adds roughage to the diet. On occasions, grass may induce vomiting; sometimes roundworms will be present. Cats kept permanently indoors and deprived of grass may start eating houseplants, possibly with dire consequences because many can prove poisonous. As a substitute, it is possible to purchase the grass seeds and other necessary items in the form of a kit to grow indoors. These are available from larger pet stores; as an alternative, lawn grass seed or even oats can be sown in a pot or tray, kept watered in a warm, dark spot such as an airing cupboard until the seedlings start to appear, and then transferred to the light. Once the shoots are well developed the tray can be placed on the floor for the cat.

One particular favourite plant of cats is catmint (*Nepeta mussinii*), also known as catnip, which can be easily grown either in pots or a garden. The chemical present in the plant, to which the majority of cats respond, is called nepetalactone, and, although not addictive, it appears to induce a transitory sense of well-being in both wild and domestic felids. Toys impregnated with this compound are also marketed, and have a similar effect.

Types of food
PREPARED FOOD The simplest and most satisfactory option for the majority of owners is to feed their cats on canned food, which has now been marketed for over a quarter of a century. The contents of the cans do vary significantly, however, and some only contain a single ingredient such as sardines. These 'speciality' items do not constitute a balanced diet; if in doubt, the labelling of the can should be checked for the contents. At present the situation in Britain is not as clearcut as it is in the United States, where descriptions such as 'balanced', 'complete' or 'scientific' on the labels of canned cat food ensure the contents include all the necessary ingredients to keep a cat in good health from weaning onwards. Many cans of complete cat food are flavoured, and a 'pilchard variety' should not be confused with a product which clearly states that it is composed entirely of pilchard.

Manufacturers have gone to considerable expense to formulate and prepare balanced rations for cats. This market in Britain alone is now worth 225 million pounds per annum for canned products. During recent years, however, the supremacy of the can has been challenged by both semi-moist and dry cat foods. While canned diets are more expensive, they do have the advantage of being generally more palatable, as they are relatively high in both fat and animal protein. It may prove difficult to transfer a cat from canned to dry food, although this depends on the individual concerned. A gradual, rather than sudden change is to be recommended. At least a fortnight should be allowed when introducing dried food so the cat has a chance to become accustomed to it.

The semi-moist products are the most recent innovation in the marketing of cat foods and contain significant levels of vegetable protein, augmented with essential nutrients. These brands appear quite succulent and contain about 20 percent water, compared to 75 to 80 percent in the case of canned food. They are treated chemically to maintain their moisture level. Especially for young cats, however, semi-moist food may not be entirely adequate to support their growth and milk must certainly be provided daily as a supplement. The provision of some fresh or canned food on a regular basis will also be beneficial, ensuring that the right level of nutrition is maintained.

Dried cat foods are the ultimate in convenience for the owner but, with only 10 percent water present, are the least palatable of the three types of prepared food and cannot be regarded as a complete diet on their own. Fluid, typically water or milk, must be constantly available to cats fed dried diets and the amount consumed should be monitored. Cats in the wild do not drink large quantities, obtaining most of their fluid intake directly from their prey, and may not readily adapt to drinking the equivalent of a large cupful daily to balance their fluid intake on dry food. Some brands had relatively high levels of magnesium included at first but these have now been lowered, since it has been shown that this might lead to urolithasis, especially if the accompanying fluid intake is low. In this condition, the magnesium crystallizes in the urinary tract as magensium ammonium phosphate, with extremely serious consequences for the cat.

In order to encourage cats fed dried food to drink adequately, manufacturers include a salt level of three percent in such products, which also serves to increase the food's palatability. The expanded pelleted forms of dried food are most acceptable, since the higher temperatures used during production gelatinizes the starch present making it more digestible. Fat is then sprayed on directly, increasing the appeal of this type of pellet, which might otherwise not be accepted.

Wild cats *(ABOVE)* kill to ensure a constant supply of fresh meat. All cats are naturally carnivorous in their feeding habits and will usually choose meat, if it is available. In domesticity, although cats preserve many of the habits of the wild *(RIGHT)*, stalking and killing birds, for instance, a balanced diet is essential. This should contain the necessary mixture of proteins, minerals, fats and vitamins required for good health. Even raw steak, if fed exclusively, will be insufficient, since it lacks certain key minerals and vitamins, such as calcium and Vitamin A.

FRESH FOOD Fresh food is readily taken by the majority of cats, but must never be regarded as a complete, balanced diet. Indeed, a cat fed exclusively on expensive steak will suffer, despite the expense, compared to one receiving a formulated canned ration. Steak is low in Vitamin A, calcium and iodine; liver, enjoyed by many cats, is an excellent source of many vitamins, but can also promote hypervitaminosis A if fed to excess. Cooked lites, another popular cat food which consists of lungs, often pigs' lungs, proves low in protein.

Feeding fish exclusively can also result in dietary imbalances. An enzyme known as thiaminase present in raw fish destroys Vitamin B1 and may cause a deficiency. Typical signs are of ill-thrift and poor appetite. The terminal stages are preceded by fits, leading to prostration and death. Recovery can be dramatic, however, within a few hours following an injection of thiamin. When fish is cooked, the thiaminase is destroyed.

When preparing fish, check that it is adequately filleted, with all bones removed. Although cats are more fastidious in their eating habits than dogs, they can accidentally ingest bones, which may then become lodged in the throat or lower down the digestive tract. Chicken bones are likely to be equally hazardous.

Excess fish oils in a cat's diet lead to steatitis, also known as yellow fat disease because of the distinctive colour change in the body's fat deposits. Vitamin E is likely to be deficient in such cases and forms part of the treatment. Affected cats may appear superficially in good condition, but show loss of agility, often preferring to remain in one place, and resent being touched. Their temperature will be elevated, and appetite declines in the latter stages. Young cats are especially susceptible to steatitis, but the disease does not occur when canned complete fish foods are fed, because the Vitamin E level is adjusted accordingly. A similar condition will result from feeding horseflesh on a regular basis.

It is important to establish a regular eating routine for a cat as early as possible*(RIGHT)*. Cats can be fussy feeders and are easily put off their foods by noise, strong light, other people and even other cats. Since they are clean animals, they are also sensitive to cleanliness; a cat's food bowl should be washed regularly with detergent and then rinsed thoroughly to remove any aftertaste, which may well discourage the cat from eating. As far as actual food is concerned, cats become creatures of habit from early on, so they should be introduced to a selection of foods as quickly as possible and never allowed to become addicted to, say, a single brand of cat meat. Meal times, too, should be fixed.

While it is preferable to cook some fresh foods, overcooking reduces the vitamin value itself. Cats will readily take raw foods such as beef mince, although there is a slight risk of transmitting some diseases, including toxoplasmosis, by this route; poultry, pig-meat and offal should never be offered uncooked for this reason. Eggs, a valuable source of both fat and protein, must also be cooked because biotin, a member of the Vitamin B group, is destroyed in the presence of raw egg white. Once hard-boiled, eggs are quite safe and can be cut up for feeding; eggs can also be scrambled with butter and milk, in the same way as for human consumption. Milk can be given directly, although it should be allowed to warm up for a few minutes if it has been kept refrigerated.

Providing sufficient variety to prevent significant nutritional shortcomings is essential when cats are fed exclusively on fresh food. While the work involved in preparation makes it a tedious task for the average cat-owner on a daily basis, feeding fresh food can prove most economical for those catering for relatively large numbers of cats. As a compromise, it is possible to obtain blocks of fresh food from many larger pet stores. These must be kept refrigerated and, again, do not constitute a balanced diet on their own, but are precooked and can be fed directly. Beef and chicken are marketed in this way.

A practical diet

Canned food, supplemented with fresh food given once or twice a week, will keep a cat in peak condition throughout its life. This diet can also be varied with semi-moist or dried foods at regular intervals. It is sensible to persuade a cat to take all such items. Cats can prove very fussy eaters, and will starve themselves rather than sample unfamiliar food later in life. Some individuals are much worse in this respect than others, and conditioning from an early age is certainly significant in this respect. A cat fed on one particular brand of canned food for much of its life may be very reluctant to try another and is likely to ignore the drier foods completely. Such preferences extend to fresh items as well. Fish, popularly regarded as being a favourite food, is not greedily accepted by all cats.

Fresh milk should be offered on a daily basis, providing it does not cause diarrhoea. (Any digestive disturbances of this nature must be taken seriously, particularly in a young cat, since infective agents are more likely to be implicated than the inability to digest the lactose component of the milk.) The cream at the top of a bottle is best, since fat is more concentrated here, but homogenized milk is also quite acceptable. A small amount of cheese can also be offered occasionally as a substitute for milk. Water must be constantly available, irrespective of the diet, although little may be drunk in the majority of cases. Indeed, when cats do drink, they often choose a stale source of water, such as a fish pond or puddle. No evidence exists, however, to suggest that they deliberately ignore domestic water supplies which are chlorinated. The chlorine at any rate comes out of solution after the water has been standing for 24 hours or so.

Various vitamin and mineral supplements are marketed for cats, in several forms. Care must be taken over using such additives, especially when the diet is based on a complete food because excessive intake of fat-soluble vitamins, in particular, can have severe consequences. If in doubt, veterinary advice should be sought. Supplements are often of value to breeding queens and their kittens; there are others on the market which, when used on the food, may tempt a sick or geriatric cat to start eating. Vitamin supplementation assumes greater importance in old cats, where failing kidneys may cause a net deficiency of the water-soluble group through excessive losses in the urine.

FREQUENCY AND QUANTITY A kitten under six months of age will need four or five meals a day, which can be reduced to three by the age of nine months. In the natural state, adult cats only eat perhaps once a day, but under domestic conditions, they are normally fed twice daily, morning and evening. Breeding queens need perhaps four meals per day because, like kittens, they cannot consume enough at one time to meet their body requirements.

The amount of food consumed at one meal varies quite widely, according to the individual cat and its physiological state. Kittens obviously eat a good deal when they are growing whereas the appetites of older, sedentary cats are correspondingly smaller. The guidelines set out by the

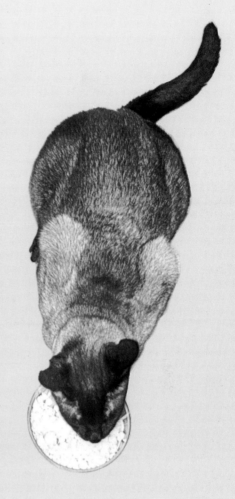

Cats vary in the amount of food they require *(ABOVE)*. The chart *(BELOW)* is based on the findings of the National Research Council and shows amounts of alternative types of food needed by cats at different ages. Dry food contains 90 percent dry matter; semi-moist 70 percent and canned 25 percent. Quantities are given in metric measurements for accuracy.

Type of cat	Weight of cat in kg	Dry food		Semi-moist food		Canned food	
		g/kg of body weight	g/cat	g/kg of body weight	g/cat	g/kg of body weight	g/cat
Kitten							
10 weeks	0.4-1.0	70	28-70	80	32-80	200	80-200
20 weeks	1.2-2.0	36	43-72	42	50-84	104	125-208
30 weeks	1.5-2.7	28	42-76	32	48-86	80	120-216
40 weeks	2.2-3.8	22	48-84	26	57-99	64	141-243

Type of cat	Weight of cat in kg	Dry food		Semi-moist food		Canned food	
		g/kg of body weight	g/cat	g/kg of body weight	g/cat	g/kg of body weight	g/cat
Adult							
Active	2.2-4.5	20	44-90	22	48-99	56	123-252
Inactive	2.2-4.5	24	53-108	27	59-122	68	150-306
Gestation	2.5-4.0	28	70-112	32	80-128	80	200-320
Lactation	2.5-4.0	70	154-280	80	176-320	200	440-800

manufacturer on the package or can should be followed in the case of prepared foods, while with high-protein fresh foods such as mince, a similar allowance in terms of weight to that recommended on cans should prove adequate. Only a relatively small amount of dry food is necessary.

Obesity is not as common in the cat as the dog, because of the higher intake of protein and fat at the expense of carbohydrate. Fat in particular slows the emptying time of the stomach, acting as a control on appetite stimulus. Neutered cats are more prone to obesity than intact animals because of hormonal changes and a less active lifestyle, but with sensible care, this need not present any problems. Certain breeds have acquired reputations for being relatively big eaters, and the Bombay is typical of this group.

Some owners leave food available throughout the day, so the cat can return to it at will. While this does not seem to encourage excessive eating, in hot weather the food will probably serve to attract flies, especially if it is fresh or from a can; milk also rapidly sours under such conditions. Cats will ignore both items once they are no longer fresh, and these will then have to be discarded. When food is constantly accessible, cats also tend to become more finicky, picking at favoured items in small amounts. This can become a problem when cats have to be boarded. Feeding may well be followed here by the general removal of dishes several hours later, so these cats will not then have had their normal daily intake. Set mealtimes are therefore preferable for all adult cats.

Once a can has been opened, it should be stored between meals in a refrigerator, as must fresh food. Bowls used for feeding need to be washed thoroughly, with adequate detergent to remove all grease and then rinsed, ready for the

Cats should not be fed outdoors especially when fresh food is being offered (TOP). Otherwise, flies will be attracted to the food bowl, bringing the risk of disease with them. Milk, in particular, will sour rapidly in hot weather and should not be left outside in the sun. Scavenging (ABOVE) should be similarly discouraged, since cats pick up diseases and parasites from rotting foods. Cats do eat grass, although the precise reason for this is not known, but care must be taken to ensure they do not consume any plants that may be poisonous (RIGHT).

next meal. They must always be cleaned separately and kept apart from normal domestic utensils. Just prior to the next feed, the meat or fish should be allowed to warm up briefly, since cats will not readily accept cold foods. They normally eat their prey at its body temperature as soon as they catch it, before the carcass has cooled significantly.

LOSS OF APPETITE A cat may lose its appetite for various reasons, which include dirty bowls or stale food. Discreet enquiries may, in fact, reveal that its appetite is quite healthy, and that it is also being fed by a neighbour. The cat might have stolen another cat's meal, entering through a cat flap to find food available. A transient disinterest in food is also quite common during the breeding season, with intact toms often losing considerable weight during this period if they are living wild. There are various medical causes for loss of appetite, ranging from a sore mouth to various infections which need veterinary attention.

Training
Housetraining
Having adopted its dirt tray, the kitten should continue using it regularly without problems. If an accident does occur elsewhere in the room, there is no point in punishing the young cat. It will not understand the reason for its harsh treatment; this will only encourage sly behaviour and a lack

Mother cats start toilet training their kittens around the age of three weeks. Licking the anal region after a meal (ABOVE) encourages the kittens to urinate and defecate. A litter tray should be provided for the kittens from around two and a half weeks; otherwise they will establish their own location, a habit that may be hard to break. The tray should be filled with a layer of clean, dry, absorbent litter, which should be changed at regular intervals. Do not worry if the kittens paw their faeces; this is perfectly natural as, in the wild, many cats conceal their faeces by burying.

of trust in its owner. After the floor has been soiled, it must be cleaned very thoroughly because the kitten attracted by its own scent may well choose to use the same area again.

A pair of rubber gloves should be kept exclusively for clearing up such mess, to avoid any contamination of the hands with faeces. The affected surface will need to be well washed, preferably with hot water and disinfectant, after any solid matter has been removed. Vinegar can then be applied to descent the area, although this will have to be used carefully, depending on the surface concerned. Chemical preparations for the same purpose can be purchased from many pet stores as an alternative. Shampoo applied to soiled carpeting, or a scented polish on furniture are other safe alternatives.

Most kittens are taught by their mothers to be clean, and it is quite natural for them to attempt to bury their faeces by scraping litter over them. Orphaned kittens are liable to prove more of a problem to housetrain successfully, but cats are clean creatures by nature. It is important to discover why a kitten is refusing to use a dirt tray, particularly if this happens repeatedly. A previously soiled box has already been mentioned as a possible cause, but if the dirt tray is unused, then its positioning could be wrong. Moving the box to a more secluded spot may resolve the problem. Alternatively, a second box can be placed elsewhere in the room. If the kitten suffers from diarrhoea, and simply failed to reach the box, veterinary treatment will be necessary.

Older cats will, on occasions, deliberately soil their surroundings with urine. Such behaviour is most likely to be encountered in intact males, but also occurs to a lesser extent in queens on heat. This habit is known as spraying and serves to mark the animal's territory. Neutered cats of either sex will only spray very rarely, when threatened or nervous, perhaps if a new individual is introduced.

There is no really effective deterrant for spraying; it is partly for this reason that cats not intended for breeding should be neutered early in life. Thorough cleaning of the soiled area to remove all trace of scent will be necessary. In order to protect a specific part of a room against spraying, the cat should be fed as close as possible to the sprayed area: cats will rarely soil close to where they eat. Apart from having to live with the pungent odour, leaving the soiled surface uncleaned will not deter future spraying to reinforce the remaining scent.

While a litter tray is essential, a cat flap may or may not be required depending on whether the cat is to be allowed outside. Cat flaps are particularly convenient, however, allowing the cat to come and go at will. They should be fitted with a latch to allow them to be secured at night.

Once the cat can be allowed out of doors safely, it should be introduced to the cat flap and taught to use it. Persuading a cat to use a swinging door of this type will require patience, because the animal will be frightened of being caught going through the flap itself. At first the hinged unit must be fixed back firmly, leaving just an entrance hole visible. The cat should be encouraged to enter and leave its home via this route. The next stage is to lower the flap partially, holding it in position by means of a stick. The cat inside should then be called through the hatch by placing a plate of milk, for example, on the ground just outside the flap as a lure. With the house door closed, it should not be too difficult to persuade the cat to venture forth through the flap. This procedure will then have to be repeated in the reverse direction, so the cat feels confident about returning back into the home through the flap. It will soon use its paw to push a cat door which hinges outwards, if this is propped open at first. Cats must always be encouraged to come in at night if they are allowed out during the day, so the flap can be closed.

Simple tricks

A cat will certainly learn to identify with its name, particularly if this is both simple and distinct. Kittens are much more responsive to training, and will soon come when they are called. To teach a kitten its name, call it before each meal, so that the sound will begin to be associated with the pleasurable sensation of food. In these early stages, the inquisitive natures of many kittens will ensure a ready response, which can be reinforced by paying a lot of attention to the cat every time it responds to a call.

While getting a cat to respond to its name is really an essential part of ownership, it is also possible to teach several other lessons without difficulty. A common trick is to instruct a cat to beg for food by holding a favoured item just out of reach above its head. The cat will then reach up of its own accord to take the morsel, which must be given to it as a reward. Although this may have to be repeated quite often at first, cats soon learn such procedures and then need no further prompting to recall the routine when the situation presents itself again.

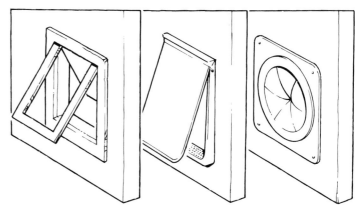

A cat can be trained to urinate and defecate outdoors quite easily, but in such cases it is important to provide it with a means of access. Cat flaps *(ABOVE)* are an ideal solution. All work on the same principle of allowing the cat to push through a swinging flap. Some models, however, are activated by a small magnet hung on the cat's collar.

This means that the flap cannot be opened by stray cats, or followers, if the cat is courting. The mother cat can play a vital part in this training; her kittens learn from observing her, as in the case of climbing stairs *(BELOW)*. Otherwise keep the flap raised until the kitten has got used to going through it and only then lower it.

Grooming

A kitten should become accustomed to being groomed by its owner from an early age, although cats do spend a significant part of their day licking and grooming themselves. While longhairs must be groomed daily, shorthaired cats only require such treatment once or twice a week unless they are moulting; excessive grooming may deter them from caring for their own coat. Prior to a show, grooming and perhaps even bathing will be necessary; on a mundane level, regular inspection of the coat provides the opportunity to check the cat's overall state of health.

Various tools are available to facilitate the task. A fine-toothed metal flea comb will be essential; some are marketed with a broader comb on the opposite surface as well. Following a thorough combing, a rubber brush will remove any additional loose hairs and will especially improve the appearance of shorthaired cats. If an ordinary brush is used, the bristles should be natural; nylon can damage the hair and create additional static electricity in the coat.

Grooming shorthaired cats is a straightforward procedure. The cat should be stood and restrained with one hand on an even surface, with a sheet of paper beneath. The paper will serve to show up any fleas which may jump off, as well as catching loose debris from the coat. The comb should be passed through the fur, starting around the shoulders or at the base of the neck and drawn backwards towards the tail, working round the whole body. The legs must be groomed as far as possible in a horizontal manner.

Loose fur will accumulate between the teeth of the comb,

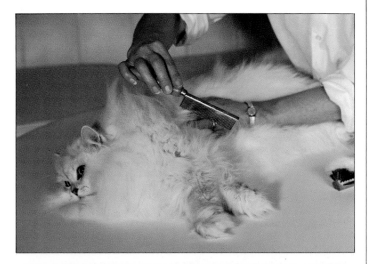

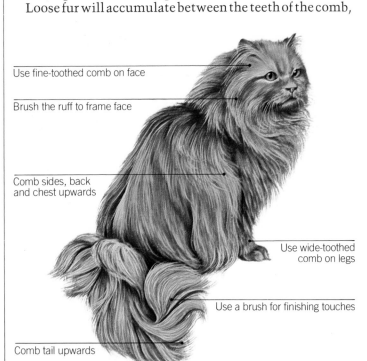

Use fine-toothed comb on face

Brush the ruff to frame face

Comb sides, back and chest upwards

Use wide-toothed comb on legs

Use a brush for finishing touches

Comb tail upwards

All cats required regular grooming, since they all moult to a greater or lesser degree, particularly in the warmer months. Longhaired cats *(RIGHT and ABOVE)* need more careful grooming than their shorthaired counterparts, since their coats quickly become matted if they do not receive daily attention. There is also the risk that fur balls will form in the stomach as a result of the cat's efforts to groom itself. Comb and brush the coat thoroughly, watching for fleas *(TOP RIGHT)*. For shorthaired cats *(FAR RIGHT)*, a rubber brush will remove loose hairs. The tail may need special attention in certain breeds *(CENTRE RIGHT)*.

and should be examined for any sign of flea dirt. Minute dark blackish spots, which are the droppings of the fleas, confirm the presence of these parasites, even if none can be seen.

After use, a comb should be thoroughly cleaned and washed. When any cat is thought to be suffering from ringworm, then it must have its own set of grooming equipment, which is not used on the other cats. Before a show, a cat's coat will benefit from being rubbed with a chamois leather pad.

Longhaired breeds need more rigorous grooming to prevent their coats becoming matted and the fur must be groomed in a different direction. If neglected, the hair can become so tangled that the cat will need to be sedated by a veterinarian in order to remove the mats, which may well have to be cut off. The coats of longhairs are groomed in a vertical direction, upwards towards the back. This causes the hair to stand up, away from the body and serves to emphasize the ruff around the neck. After an initial combing the procedure needs to be repeated with a brush. A crescent-shaped brush is ideal for this purpose, while an old toothbrush can be used around the face. Exceptions include Maine Coons and the Turkish breeds which should be groomed like shorthairs, but on a daily basis.

Moulting occurs mainly in the spring, although shedding may increase for a period just before winter. All cats should be groomed more regularly at this time. When moulting, cats will shed many more hairs than usual, which can lead to the formation of fur balls, especially in longhairs. As the cat licks itself, it will ingest large quantities of loose hair, which can accumulate as a mass in the digestive tract causing a blockage. The fur ball may be vomited successfully, depending on its location, but those which pass lower down the intestines and away from the stomach may cause constipation. A laxative, such as sardines in oil, medicinal or liquid paraffin (which is not the same as combustible paraffin used for heating purposes) given directly on to the food (about a 5ml spoonful twice daily for two days) should ensure any accumulation of fur is passed without difficulty.

Bathing

Most cats dislike water and are content simply to paw at drops falling from a tap. Only the Turkish breeds do not show such an aversion. Rather than wetting the cat's fur, it is better to try other forms of bathing in order to remove excess grease and dirt from the coat. Bran baths are commonly given for this purpose and cats appears to enjoy them. The bran, which is in fact derived from grain husks, can be obtained from many pet stores. Warm it in an oven beforehand and rub it thoroughly into the cat's coat. This will prove a rather messy operation and is best carried out on newspaper outside. Afterwards, groom the coat.

Certain cats produce excessive amounts of grease from sebaceous glands located around the base of the tail, which can give rise to the condition known as stud tail, especially in pedigree toms. The hair in this region becomes matted and unsightly, providing a focus for infections. Veterinary

SELF-GROOMING Cats groom themselves by licking their fur fastidiously.

As cats are so flexible, they have little trouble reaching inaccessible places.

The forelegs will be licked and used to clean the face and head.

GROOMING A SHORTHAIR 1. Stand the cat on a sheet of paper and work carefully through the fur.

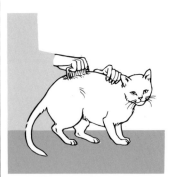

2. Work with the fur, not against it. Start at the shoulder and work towards the tail around the body.

3. Rubbing down with a chamois leather pad brings up the coat and is often done before showing.

GROOMING A LONGHAIR 1. Start by combing vertically upwards towards the back.

2. After combing, brush thoroughly in the same manner. Keep an eye out for flea dirt on the brush.

treatment may be needed but a regular bran bath helps to remove the secretions before serious problems arise.

Other effective dry shampoos include talcum powder and cornflour. These should also be sprinkled on the coat, rubbed in well and then brushed out, finishing with grooming. Talcum powder is especially popular for paler longhaired breeds, such as the White Longhairs.

Show cats may be washed occasionally, using water and a suitable shampoo. Other cats may also need washing if they are infested with parasites; a medicated preparation will be prescribed for treatment. If a cat is likely to require regular bathing at any point in its life, it should be given a wash by the age of six months to lessen its subsequent fear of the ordeal. The task will be easier with two people; the person holding the cat should wear gloves for protection. A large bowl makes the best receptacle, placed on a firm surface. It should be filled with tepid water. Scoop the water over the cat's body, either by hand or using a disposable plastic container such as an old yoghurt carton. Soap the cat with a mild baby shampoo, taking great care to ensure that none actually enters the eyes; this will be extremely distressing to the cat and difficult to rinse out. After washing, the bowl should be emptied and refilled with tepid water so that the cat's coat can be thoroughly rinsed. Once this has been completed, the cat should be wrapped in a towel and dried by hand as far as possible. It must be kept warm until its coat is completely dry and then it can be groomed. Rinsing is not always advised if the shampoo is medicated. In such cases, the instructions must be followed implicitly.

Common Problems
Chewing and scratching

The young cat will have replaced its first set of deciduous or 'milk' teeth by the age of six months. The incisors are renewed first, followed by the canines and finally the premolars. It is quite usual to find discarded teeth on the floor, when the kitten is between the ages of three and six months. A certain amount of accompanying bleeding may also be noticed during this period, but is unlikely to prove serious. The kitten is, however, liable to start chewing objects to ease the discomfort of teething, and will not discriminate sufficiently to avoid gnawing on electrical cables. All appliances within reach must at least be switched off at the power point when not in use, and preferably disconnected.

It is a good idea to provide suitable chewing blocks to discourage damage to household items. The sole of an old shoe is ideal for the purpose, providing there is no risk of pieces being accidentally chewed off and swallowed. Shin bones from cattle are another possible alternative, although these should be checked for any flaking pieces of bone, especially at the ends. The thick chews marketed for dogs also prove acceptable to many kittens. Close supervision or separation will be necessary if there is a dog in the household as well, because jealousies may break out over such items.

Some milk teeth may be swallowed rather than spat out. They are not harmful and pass through the digestive tract without problems. The teething phase normally proceeds

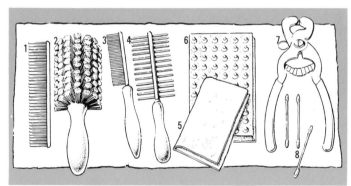

Natural claw control enables a cat to climb (LEFT) and also to catch prey, but scratching to keep the claws sharp can cause considerable damage. It is not necessary to go as far as declawing the cat; regular clipping of the claws and the provision of a scratching post, which the cat is trained to used, should be sufficient. Grooming equipment need not be elaborate (ABOVE). All cats will require a wide-toothed comb (1), a fine-toothed flea comb (3), or a combination wide- and fine-toothed comb (4), a natural bristle brush (2) and cotton buds for cleaning ears (8). For shorthaired cats, a chamois leather (5) and rubber brush (6) are useful. Nail clippers (7) should be used with care.

with no worries, but if the kitten's mouth appears to be getting overcrowded, a veterinary check will be necessary. It is a relatively simple matter to extract any remaining teeth which should have fallen out of their own accord.

Scratching is not, however, a transitory problem in cats, and may result in serious damage if uncontrolled. This activity serves to sharpen the front claws and may help to prevent them becoming overgrown. Scratching is also another way of marking territory. Cats possess sweat glands between their pads, and the exercise afforded by scratching may well promote secretion of a scented marker, which is transferred to the site itself. It is noticeable that cats acquire regular scratching places and do not scratch randomly. The marks also serve as a visual reminder for any other cats in the vicinity.

The undesirable effects of scratching in the home soon become apparent, particularly if the cat is never allowed outdoors. Furniture is most commonly assaulted in this way, but even thick rugs on the floor cannot be considered immune. Providing a kitten with its own scratching post from an early age is to be recommended. The post does not need to be an elaborate structure, just a piece of softwood about 3in (7.5cm) square and 2ft (60cm) or more in height, mounted vertically on a sound base. A piece of bark or thick matting nailed on to one face of the wood increases the appeal of the post. Scenting the wood by rubbing the crushed leaves of catmint over it is likely to attract the cat's attention. A kitten should be introduced to a scratching site by gently raising its front feet off the ground and positioning them against the wood. It should soon start to scratch here of its own accord. With older cats, any items which have been scratched previously should be removed to divert attention to the new site.

Cats can inflict considerable damage in the garden by scratching the trunks of fruit trees or shrubs. If this occurs, a protective tube of wire mesh should be staked into the ground around the bush by means of canes. Providing the mesh is set several inches away from the bark itself and does not come into contact with it, further scratching at this site will be prevented.

DECLAWING (ONYCHECTOMY) Certain cats are more destructive with their claws than others. To remedy this, a declawing operation known as an onychectomy can be carried out to actually remove the claws. This is more common in the United States than elsewhere: more cats are kept indoors on a permanent basis where not only can they cause more damage, but they are also less handicapped following an onychectomy. Nevertheless, there is considerable opposition to such surgery, both from many veterinarians and from within the ranks of the cat fancy itself. The CFA and most other American associations, as well as the GCCF in Britain, refuse to accept declawed cats in any exhibition class.

Without doubt, the operation does handicap the cat. For this reason, only the claws on the front feet are generally removed. This is not the same as removing dew claws from puppies; dew claws are vestigial, and serve no purpose. They may, in fact, hinder the dog, causing it injury if the nails get caught. Cats, however, are very dependent on their claws both to climb effectively and to catch their prey. Although when fighting seriously, cats bite their opponents, the preceding baring of claws and preliminary sparring may well deter a potential aggressor. Once a cat has been declawed it is not well adapted to roam free out-of-doors. Considerable thought on the part of the owner is required to justify what may be cosmetic surgery.

The operation should preferably be carried out only when the cat is about four months old, when it will adapt better to the handicap. An onychectomy requires a general anaesthetic and the feet will be sensitive for a week or so afterwards. Providing all the claw and associated tissue is removed, there is no likelihood of any regrowth at a later date. A much less drastic alternative is to have the cat's claws cut regularly by a vet. so that the sharp ends are removed; this, coupled with a scratching post, should be adequate in the majority of cases.

Hunting

The hunting instinct in domestic cats remains strong, even in individuals which are adequately fed, often much to the

HUNTING BEHAVIOUR Domestic cats are still predators and, even though fed well and regularly, will naturally hunt for prey. The kitten learns hunting skills from its mother — at first in play — and soon puts them into practice. Through play, the kitten stimulates its natural inquisitiveness. It learns how to coordinate its movements and how to climb, run, spring and pounce. These skills are not only valuable in hunting, but are also important in territory keeping.

Cats are very agile and alert creatures, a result of both the adaptation of their musculoskeletal system and their brain development. A flexible skeleton enables them to stretch their bodies into a wide range of postures and an efficient nervous system gives them excellent reactions. The natural hunting instincts of the cat are always in evidence, even in play *(ABOVE)*. Objects such as catnip mice will be stalked and pounced; insects such as butterflies may even be caught.

distress of their owners. Small rodents, especially mice, and birds, are favoured prey. Kittens are taught to hunt by their mothers; some prove more adept than others in acquiring this skill. Hunting ability appears to be inherited to a certain degree; for controlling a plague of mice, acquire a kitten from a dam who is herself a good hunter. Perhaps not surprisingly, farm stock is much sought-after for this purpose.

Cats are extremely patient hunters, and are content to remain motionless for long periods near a mouse hole, waiting for an unsuspecting animal to emerge. Their approach when preying on birds is different; stalking assumes greater importance than waiting. In either case, however, the final pounce must be precisely timed to catch the creature unawares. Whenever possible, the forelegs alone are used to grab the prey, while the hindlimbs remain on the ground for stability. The killing blow is a bite on the back of the creature's neck — the long canines penetrate and cut the spinal cord precisely between two vertebrae. The whiskers have an important sensory function in locating the vulnerable spot; if they are cut or otherwise damaged, the cat may have difficulty in killing its prey. Larger prey can present more of a problem and are likely to be pounded first by the feet until the cat achieves its deadly grip on the animal's neck.

Cats are notorious for playing with their prey, especially small mammals like mice. The shocked, disorientated rodent will be released and allowed to run for a short distance before being leapt upon again. It is poked and prodded into further activity, until it either dies of shock or is finally dispatched by its captor. Even then, the cat may continue playing with the corpse, tossing it into the air before actually consuming it.

Depending on the animal concerned, the cat will eat part or all of the body. Mice are typically swallowed whole, head first, being chewed in the process. Their fur will not stick in the throat when ingested in this manner. Feathers, however, are often torn from a bird, which has a thinner skin. Most of the body is consumed, although the legs and skeleton are usually left. Unfortunately, a cat will often return home carrying prey in its mouth for its owner. The cat is identifying with its owner as a member of the colony, who will want to share the kill. The offering should be taken gracefully, and the cat itself rewarded with food.

It may sometimes be possible to rescue a live bird from a cat. Unfortunately the bacteria present in the mouth of cats tend to be noxious to other species; a bird may well die from a *Pasturella* infection introduced by the cat's teeth, even though the initial injury itself appeared relatively slight. In addition, certain birds are more likely to succumb from shock than others, with starlings dying much more readily than pigeons. Handling the rescued bird should be kept to a minimum, and it must be transferred to a closed darkened box lined with paper tissue while advice on its care can be sought either from a veterinarian or a wild bird welfare organization. The number of birds caught by cats rises significantly during the fledgling season, when a large number of unsuspecting young birds emerge from their nests.

Preventing cats from hunting is virtually impossible, and their instinct is reinforced by successive captures. There are nevertheless several steps which can be taken to reduce the chances of the cat making a successful kill. Birds, for example, should only be fed in the open, where a cat cannot creep up on them unnoticed. Nesting boxes need to be placed in similarly secure locations. Some owners attach small bells to their cats' collars, warning birds of their movements. Studies show that the odds favour the prey, however; even experienced cats catch less than 10 percent of the birds which they actually stalk. Older, or sick individuals are most likely to be taken throughout the years, and in this way, the cat helps to ensure that the overall population remains healthy, and has an adequate supply of food. The role of felids in maintaining the overall ecosystem of an area is, of course, particularly apparent in Africa, where the big cats prey on the herbivorous creatures, and thus exert a control on their numbers.

Other behaviour problems

Some cats, notably Siamese, are great climbers and in the home they may knock over ornaments in the process. The only solution in such instances is to remove all loose ornaments from the room, and invest in a protective cabinet for any valuable pieces.

Certain cats have the annoying habit of pounding repeatedly up and down with their claws extended on their owner's lap, prior to settling down. This behaviour extends back into kittenhood, with the movement originally stimulating milk flow in the dam. A piece of thick material laid over one's knees should prevent scratching but claws can also become caught up on chair covers, causing damage. Most cats will tread lightly before settling down on a soft area, but when such behaviour is carried to excess a blanket should be placed on the chair to prevent damage to the underlying cover. If the cat starts dribbling once it has settled and is purring contentedly there may be some inflammation in the mouth and this should be checked accordingly.

Moving Cats

Cats can become distressed when being moved from place to place, especially if they are unused to travelling. Show cats are likely to travel a good deal during their lives, and all cats will need to be taken to a veterinary surgery or boarding cattery at some stage. For this reason, it can be helpful to let them experience the sensation from an early age, perhaps by taking them out in a car occasionally. In the case of a persistently bad traveller, a veterinarian may prescribe a suitable sedative. Under no circumstances should any cat be left in a vehicle with the windows closed on a sunny day, because death from hyperthermia, or overheating, may well result.

Carriers

A cat should be confined in a secure carrying box or basket to move it from place to place. Although a cat may be very amenable to handling in its normal surroundings, it is liable to become very upset when travelling, and can scratch or even bite before escaping from its owner. During a visit to a veterinary surgery, for example, cats often become scared by the other animals present and will run off given the slightest opportunity. It is a good idea to get the kitten accustomed to its travelling box regularly from an early age. This makes future journeys less distressing, and also avoids the unpleasant task of having to remove a spitting, scratching cat from the back of its basket, either in a veterinary surgery or boarding kennel. Such cats, as their owners point out apologetically, are not usually vicious,

but just very scared of being confined and moved in a box.

It is well worth buying a special carrier for the cat, because makeshift containers often prove inadequate. Cardboard boxes tied up with string fall into this latter category, as cats can escape without difficulty, simply by pulling a flap down with a paw and then squeezing out. In an emergency, wooden orange boxes, which can be closed firmly by means of wire loops, are preferable.

Special cardboard carriers for cats can be purchased from larger pet stores and are cheap yet relatively safe. They are sold flat with ventilation holes already punched out, and

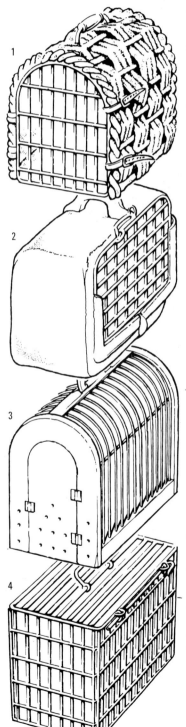

Cats are keen climbers. While climbing outdoors is unlikely to cause any difficulties for the cat — cats rarely become stranded up trees — in the home such behaviour can lead to damage. The cat may rip curtains or furnishings with its claws if allowed to climb freely; it may well scratch if allowed to climb over people (ABOVE). Attempts to dislodge the cat will only encourage it to increase its grip. Cat scratches can be very painful, so it is better to discourage this behaviour from the outset. There are a number of different types of carriers and baskets designed for moving cats from place to place (LEFT). For durability, wicker (1) and fibreglass (2) baskets are preferable. Metal carriers with mesh fronts (3) are easy to clean and disinfect. A wire basket (4), open on all sides, has good ventilation. All baskets must provide adequate space and air. Line the base of the carrier with newspaper or bedding.

BOARDING When selecting a cattery for a cat, always choose one that is licensed and recommended by a breeder, veterinarian, or reliable friend. If you have the time, visit it yourself before confirming a booking — advance booking is usually necessary in any case, particularly during the busy holiday season. The first test of a good cattery is whether or not you are asked for certificates to show that your cat has been innoculated against the common cat ailments, particularly cat flu . The chief risk to your cat and the others in the cattery may well be cross-infection, which is obviously heightened if proof of innoculation is not demanded. The cat houses should be clean, airy and, together with the runs, spaced well apart to minimize the risk of infection *(CENTRE LEFT)*. Ideally, every cat should have its own enclosure, which should be well wired to be escape-proof *(BELOW LEFT)*. Check that interior conditions, too, are hygienic *(ABOVE LEFT)* and look for the little extras, such as heating lamps *(ABOVE RIGHT)*, which show that the cattery has the welfare of your cat at heart. When you take your cat to the cattery, it may well by unhappy and unsettled at first *(FAR LEFT)*. This is primarily due to lack of familiarity with the territory, since cats rarely pine, and the majority of them adjust within a few days.

once folded into shape have no loose flaps to give a possible exit. Particular attention should be given to the base though, which will collapse if the folding is incorrectly carried out or if the cat is heavy. There should be a cardboard liner to fit inside the carrier, and it is a good idea to add paper on top of this because if the base becomes wet the cardboard will rapidly disintegrate. As an additional precaution, string can be tied round the box, passing through the handle, once the cat is inside. These carriers are not suitable for repeated use, as they may be scratched and weakened by the cat.

Wicker baskets prove a much safer alternative, although straps on the doors can wear and break especially if the ties are plastic rather than leather. Designs with metal rods for holding the door shut are preferable for this reason. The door may be located either at the front or at the top of the basket. The latter are easier to use because the cat can be simply lifted into the basket and the lid swiftly closed, whereas it may need to be bundled, sometimes with difficulty, into a basket with a door at the front. As with all carrying containers, these baskets should be lined with a thick layer of paper, because the cat may well urinate or defecate during the journey if it is upset.

Plastic or fibreglass cat carriers are expensive, but can always be cleaned more easily than the wicker type, using a hose if necessary. This factor may be particularly important when moving cats to and from shows or a veterinary surgery, where diseases can be picked up and brought home to other cats. Closed boxes offer a greater sense of security than all-wire models, which are coated with a layer of epoxy resin giving them a white, shiny finish.

Holiday Periods

Cats are never as much trouble as dogs over a holiday period, particularly if a friend or neighbour can be persuaded to call in and feed them daily. One of the major advantages of dried food is that a quantity can be put out, and will not deteriorate like fresh or canned food. There should always be adequate water available, and milk, although this tends to sour in hot conditions. When provided with a cat flap, the outdoor cat will hardly notice the absence of its family, although it will miss their companionship and may wander further afield as a result.

The obvious drawback of leaving a cat on its own with someone calling in to feed it, is that it may fall ill or be involved in an accident without the owner's knowledge. For this reason, it is safest to keep the cat permanently inside with a litter tray, and ask its temporary mentor to attend to this as well. If the owner supplies canned food, then a suitable can-opener should be left readily available, along with other items such as litter and the feeding bowls. The name, address and telephone number of the veterinarian where the cat is registered should be written on a piece of paper and displayed prominently, in case of emergencies.

Some owners like to take their cats on holiday with them whenever possible. There may, however, be restrictions on the movement of such animals, especially from country to country, making this impractical for many holiday-makers. Cats returning to Britain, for example, are required to undergo an obligatory six months' quarantine in special premises. Advice on this aspect of moving cats should be obtained from the Department of Agriculture in Britain, or a similar body in the country concerned.

Cats should never be allowed to wander free while on holiday, but are best kept in a small pen unless someone is present. If by any chance a cat escapes and does not return, as is likely in a strange environment, then the holiday will probably be ruined. Cats travelling in this way should always have an identification tag on them, so that if they do disappear by accident it will be possible for the finder to contact the owner. Cats which will accept a harness and lead can be exercised, preferably in quiet surroundings where there are no dogs in the vicinity. Once a cat has been scared, it will be hazardous to try and pick it up immediately, and it should be encouraged to walk back to safety whenever possible. If you do attempt to pick it up, it will probably scratch or bite.

Boarding

Catteries provide the most obvious means of coping with a cat over a holiday period, but they should be approached with initial caution. In Britain there are licensing requirements for such institutions, but no standardized system of management or fees. It is therefore advisable to seek out a boarding cattery well in advance of the holiday period. As a rule, most satisfied owners return to the same cattery with their pets each year, which may leave few vacancies during peak holiday time, such as Christmas, Easter and during the summer.

Recommendations for catteries can be sought from breeders or friends, or even a veterinarian. It would be unfair to ask a vet for comments on a particular establishment, but a recommendation can generally be accepted without worry. If time is short, however, it may be necessary to refer to the telephone book, in which case, consideration of the following points may give a guide to the standard of the cattery concerned. All catteries should insist on seeing vaccination certificates for every cat. Those which ignore this precaution are likely to have lower standards; cat flu outbreaks will almost certainly occur on such premises where large numbers of cats are constantly moving in and out. An appointment to view the chosen cattery, prior to making a firm booking, should be quite acceptable to the staff. Some catteries produce brochures listing their facilities and fees, which can be useful, but these rarely give any indication of the people actually responsible for caring for the cats, and cannot substitute for visit. Boarding catteries usually have pens, perhaps connecting to outside runs, for individual cats. The quarters should appear clean and spacious, while the building itself should be well ventilated and have either air-conditioning or heating, whichever is relevant.

The fees vary according to the individual establishment and the services offered. Heating during the winter months and extra services, such as medication, are likely to lead to supplementary charges. It is becoming routine practice for catteries to request payment in advance, because certain owners have used them as a dumping place for unwanted pets, giving false details and then disappearing without trace. Many catteries also have a standard list of conditions for their protection, which the owner accepts and signs accordingly, prior to leaving the cat behind. It is important for both sides to understand their responsibilities.

The only item likely to be required is the cat's bed, although some catteries prefer owners to supply food, and adjust their fees accordingly. Cats can prove very fussy about eating, particularly when transferred to unfamiliar surroundings. The owner of the cattery should therefore be provided with a diet sheet and, if possible, details where the owners or a friend can be contacted, along with the veterinarian's telephone number. A small proportion of cats do not settle well in a cattery, irrespective of the care lavished upon them, and may appear in relatively poor condition when collected at the end of the holiday. Younger cats usually prove more adaptable, but even they may refuse to eat for the first day or so, due to the disruption in their routine.

Keeping Many Cats

If many cats are kept an outdoor cattery is likely to be needed. Such structures generally comprise an outdoor wired area which acts as a run and a connecting shelter where a bed, food and a dirt box are located. There may also be a heating lamp, although the type of electrical tubular heaters used in greenhouses are probably safer. These can be protected by a mesh screen so that the wires are out of reach, and can be linked to a thermostat. The minimum temperature should be approximately 50°F (10°C), rising to about 60°F (16°C) for Rexes and similar breeds, although many American catteries are maintained at a temperature of 68°F (20°C), which is to be recommended for breeding queens.

A cat flap is usually fitted to the connecting door leading to the run, which can be furnished with thick tree trunks or platforms for climbing purposes. These fittings must be adequately secured and can be set in concrete. The floor should be made of concrete or covered with paving tiles so that it can be washed thoroughly whenever necessary. A slope away from the sleeping quarters is recommended for drainage purposes. As an additional protection against bad weather, corrugated plastic sheeting should be fixed over part of the roof and sides of the run.

In large units, there may be a corridor running down the back of the indoor quarters to prevent cats escaping — this allows the outside door of the cattery to be closed before an individual pen is entered. External doors in the outside runs are not strictly necessary and may lead to escapes unless there is a similar double-door safety system.

Various firms advertising in cat periodicals manufacture outdoor catteries, offering either a metal or wooden framework for the outside run. Metal is likely to have a longer lifespan; if wood is used, it should be relatively thick timber — ideally 2in (5cm) square. In either case, it pays to check that there are no loose edges of wire on which the cat could injure itself.

Outside catteries may require planning permission; those which are maintained for business purposes, either as breeding or boarding units, may require additional consents.

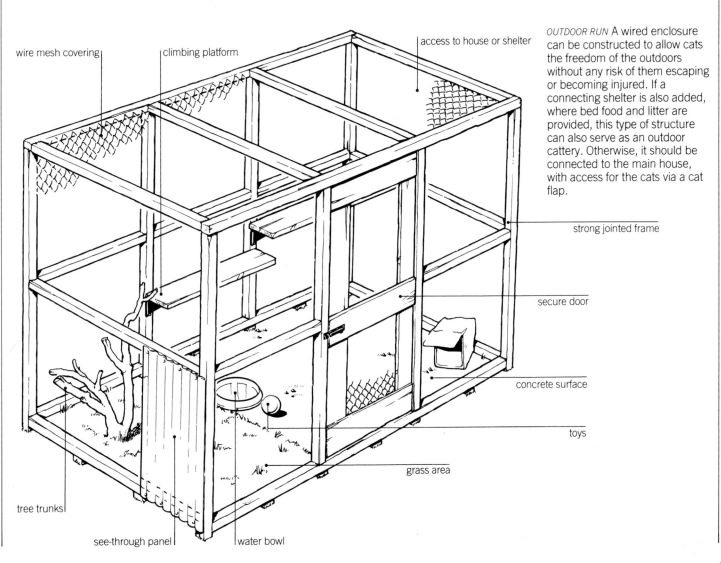

wire mesh covering

climbing platform

access to house or shelter

OUTDOOR RUN A wired enclosure can be constructed to allow cats the freedom of the outdoors without any risk of them escaping or becoming injured. If a connecting shelter is also added, where bed food and litter are provided, this type of structure can also serve as an outdoor cattery. Otherwise, it should be connected to the main house, with access for the cats via a cat flap.

strong jointed frame

secure door

concrete surface

toys

grass area

tree trunks

see-through panel

water bowl

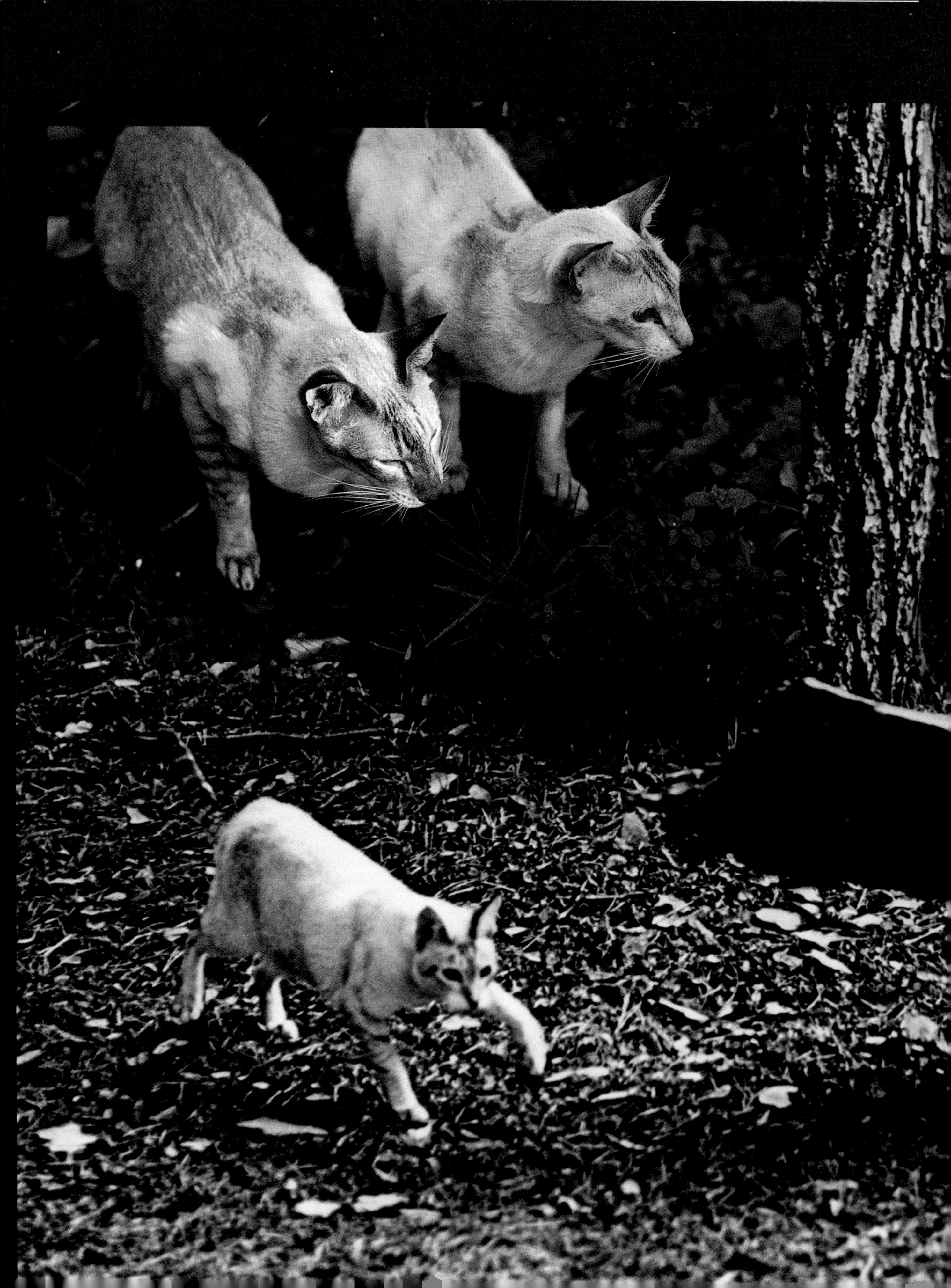

Health Care

The best health care is preventative. As well as regular visits to the veterinarian for vaccinations and check-ups, prevention includes providing a clean environment and a good diet, combined with a degree of vigilance. In emergencies or if the cat exhibits any distressing or unusual symptoms, a vet should be consulted at once — complete recovery is more likely if problems are dealt with early. Routine worming and parasite control will also help to ensure that the cat is troubled with few ailments during its lifetime. Age will bring failing health, as with all creatures, but there is much the owner can do to alleviate these problems by adapting diet and general care to suit the cat's changing needs.

Some cat diseases can be transmitted to humans, but extreme measures do not need to be undertaken to ensure that this does not happen. Nevertheless, it is sensible as well as humane to make every effort to maintain the cat in the best possible condition.

Consulting a Veterinarian

After acquiring a new kitten or cat, it is sensible to make an appointment with a veterinarian as soon as possible. The choice of veterinarian will be influenced by various factors, such as personal recommendations and proximity to the surgery, but all veterinarians have undergone a rigorous and extensive training, and this decision will not be critical to the cat's subsequent welfare. Once the cat is registered with a particular veterinarian, it is sensible to continue the relationship if at all possible. The records kept at the surgery are likely to be helpful in treating any subsequent illness, in the same way that medical records of patients can assist a doctor.

The first contact with the veterinarian is likely to be for vaccinations. Vaccines may seem expensive, but they offer protection against some of the most widespread and significant viral diseases to which cats are susceptible. The cost of treatment is likely to be much higher if the cat falls ill, quite apart from the risk of the animal dying after contracting such an infection.

Routine vaccination is generally carried out against feline infectious enteritis and respiratory disease viruses, including a calici virus; where rabies is endemic, vaccinations are also given for this disease. Various types of vaccine are produced, some of which are not recommended for pregnant cats; the veterinarian must be informed if the cat could have been mated before vaccination. Certain respiratory vaccines come in the form of a nasal spray, but generally an injection is given, either in the scruff of the neck, or in the muscle of the hindlimbs which is slightly more painful. The discomfort is relatively minor and there are no serious side-effects in the vast majority of cases. Some cats may be sleepy and slightly off-colour for a day or so afterwards, but this is by no means general.

Many owners do not like being present while their cat is being vaccinated; the veterinarian will not be offended if this is explained at the outset. A nurse will then assist in holding the cat while the vaccine is administered. This method is much simpler (and less embarrassing for all parties concerned) than having to revive an owner who has fainted at the sight of the syringe and needle. Most vaccines need to be repeated annually; a card recording the vaccination and giving the date when the next one is due will usually be given to the owner.

As well as arranging a programme of vaccinations, the vet will be able to give advice on worming and other routine health procedures. Always consult the vet if there are unusual symptoms or odd behaviour; as with all illnesses, the earlier the treatment is begun the better. Yearly check-ups when vaccinations are repeated will also help to detect

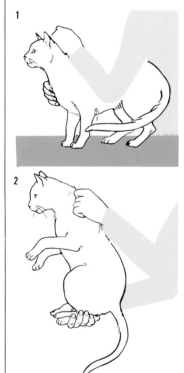

Handle a sick or injured cat with extra care to prevent distress (BELOW). Restrain the cat gently while it is being examined (1). If the cat is frightened and struggling, it may have to be picked up by the scruff of the neck (2). A visit to a veterinarian, shortly after obtaining a new cat or kitten, is recommended — for advice, vaccination, worming and general health check (RIGHT).

1

2

any health problems at an early stage.

Many owners now insure their cats to cover veterinary fees, loss or accidents. Most veterinary surgeries carry details of such insurance schemes or will be able to advise on brokers. This protection can be particularly valuable for those with show cats or people with large numbers of cats in their care. Insurance will not, however, cover 'routine' costs such as vaccinations; as always, the details of cover should be closely scrutinized before a particular policy is taken out.

Signs of Illness

Grooming or bathing the cat provides an opportunity to carry out an overall health check. Starting at the head, the eyes should be clear, although tear-staining may well be noticeable on the fur beneath. This is particularly obvious in light-coated longhairs; the marks should not be treated with shampoo because they are dangerously close to the eyes, but gently bathed with cottonwool soaked in warm water. The ears will also benefit from regular cleaning with cottonwool buds, providing these are not thrust down deep into the ear canal itself, but used in the vicinity of the flap. If there is an unpleasant odour, it is likely that an infection is developing which will need prompt veterinary attention.

Grooming the sides of the face and under the chin may reveal signs of soreness around the gums. These areas will appear reddened and inflamed. Accumulations of tartar can cause such inflammation, encasing part or all of a tooth in a yellowish-brown deposit. This will need to be cleaned off by a veterinarian, who will be able to check whether the underlying tooth has decayed as well. Tartar is a possible cause of bad breath, although another more serious reason may be kidney failure, especially in an older cat. Both are likely to lead to a loss of appetite. Any swelling on the lips themselves, particularly in white cats of any breed, must be viewed with concern. Rodent ulcers, possibly caused by an infection or tumours, may be the underlying cause. Abnormal swellings over the other parts of the body may first be noticed during a grooming session. These may be abscesses resulting from a fight with another cat and need not necessarily be tumours.

The claws should also be checked by gently holding the pad and pressing the retracted claws out. Cats normally keep their claws in good shape, but if they seem long, it is advisable to have them clipped by a veterinarian. The claws receive a blood supply; if too much dead nail is removed, they will bleed quite profusely. It is important to use an adequate tool for cutting purposes and not just scissors, since these may actually cause the nail to split, rather than cutting it cleanly.

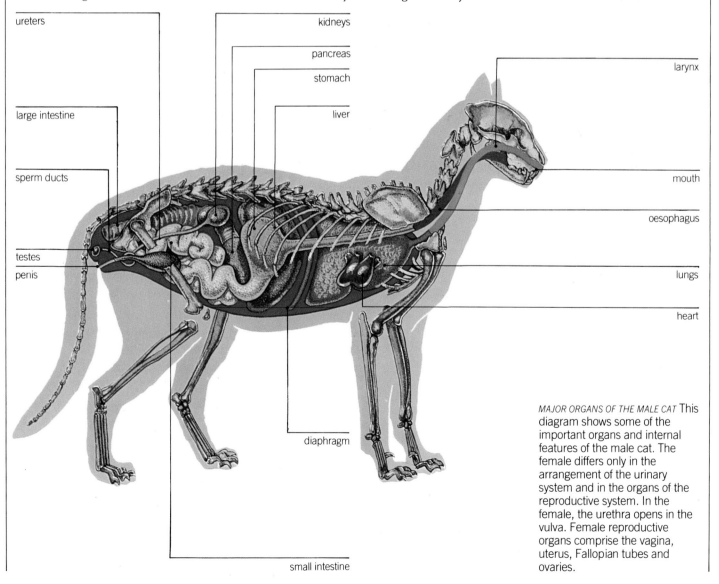

MAJOR ORGANS OF THE MALE CAT This diagram shows some of the important organs and internal features of the male cat. The female differs only in the arrangement of the urinary system and in the organs of the reproductive system. In the female, the urethra opens in the vulva. Female reproductive organs comprise the vagina, uterus, Fallopian tubes and ovaries.

TAKING A CAT'S TEMPERATURE Shake the thermometer down and then lubricate it with oil or jelly before gently inserting it in the anus. Leave it in place—about one-third should be inserted—for about one minute. Normal temperature is about 101.5°F (38.6°C) but a degree higher is not uncommon.

TAKING THE PULSE There are various sites on the body where the pulse can be taken. The femoral artery, at the top of either hindleg on the inside, is the most common place. Press lightly with your fingertips. Normal pulse rate for a cat at rest is between 110 and 140 beats per minute.

ADMINISTERING PILLS 1. Hold the cat's head and tilt it well back, easing open the jaws by pressing on the corners of the mouth. This is easiest if another person is restraining the cat.

2. Drop the pill as far back on the tongue as possible. Hold the mouth closed and stroke the throat until the cat swallows the pill.

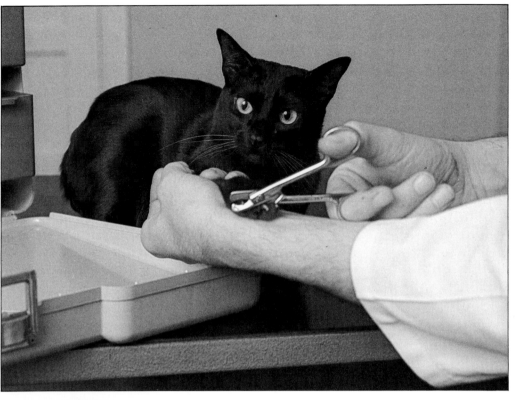

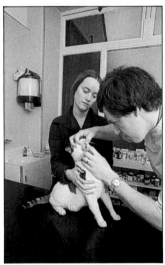

CLIPPING THE CLAWS In general, cats do not need to have their claws clipped very frequently, but if they do become overgrown, it is a good idea to leave this task to a veterinarian, who will also have the correct clippers *(TOP)*. Only the tips of the claws should be cut; care must be taken not to cut into the quick.

CLEANING THE TEETH Debris in the form of a brown deposit known as tartar may collect around a cat's teeth, causing bad breath. This can be removed by a veterinarian, who will also check for other mouth disorders, such as sore gums or decaying teeth *(ABOVE)*.

External Parasites
Fleas

Fleas are without doubt the most common skin parasites found on cats and will almost certainly be picked up at some stage during a cat's life if it is allowed outside. Likely sources of infection are other cats, dogs, hedgehogs and even rabbits. The rabbit flea is unusual in that it remains attached, usually to its host's ears, until the breeding season and does not move through the coat. In cats which accidentally pick up such fleas, the distribution of these parasites is largely confined once again to the head and ears.

During the warmer months of the year, the flea population increases and infections become much more common. Cats infected with fleas scratch themselves repeatedly, but there is no correlation between the number of fleas present on the body and the degree of irritation which they cause. Some cats become sensitized to a component of the flea's saliva and one single bite may produce a great degree of discomfort. Flea bite allergy is now accepted as a significant predisposing cause of the skin condition known as miliary eczema.

The major natural factor controlling the flea population is low humidity, rather than temperature; even in centrally heated homes during the winter, the relative humidity is usually too low to enable the fleas to complete their life cycle. An average humidity is in the range of 38 to 44 percent, whereas the cat flea (*Ctenocephalides felis*) cannot effect development at a relative humidity of less than 50 percent, and even at this figure, only a quarter of the fleas will mature successfully.

The presence of fleas on a cat will be confirmed by grooming with a fine metal flea comb which should be purchased for this purpose. The fleas have predilection sites on the body, often just in front of the tail, and this area should always be combed carefully. Combing a cat for fleas should be undertaken outside, so if any fleas jump off they

SCRATCHING Repeated scratching of various parts of the body is a common sign of fleas.

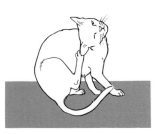

If the ears are scratched a great deal, this may indicate an ear infection.

Notoedres mites often localize around the face, causing irritation.

Combing or brushing the cat outside on a piece of white paper will show up fleas.

do not infest the house. When this is not possible, a disused margarine tub or similar container half-filled with water should be on hand to immerse loose fleas in, until they can be flushed down a toilet. Fleas are extremely difficult creatures to kill; the only sure method is to squeeze them hard with a fingernail to block their respiratory pore, which causes them to explode with a slight popping sound. Humans can be quite badly bitten by fleas from both dogs and cats; conversely, the flea typically associated with man, *Pulex irritans*, can be transferred to domestic pets. Precise identification of the species concerned requires microscopic examination of the flea itself.

In cases where fleas are not discovered during combing, the fur collected in the comb may reveal traces of their blackish dirt. If in any doubt as to whether or not flea dirt is actually present, a simple test can be carried out to revolve the matter. The debris should be pressed on to damp white paper, and if reddish deposits form, this confirms the presence of fleas. The minute granules contain haematin, a component derived from the blood on which the fleas feed, and this dissolves in the presence of water. Fleas only consume very small volumes of blood, less than a drop, once or twice a day.

Control of fleas necessitates both treatment of the cat and also of its bedding. Any dogs sharing the same household must be dealt with simultaneously, because fleas can be transmitted from one creature to another. Powders provide the most direct means of reducing the flea population present on the cat. Care must be taken to ensure that the preparation chosen is safe for cats and, if necessary, can also be used on kittens. Cats are especially susceptible to the toxic effects of such insecticides because of their licking and grooming habits. Aerosol sprays are also available, but often prove considerably more expensive than powder; apart from the unpleasantness of using them, aerosols are liable to scare the cat more than applying powder.

Fleas typically lay their eggs away from their host, although *Ctenocephalides felis* is an exception: its eggs rub off the body very easily and are often transferred to the cat's bedding. It is quite possible for a single female flea to lay up to 800 eggs in its lifetime, although 500 is an average figure, with the complete life cycle taking four to five weeks. In order to break the cycle, the cat's blanket should be either discarded or thoroughly washed and treated as necessary. While sprays may be easier than powder to use around the home, care should be taken if there are other creatures such as fish in the same room. Fish may be inadvertently poisoned unless their tank is adequately covered before and after treatment, until the particles have settled out from the air. Vacuuming will not remove all flea eggs from a carpet and eggs may occur in large numbers right up to the walls. Faced with a heavy domestic infestation of fleas, it is sensible to call in pest control agents to treat the home. Some local government authorities run a service of this nature and the treatment should keep the home free of fleas for some months.

Special flea collars impregnated with toxic compounds are available for cats, but need to be used with the utmost caution, preferably only under veterinary advice. They can produce local skin irritation around the neck itself and have been linked with the recently diagnosed nervous disease known as the Key-Gaskell Syndrome. Furthermore, these collars are usually not elasticated and a cat may become caught up while out climbing for example, with little hope of freeing itself. Impregnated medallions, which attach to standard collars, are marketed in various parts of the world, but are not widely sold in Britain. These are safer than flea collars, but may not prove as effective. In both cases, the chemical compound involved is released over a period of several months, but neither is completely reliable.

Fleas are responsible for transmitting another parasite, *Dipylidium caninum*. This is a tapeworm which can affect both dogs and cats and potentially humans. The segments of the tapeworm containing the eggs — resembling fine grains of white rice — are passed out of the cat's anus and stick around the perimeter. The eggs are often brushed off onto bedding, where they are ingested by immature fleas. The tapeworm begins its development once the flea larva starts to pupate. They may kill some fleas; on emerging from pupation, the surviving fleas affected with *Dipylidium caninum* are believed to be less active. This in turn means that they are more easily caught by the cat, which, on swallowing them, completes the cycle, with the tapeworm then developing in its gut. A child could be infected by the same route. *Dipylidium* does not appear to cause a great deal of harm, but should be treated, if only for aesthetic reasons, with a suitable medication obtained from a veterinarian.

Ticks

Cats living in rural areas, especially where there is a high sheep population, may accidentally pick up ticks, which attach to the skin and swell in size as they feed on blood. The cat's head and neck are the most common sites of attachment. Under normal circumstances, only one or two ticks will be encountered, but for one cat to have as many as 100 is not unknown. In such large numbers, these parasites are likely to cause anaemia. Ticks are detached by dabbing the areas close to their heads with alcohol, which loosens their grip. After a few moments, each tick can be removed

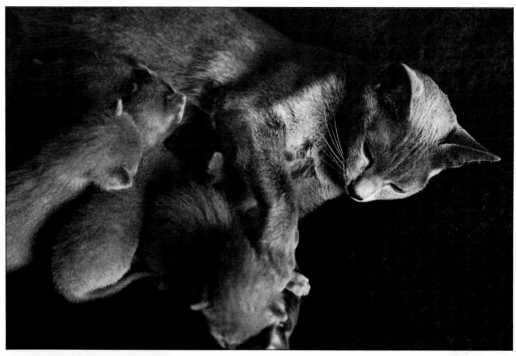

INTERNAL PARASITES Cats can suffer from a number of different internal parasites, which are transmitted in a variety of ways. Some tapeworms are passed on via the cat's prey. One in particular uses rodents as its intermediate host; cats become infested after eating such creatures *(ABOVE)*. In the same way, wild relatives of the cat, such as the lion, may also pick up infestations from their prey *(LEFT)*. For cats kept indoors and who do not hunt, only the tapeworm *Dipylidium* poses a threat. This parasite is carried by fleas. Roundworms, unlike tapeworms, can be transmitted directly without the need for an intermediate host. Kittens may pick up the infection from their mother's milk.

with tweezers, but often the head or capitulum remains stuck in the skin and can cause irritation. To prevent this, the area should be dabbed with a safe, non-toxic ointment.

Mites

Various mites can affect cats, with skin mites giving rise to the condition commonly referred to as mange. These microscopic creatures cause local irritation, leading to excessive washing or scratching of the affected area. Baldness and spots are also associated with cases of mange. *Notoedres* mites occur especially on the sides of the face in the region between the eyes and ears, but can spread up to the neck and down the back if left untreated.

A mite which causes no noticeable symptoms in cats and yet can give rise to an unpleasant dermatitis in humans is *Cheyletiella parasitivorax*. As with other mite infections, the parasite responsible can be detected by means of a skin scraping carried out by a veterinarian. This involves scraping the surface of a suspected area of skin with a sharp blade and examining the sample under a microscope. Obtaining a scraping is not a painful procedure and no sedation is normally necessary.

Mites remain in close proximity to their hosts throughout their life cycles, but *Trombicula autumnalis*, commonly known as 'chiggers', is an exception. The adult form of the mite is free-living, and resembles a minute red spider, but the larval form is parasitic and will attach to the cat, often between the toes, causing a great deal of irritation. The larvae appear as minute orangish-red spots and may be seen elsewhere on the body where the skin is both relatively thin and hairless. Infection with these larvae only occurs during the summer months and is localized to particular regions where the adult mites naturally occur.

Veterinary advice should be sought without delay in cases of suspected mite infections. Treatment consists of the application of a suitable preparation to kill the mites and soothe the affected skin, so the cat will not mutilate itself by continually scratching at the site of irritation.

Mite infections of the ear are also extremely common; if a cat rubs its ears repeatedly, they should be examined carefully with a torch. Grass seeds may occasionally become lodged in the ear, but if dirty, brownish deposits of wax are visible in the ear canal, then the mite known as *Otodectes* is likely to be responsible. An unpleasant smell is usually associated with such infections. Treatment in this instance is likely to be prescribed in the form of drops or a lotion, containing an aracicide to kill the mites and an antibiotic, because bacteria are also often involved in the infection. Steroidal compounds are also included in many ear preparations and serve to soothe the irritation.

As these ear infections are often stubborn and are likely to recur, the ears should be checked regularly. Delay in seeking veterinary help can lead to haematomas — blood-filled swellings — developing on the ear flaps: scratching and shaking the ears repeatedly causes local blood vessels to rupture and the ears swell up as a result of the internal haemorrhaging. Haematomas are extremely painful and should not be touched. They may require surgical treatment to drain them, otherwise the ear will be permanently crumpled.

Another serious complication can arise if infection spreads from the external ear or enters via the eustachian tube. This disorder is referred to as middle-ear disease and results in very distressing symptoms. The cat is likely to start moving in circles with its head tilted to one side, while its sense of balance may also be lost. The chances of successful recovery are not always good, in spite of antibiotic treatment, especially if the inner ear becomes involved.

Fly strike
Fly strike is seen more commonly in older, neglected cats or among members of a feral colony. Flies, typically the green bottle (*Lucilia sericata*), are attracted either by faeces or blood sticking to the fur, laying their eggs nearby. When the larvae hatch, they not only penetrate the skin, worsening any wound, but also produce a toxin which, once released into the general circulation, can rapidly prove fatal.

All maggots must be removed from an infected area with tweezers and soiled fur cut off as necessary. To carry out a proper search may well require sedation of the cat as maggots will rapidly disappear into other areas of fur once they are exposed to light. The affected region is then washed with hydrogen peroxide; a course of antibiotics may also be necessary to prevent any risk of subsequent infection. Flies are not normally attracted to cats with healthy, clean coats; if an individual is at risk for any reason, such as the presence of a sutured wound, a close watch should be kept for maggots.

Internal Parasites
Worms (helminth infections)
Cats are affected by a number of worms, which fall into three main categories: tapeworms (cestodes), roundworms (nematodes) and flukes (trematodes). The life cycle of the tapeworm *Dipylidium* proceeds via fleas, whereas another, *Taenia taeniaeformis* uses rodents as its intermediate host, with cats becoming infected by consuming such creatures. Wild felines can also acquire similar parasites from their prey. These tapeworms do not usually produce serious disease, but can lead to a noticeable loss of condition and may cause mild diarrhoea. Cats which do not hunt are unlikely to encounter tapeworms such as *Echinococcus multilocularis*; for those living indoors, *Dipylidium* is the only real threat.

Roundworms, or nematodes, are more common than the cestodes in cats, and can be passed on directly without the need for an intermediate host. Even young kittens can suffer from roundworms, picking up the infection from their mother's milk. *Toxocara cati* occurs in at least 20 percent of cats, whereas *Toxaxaris leonina* is only encountered in 1 percent of cases. Roundworms develop in the intestine, reaching a length of about 4in (10cm), and lay eggs which are passed out in faeces. When these eggs are ingested by another cat, they hatch into larvae and enter the circulation, before returning to the gut where they complete their development. Larvae which migrate into the mammary tissue are then passed out in the milk. Kittens are especially susceptible to roundworm infection, which can prove very debilitating and will result in a characteristic pot-bellied appearance, with a 'staring' coat.

Other worms occur in the warmer parts of North America and Australia. Both threadworms (*Strongyloides* species) and whipworms (*Trichuris* species) are in this category, but respond well to treatment. Diagnosis of such infections is based on examining the faeces of a cat for eggs. Tablets are the normal method of dosing at present, although injections may be developed in the near future, a treatment becoming more routine for controlling such parasites in farm livestock.

Treatment of helminth infections, along with regular preventive worming, is best undertaken with veterinary guidance, although preparations can be purchased in pet stores. It is important to select the correct medication for the particular parasite concerned, and if any course of treatment is purchased from a pet store, it is important to follow the instructions on the packaging. Some effective new products have recently been introduced on to the market. Praziquantel has proved very active against all the cestodes which can infect cats in the relatively short time it has been available, whereas for roundworms, piperazine salts have been used for many years. Piperazine, although a relatively safe compound, will only kill 80 to 90 percent of the nematodes and treatment must be repeated for maximum efficacy. Dichlorvos is a potentially more dangerous anthelmintic for cats.

Apart from helminths which localize to the gastro-intestinal tract, there are those which prefer other sites. The lungworm, *Aleurostrongylus abstrusus*, has become more widely recognized in cats during recent years. One survey found a level of infection of 9.6 percent, based on a sample study of 125 cats. A mild case of lungworm may produce few apparent symptoms, but coughing and signs of respiratory difficulty, such as laboured breathing, could be indicative of this parasite. The disease has been seen in both domestic and wild cats and can be treated, although the drugs used are rather toxic. Examination of the faeces for the lungworm eggs, together with perhaps a blood test, should serve to confirm a diagnosis before treatment. As with many other parasitic infections, the eosinophils, which form part of the white cell group, are raised in number in such cases. Various other lungworms may occasionally be seen in cats in other areas of the world.

Another localized helminth is the heartworm, (*Dirofilaria immitis*), which is much more commonly encountered in dogs rather than cats. These helminths occur in the vicinity of the pulmonary artery, as well as the right ventricle of the heart. They may actually block off the circulation, leading to sudden death, or cause circulatory disorders such as fluid collecting in the tissues, a condition which is technically referred to as oedema. Transmission occurs by means of insect bites, with mosquitoes picking up the immature larval forms (microfilariae) from the blood of an infected animal. The microfilariae develop in the insect for about two weeks to form third-stage larvae. These are then passed into the circulation of another host when the mosquito feeds again, and the cycle of infection is completed. Treatment of heartworms is extremely hazardous, because destroying the adult worms *in situ* can itself cause an obstruction. Regular preventive dosing of both dogs and cats is therefore carried out in areas where the infection is present, typically Australia, the Mediterranean region and the warmer parts of North America.

Flukes, which are classified as trematodes, do not usually affect cats, although they can be a problem in certain areas of North America. The intermediate infective hosts are usually fish and where flukes are endemic in the local fish population, such food must be cooked before being offered to cats. Flukes develop in the bile ducts of the liver and can cause jaundice, as well as affecting the pancreas in some cases. Treatment with praziquantel is extremely effective against *Opisthorchis felineus*, but *Metorchis conjunctus* infections do not respond well, and are likely to prove fatal.

Protozoal infections

Protozoa are one-cell organisms which can only be seen under the microscope. *Isospora catis* gives rise to the disease known as coccidosis. When present in large numbers it causes diarrhoea which may be tinged with blood, and also fever and general depression. Coccidosis occurs most commonly in cats living together in cramped, dirty conditions, since it is spread by faecal contact. Treatment of coccidosis can be carried out quite successfully with sulphonamide drugs, although the dehydration resulting from the diarrhoea can prove fatal, especially in kittens, unless it is corrected early.

The protozoan *Toxoplasma gonadii* is particularly significant because it can be transmitted to humans with pregnant women especially at risk. Symptoms of infection in the cat are rather vague and may resemble those of panleucopaenia or bronchopneumonia, even if they become apparent. Clinical tests will be necessary to confirm this illness. After becoming infected, either by consuming contaminated raw meat or rodents, the cat then excretes the oocyst or dormant stage in its faeces four or five days later, and may continue to do so for up to three weeks. The oocysts themselves, once outside the body, take between two and four days to become infective. They may then survive in the environment for months, although they can be destroyed by boiling water and certain chemicals. The risk to humans comes when these oocysts are accidentally ingested, once they have had an opportunity to become infective.

In order to prevent this hazard, contact with cat faeces should be kept to an absolute minimum. Gloves should always be worn when emptying a dirt tray, the contents of which should be disposed of before sporulation can occur. Infection may also occur in sand pits or gardens where cats are known to have defecated. It is particularly sensible for pregnant women to wear gloves when working in such areas because of the possibility of the protozoan crossing the placental barrier in the body, to affect the unborn child in the uterus, perhaps even causing a miscarriage. If possible, cats should also be prevented from gaining access to sources of *Toxoplasma*, but in practice this is often not feasible if they are allowed outside at all. If toxoplasmosis is diagnosed as a clinical condition in a cat, treatment can be given, but this will not guarantee that no oocysts will be produced in its faeces.

An insect-borne protozoal infection, with a worldwide distribution seen in cats is feline infectious anaemia. The organism itself, known as *Haemobartonella felis* or *Eperythrozoon felis*, is transmitted by biting insects such as mosquitoes. Male cats for some reason appear more at risk than females, especially those between four and six years of age according to one study. The parasites destroy the red blood cells, giving rise to the anaemia and causing debility and fever in the process. The disease itself can be easily confirmed by means of a blood smear, which has to be stained and then studied under a microscope. Treatment may necessitate a blood transfusion, coupled with tetracycline antibiotic therapy.

Accidents and Injuries

Road accidents

In urban areas particularly, injuries to cats resulting from involvement in road traffic accidents are sadly common. After a cat has been hit by a vehicle, it must be handled very carefully. The animal will be in a state of shock and will not hesitate to bite or scratch its owner. The extent of injury will not be known and there may be severe internal complications. The injured cat should be picked up cautiously, with one hand holding the scruff of the neck, while the other is slid under the hindquarters. A blanket makes an ideal stretcher; the cat can be laid out flat on its side. Under no circumstances must the body be allowed to hang down head first, since a relatively common injury after an accident of this nature is a ruptured diaphragm. The resulting tear in the diaphragm, which separates the abdominal and thoracic chambers will then allow the intestines, or other abdominal organs to penetrate through to the thorax in the direct of gravity.

The cat should be kept wrapped up and warm until it is examined by a veterinarian. It will probably be quicker to take the cat to the surgery for assistance, rather than calling out the veterinarian to attend the accident. Diaphragmatic tears can be repaired by surgery; with professional assistance, even severely injured accident cases can often be restored to health. Pelvic injuries are another common result and X-rays are often necessary to determine their full extent. Fractured limbs can be splinted externally, while internal fixation by means of a variety of plates, pins and wires may be recommended depending on the site and severity of the break.

Drowning

Cats can swim, despite their apparent dislike of water, but may occasionally get trapped in a pond or river and start to drown. After being rescued, a nearly drowned cat should be held head downwards by its hindlimbs and swung gently back and forth to drain ingested water from its body. The mouth must be kept open; if the tongue is pulled forwards, breathing will be assisted.

HANDLING AN INJURED CAT 1. After an accident, the cat may scratch. Place one hand on the neck, the other around the chest.

2. If the cat is strugggling badly, hold it upright by the scruff of its neck, with one hand supporting the hindquarters.

3. An alternative method is to hold the forelegs securely with one hand, while supporting the hindquarters with the other.

4. In cases where the cat has been badly hurt, wrap it in a blanket to keep it warm and prevent struggling.

STOPPING BLEEDING Pressure on the site of an open wound will often serve to stem the blood loss.

BANDAGING Wrap the wound with surgical gauze. Cover this with cottonwool and then bandage securely.

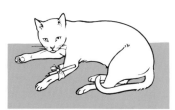

APPLYING A TOURNIQUET In severe cases, apply a tourniquet above the wound. Twist a handkerchief with a pencil, loosening often.

SPLINTS Depending on the site, a splint may be necessary if a bone is fractured. Use two flat pieces of wood, secured with tape.

EMERGENCY AID In an emergency, if the cat is showing no signs of breathing, it is possible to attempt artificial resuscitation. After rescue, a cat that has been drowning should be held head down by its hindlegs to drain water from its body. The mouth should be open; check that the airway is clear and pull the tongue forward. The cat should be swung up to a horizontal position and then down between the legs. A firm grip above the hocks (knees) of both hindlegs is essential (1). This routine may stimulate breathing but, if not, either mouth-to-mouth or manual artificial respiration can be attempted. To stimulate breathing manually, lay the cat on its right side and position both hands, one on top of the other, on the chest behind the shoulder. Press down rapidly several times and then check to see if the cat has begun breathing (2). If the heart has stopped, press the chest, behind the elbow, using fingers and thumb. Repeat twice a second until the heart can be felt beating again (3).

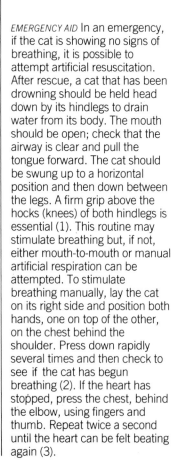

1

2   3

It is possible to give artificial resuscitation to a cat which has stopped breathing, with mouth-to-mouth proving the most effective method. The hands will need to be used to form a cup around the cat's open jaws, with the cat's tongue again held extended. Alternatively, with the cat lying flat out on its right side, the hands, on top of each other, should be positioned on the chest just behind the shoulder and pressed down on the body several times rapidly in succession. This should be followed by a brief pause of several seconds, to check whether the cat has now started to breathe of its own accord. If this proves to be the case, there is no need to repeat the treatment, unless the animal stops breathing again. It is worth continuing for two or three minutes if no immediate response is evident, although as time elapses, the chances of success will almost certainly be reduced.

Swallowed objects

Kittens are especially likely to swallow dangerous objects which may, in the first instance, become caught in the throat, causing gagging and retching. The mouth must be opened at once and the foreign body should be carefully removed, providing it is within easy reach. Rapid veterinary

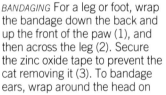

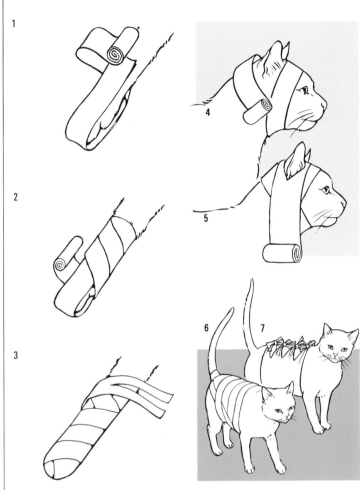

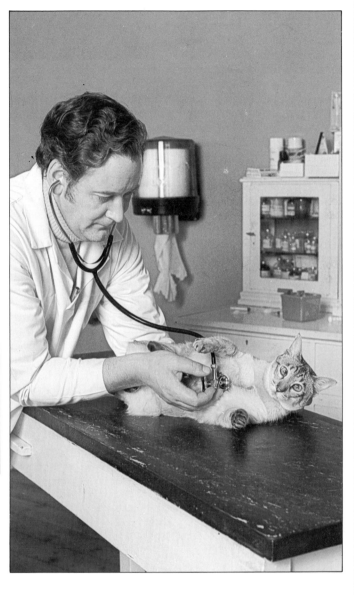

BANDAGING For a leg or foot, wrap the bandage down the back and up the front of the paw (1), and then across the leg (2). Secure the zinc oxide tape to prevent the cat removing it (3). To bandage ears, wrap around the head on either side of the ears (4), cut holes and pass the bandage over the ears (5). Abdominal bandages may be secured at the tail (6) or along the spine (7). After first aid, consult a vet for advice on care *(RIGHT)*.

help will be necessary where this is not practical and also in cases where sharp objects such as pins or bones are completely swallowed; these could lodge lower down the digestive tract and might perforate the gut. Radiology will often serve to locate the position of such items, so that surgery, if deemed necessary, can be undertaken with precision.

Snake bites and insect stings

In Britain, only the adder has a poisonous venom but elsewhere, in parts of Australia and North America for example, snake bites are a regular hazard for cats living outside and will require urgent veterinary attention. Placing a tourniquet around a bitten limb will prevent the poison entering the general circulation, while the swollen area itself should be covered with an ice-pack. Treatment with the appropriate antiserum will then be required as soon as possible. In tropical areas especially, other poisonous creatures such as spiders can present a danger to cats and similar action as for snake bites is advisable. When a cat is stung by an insect such as a bee, which leaves its sting behind, then this should be pulled out at once, before the irritant substance can be released into the tissues. A careful application of a blue bag, or a similar preparation, may then prevent the sting from having a severe effect.

Foot injuries and lameness

An unsuspecting cat may tread or land on broken glass or other sharp objects, cutting its foot as a result. The pads always bleed profusely, even after a relatively minor cut, and such wounds always appear serious for this reason. The first action must be to stem the bleeding by bandaging the area as tightly as possible. The bandage should first be positioned in a U-shape, extending around the paw and up the opposite side of the leg, before wrapping it firmly round to encompass the leg and paw. A veterinarian should examine the wound and will be able to remove any object which is embedded and suture the tissues if necessary.

When a cat appears lame but there is no obvious injury, it is possible a grass seed may have penetrated between its toes. These seeds are difficult to see and can work their way right up the leg, creating an abscess elsewhere. They are also often intensely painful for the cat and sedation will probably be necessary to allow a veterinarian to find and remove the offending seed. Pieces of grass can enter other parts of the body as well, including the ears and eyes.

Cats in rural areas may fall victim to traps or snares set for other creatures, and suffer horrific injuries as a consequence. They can, however, adapt reasonably well to living on three limbs, if one is lost in this way. Gangrene, because of the prolonged loss of circulation to the ensnared leg, often occurs, even if the limb is not amputated.

Shooting injuries are now increasingly common in certain parts of town, where youngsters have airguns and get bored of using stationary targets. Such pellets do not always cause serious injury, unless they enter an eye for example, and the fact that the cat has been shot might not even be apparent to its owner. In some cases, the pellets only show up when the cat is radiographed, perhaps for a completely unrelated problem. Shotgun or bullet wounds are much more serious; apart from external tissue damage and bleeding, there may also be internal complications such as fractured bones. A thorough veterinary examination will be necessary to assess the extent of the resulting injuries.

Heights

Contrary to popular belief, cats do not get trapped in trees or similar locations very often, but following a bad scare they are often reluctant to come down from a height immediately. Left to their own devices, such cats will eventually return to the ground, perhaps even a day later. If it is, however, decided to retrieve a cat from a tree,

considerable care will be needed. The ladder should be positioned on firm ground, preferably with someone holding it at its base. A pair of gloves will offer some protection against being scratched or bitten by the cat while handling it.

Cats have the ability to fall from a considerable height, perhaps as much as 20ft (6m), with relatively slight injuries or none at all. This is because they are able to swivel their bodies rapidly into position and land on their feet. Cats living in high-rise apartments are obviously at risk from falls. Kittens are particularly liable to overbalance on a window sill, tempted by passing birds, a butterfly or other insects. If in any doubt after such a fall, then the cat concerned should be checked by a veterinarian. Head injuries are most common in such circumstances and may have to be repaired surgically, depending on their severity.

Bites

When cats bite each other during a fight, bacteria from their mouths is introduced into the resulting puncture. There is often very little accompanying bleeding, although the fur around the bite may appear wet. Over the course of several days, however, an abscess, resulting from the local bacterial infection set up by the bite, will gradually develop. It appears as a noticeable swelling, which will contain pus. The affected area will be very sensitive, and the cat may appear generally off-colour. If the bite is noticed before any

Cats are well known for their ability to climb and rarely become stranded in trees or similar locations (RIGHT). To climb, a cat will leap onto the trunk of a tree, holding on with its claws. It will move up using its forelimbs, anchored by its claws. To descend, the cat prefers to turn and jump, rather than ease down backwards (LEFT).

swelling is evident, it may be possible to prevent an abscess by injecting with antibiotics.

If left untreated, the abscess will eventually come to a head and burst. This is obviously undesirable; the cat should be taken to a veterinarian, who will open and drain the abscess and almost certainly prescribe a course of antibiotics. If an abscess bursts before the cat can be taken to a vet, the pus should be wiped away using cottonwool or paper towelling soaked in hot water. The wound must then be washed out thoroughly with hydrogen peroxide, although another abscess may well form if antibiotic treatment is not given.

Apart from discomfort, the abscess will also ruin the exhibition potential of the cat for a period, particularly if any fur needs to be clipped so the area can be thoroughly cleaned. Intact toms fight more than other cats and are thus most likely to develop abscesses, although any cat can be afflicted, particularly those roaming free.

Burns

Cats are especially at risk in a kitchen, where they may walk across a hot surface or be splashed with cooking oil. They may also lie too close to a fire, singeing their coats or actually burning themselves. In severe cases, shock will soon be evident and a pad soaked in cold water should be applied to the affected area as soon as possible after the injury. This will help to decrease the inflammation; veterinary advice must then be sought without delay. Similar treatment, with washing, is necessary in cases where caustic chemicals have contaminated a cat's coat.

Poisoning

Cats are susceptible to a wide variety of poisons, which include certain houseplants and other common household items, as well as specifically toxic products. It is particularly important to be aware that the metabolism of the cat is not adapted to cope with acetyl salicyclic acid, more commonly known as aspirin. Aspirin is toxic to cats even in small quantities: as little as just under 2 grains (120mg) of acetyl salicyclic acid can promote toxic hepatitis. Cats also react differently from other creatures to the sedative morphine; this drug will cause excitation when used at a corresponding dose level in cats. Benzoic acid, often included as a preservative in prepared meat products, is another chemical which produces an adverse reaction when ingested by cats. It promotes aggression and may cause hyperactivity. Any human food containing this compound should not be fed to cats.

When bathing wounds, care must also be taken to use only the classes of disinfectant recommended as safe for cats. Others, such as those containing phenols, are likely to lead to convulsions and even death. Cats are particularly at risk from toxic substances on their coats; these may either pass through the skin directly or be licked off the fur with dire consequences. Apart from disinfectants, cats can become covered in a variety of noxious chemicals, ranging from tar and paint to turpentine. Before attempting to clean the coat, veterinary help should be sought, especially if the contamination is widespread. Incorrect treatment in some cases can also have serious side-effects, while sedation may be necessary to facilitate thorough cleansing. The cat's mouth should, whenever possible, be taped as soon as possible after the contamination is noticed, so that the animal cannot lick its fur. A simple muzzle will be much

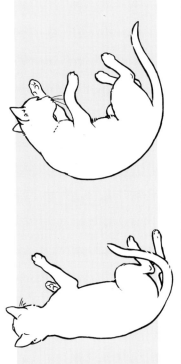

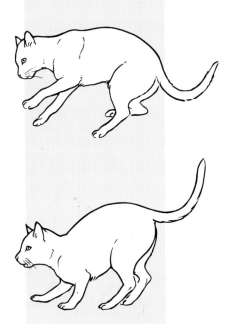

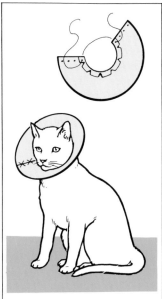

ELIZABETHAN COLLAR These collars, produced in various sizes and generally made of plastic, can be tied around the neck of the cat to prevent it scratching, removing sutures or licking its fur after contamination with a poisonous substance.

FALLING The flexible skeleton of the cat, and its remarkable agility, enables it to fall from considerable heights without injury. When falling, the cat will swivel its body in mid-air to land on its feet. If a cat falls from a great height, injuries to the head and jaw are most common.

harder for the cat to remove and probably less distressing, as it simply fits around the mouth, affixing behind the ears. It does not prevent the cat from opening its mouth, as taping must do to be effective.

Cats are actually attracted to certain poisons. In colder climates, where anti-freeze products are used in car radiators during the winter months, cats will readily drink the treated water if given the chance. The dangerous chemical in this instance is ethylene glycol, which is not itself toxic until converted in the body to oxalic acid. This compound will then crystallize out both in the cat's brain and kidneys, with fatal consequences. Treatment necessitates the injection of pure ethanol.

The most likely source of poisoning for cats comes, however, from widespread and indiscriminate use of rodenticides, although certain insecticides can also be dangerous. Metaldehyde, commonly used in slug baits and related products, is another toxic chemical which appeals to cats as well as dogs. If ingested, metaldehyde causes weakness and incoordination, as well as an excessive production of saliva leading to frothing at the mouth. This poison also affects the circulatory system, with death usually resulting from respiratory failure. It is sensible to avoid the use of such compounds in gardens where cats are allowed to roam free. Shallow dishes set in the ground filled with stout will attract and kill slugs and snails without presenting a hazard to the cat's health.

In the case of rodenticides, cats may be poisoned directly by swallowing the bait or by eating ailing rodents. Anticoagulents such as Warfarin result in spontaneous haemorrhages in the body and cause other unpleasant side-effects, such as anaemia and lameness. The presence of this poison can be detected in a urine sample, while treatment, including Vitamin K therapy, may prove effective if begun early. A repeated intake of small doses of Warfarin is likely to be more serious than a large quantity taken at one time.

Organo-phosphorus compounds are widely used in a variety of products including most insecticides, with controlled amounts being present in flea collars. They act by inhibiting an enzyme, cholinesterase, which is responsible for breaking down a chemical transmitter known as acetylcholine. This leads to muscular tremors and excessive salivation, as well as vomiting and diarrhoea. In the latter stages, convulsions may occur, leading to a coma and finally death. With veterinary help, it is possible to reverse these effects and promote a full recovery.

Treatment is not possible in all cases of poisoning because some compounds have no reliable antidote. Paraquat has attracted much attention because of its fatal effects in humans, but can also prove deadly to cats. The rat bait ANTU (Alpha napthyl-thiourea) is another member of this group, along with zinc phosphide. Some of these more unpleasant chemicals, such as sodium fluoroacetate and strychnine, have been banned from use but cases of such poisoning do still come to light; usually the baits have been used illegally.

There is a wide range of chemicals which are potentially lethal to cats; given the speed of onset of symptoms in some cases, treatment is very difficult, unless the precise nature of the agent responsible is known with certainty. If a cat suddenly becomes very ill, and could have had access to poison, then this knowledge is likely to be of very significant help to a veterinarian. While vomiting and diarrhoea can occur as a result of poisoning, they may also result from a variety of other causes, and so these symptoms are not in themselves diagnostic.

Although it is possible to use an emetic to promote vomiting, this has to be carried out within about half an hour following ingestion of the poison, to be of any assistance. The best course of action is to telephone a veterinarian immediately explaining the predicament, giving the name of possible chemicals involved. Emetics are not, in fact, recommended for all poisons, and the veterinarian will be able to advise accordingly for a particular case.

Skin Disorders

Certain skin complaints are not caused by parasites or micro-organisms and are thus non-infective, although the symptoms may appear similar to infestations in some cases. The skin may still become inflamed, causing the cat to scratch and lose hair from the affected regions.

Allergies are recognized in cats, but it is not always easy to discover the predisposing factor. A process of elimination is often necessary, taking away one item, such as milk from the diet, and then noting any improvement. Confirmation can be achieved by reintroducing a small amount of the substance held responsible, and seeing if the condition then reappears.

Sunburn can also cause skin irritation. This is most common in white cats, with the ears often becoming inflamed following prolonged exposure to the sun's rays.

The condition of hormonal alopecia is another skin disorder of the coat which is not contagious. The alopecia, or hair loss, starts in the abdominal region and may spread up the thighs to affect the flanks in severe cases. It is associated predominantly with neutered cats of either sex. There is no irritation or dermatitis present with this complaint, the effects of which are noticeably symmetrical. Hormonal treatment is required to correct the imbalance present in the cat's own hormonal system, and may need to be repeated as necessary.

Ringworm

Infectious skin diseases are of particular significance both for a cat and its owner. Ringworm, caused by fungus, affects both skin and hair, but does not always produce recognizable symptoms in cats. However, the condition is easily transmitted to humans either by handling an infected cat or from its environment. The situation is further complicated by the fact that certain cats can carry ringworm without actually having the infection themselves.

There are three recognized types of ringworm which may affect cats, the most common being *Microsporum canis*. Distinction between these forms is of more than academic interest. In cattle, ringworm infection produces typically distinct whitish circular patches on the coat, whereas the only trace of infection in cats may be a few broken hairs, barely noticeable without a very close inspection. By means of a special device known as a Wood's lamp it is often possible to confirm a suspected case without having to resort to tedious skin scrapings and cultures. The lamp emits ultraviolet rays which are passed through glass containing nickel oxide. The affected region will fluoresce, appearing apple-green if *Microsporum canis* is present. False positives may occur occasionally, but are quite unusual. Unfortunately, in two percent of cases, the other ringworm fungi are responsible and these do not fluoresce. Microscopic and culture tests will then be necessary and it may be several weeks before a definite result is available.

Treatment of ringworm is also long and laborious, requiring probably a month or more of dosing with the antibiotic griseofulvin, often in conjuction with fungicidal shampoos for the coat itself. Griseofulvin cannot be used with safety in pregnant cats, since it may well cause malformations in the developing kittens. Shampooing is necessary because,while griseofulvin works up to the skin surface, it will not act against fungal spores actually present on the hairs. Even when a case appears to have resolved successfully, tests are advisable to ensure that no trace of the fungus remains.

Ringworm is a major scourge if it enters a cattery and stringent disinfection is required to prevent spread from an infected individual to other cats. All bedding must be destroyed and the pen concerned washed as recommended by a veterinarian. This must be carried out very thoroughly, not forgetting the bars at the front of a wooden or plastic pen where spores may have been deposited by rubbing. All infected cats will need to be kept completely isolated from others, until they receive a clean bill of health, and handled only with rubber gloves. Feeding bowls and dirt boxes are also potentially hazardous.

Ringworm infections in humans do not always prove severely irritating, but are nevertheless unpleasant. If an infected cat has been handled accidentally without gloves,

washing with soap using cold water is recommended. This is thought to lessen the risk of the disease developing, since the skin pores will not open so readily when cold water is applied to them, and the fungus will not gain easy access to the skin itself. If circular red patches do appear, particularly on the hands or arms, medical advice must be sought. Human treatment is also likely to involve a prolonged course of griseofulvin.

Ulcers

Rodent ulcers are relatively common in cats, although the cause remains obscure. Such lesions occur usually in the region of the lips, often starting on the upper lip itself, and are seen largely in adult cats. It used to be thought that they resulted from an infection derived from catching rodents. The ulcerated area will both enlarge and deepen if left untreated. Various methods have been used successfully for this purpose, ranging from a cautious application of gentian violet to cryosurgery. This latter technique entails freezing the affected area using a liquid nitrogen probe, to kill the diseased tissue, hopefully ensuring subsequent healthy resolution. Healing in all cases is likely to take several weeks, and recurrences are not unknown. Other treatments may entail the use of steroidal compounds and irradiation. The condition, more correctly described as an eosinophilic granuloma, is not malignant like the rodent ulcer encountered in humans, although cancerous growths actually within cats' mouths are not uncommon.

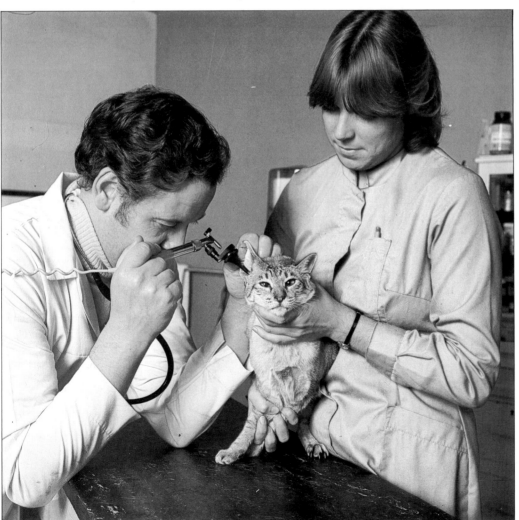

Symptoms of ear trouble include constant shaking of the head and repeated scratching. Rather than attempt treatment at home, it is better to seek veterinary advice. A vet will be able to examine the ears using an auroscope, detecting foreign bodies such as grass seeds or infestations by ear mites *(LEFT)*. Appropriate treatment can then be undertaken with the minimum of delay.

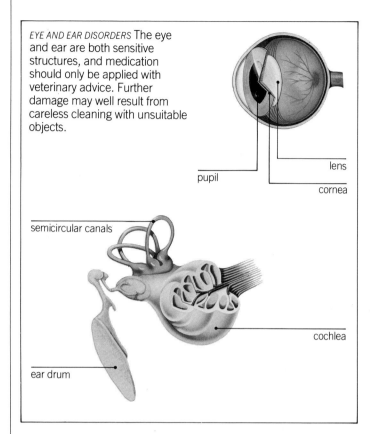

EYE AND EAR DISORDERS The eye and ear are both sensitive structures, and medication should only be applied with veterinary advice. Further damage may well result from careless cleaning with unsuitable objects.

pupil

lens

cornea

semicircular canals

cochlea

ear drum

CLEANING EARS Use moist cotton buds to remove wax or dirt inside the ear but do not probe deeply.

EAR DROPS Restrain the cat and turn its head to one side. Apply drops and massage behind ear.

CLEANING EYES Use cottonwool moistened with warm water and wipe gently.

Clean the eyes first, then apply ointment or drops directly to the cornea.

Eye and Ear Ailments

Eye ailments are relatively rare in cats, but in some cases can be linked with nervous disorders. Any sign of discharge from the eyes should be taken seriously, as this may indicate a viral infection. Injuries, or a noticeable change in the colour of one or both eyes will also require immediate veterinary advice. It is quite possible for ophthalmic surgery to be undertaken successfully in many cases, if medical treatment alone will not correct the condition. When using ophthalmic preparations, it is important to use them as regularly as it states on the container because drugs are liable to be washed out fairly rapidly from the eyes by tear fluid. Repeated applications help to ensure that a therapeutic dose is maintained at the site of infection.

Treatment of ear disease in cats will also require persistent application of various preparations, as directed by a veterinarian. It is important to continue using the drug concerned for the period stated to eliminate the infection totally and prevent recurrence. Antibiotic resistance can also develop otherwise, making it even harder to effect a satisfactory cure.

Serious Illness
Digestive tract infections

Diarrhoea is a symptom associated with a variety of diseases, particularly those of the digestive tract, and is not a disease itself. Nevertheless, as a condition it should be taken seriously and veterinary advice sought early, both to establish the underlying cause of the disorder and to prevent excessive dehydration, an effect which can be particularly debilitating in kittens.

Constipation, on the other hand, is much rarer in cats. A laxative, such as one recommended for fur balls, will relieve most cases. Cats allowed outdoors which are seen squatting and straining over a dirt box in pain may not be suffering from constipation at all, but a blockage of the urinary tract.

The most important and serious infection for cats which affects the digestive tract is known as either feline infectious enteritis (FIE) or feline panleucopaenia. All members of the cat family can succumb to this disease, which is often fatal in unvaccinated animals. Up to 90 percent of young cats may die in an outbreak, although those which recover will be permanently immune.

The incubation period is between four and 10 days; the cat will lose its appetite as its temperature rises and may start vomiting. After this stage, severe diarrhoea occurs resulting in serious dehydration, despite the cat's attempts to drink to compensate for the loss of fluid. The term 'panleucopaenia' refers to the characteristic alterations in the numbers of white blood cells (leucocytes) present in the circulation during the disease. The leucocyte count falls sharply and very few cells of the lymphoid group remain in severe cases. All rapidly dividing cells in the body are attacked by the virus; the resulting damage to the intestinal cells can be so severe that absorption of nutrients is permanently impaired. The cat may suffer intermittent bouts of diarrhoea for the rest of its life, if it manages to survive at all.

The infection is particularly dangerous for unborn kittens because the virus will also attack their developing nervous systems during the latter part of their dam's pregnancy, damaging the cerebellum. As a result, when the kittens are born and start to walk, they have an unsteady gait and cannot coordinate their movements effectively. Newly born kittens can also be infected. To ensure a good level of protective immunity is present in the dam's colostrum or first milk, she should have been vaccinated with a killed preparation, preferably just prior to mating. There is no treatment available for feline cerebellar ataxia, as the condition is known, after the infection has occurred.

SIGNS OF STRESS 1. An anxious or depressed cat may be reacting to a sudden change in its environment.

2. Another behavioural abnormality associated with stress is defecating in inappropriate places.

3. Compulsive grooming can lead to self-mutilation and is typical of bored or neglected cats.

4. Chewing wool is an annoying habit particularly associated with Siamese and other pedigrees.

5. Sudden incidents of aggression may well indicate a nervous disorder or illness.

URINATING 1. Normally cats squat quite low in their litter trays to urinate.

2. If there is an obstruction, the cat will crouch rather than squat and may refuse to leave the tray.

Since feline panleucopaenia is caused by a virus, it will not respond to antibiotics, although these will help to prevent secondary bacterial infection. Antibiotic treatment is of particular value since the cat's own defence system cannot function effectively with low levels of leucocytes. Fluid and electrolyte replacement to offset the effects of the diarrhoea, given as a drip and coupled with a blood transfusion, generally offers the best hope of recovery.

In a household where an outbreak has occurred and other cats are at risk, it may be advisable to give antiserum in the hope of protecting apparently unaffected individuals. If a kitten or cat dies as a result of feline panleucopaenia, all items associated with it should be disposed of, preferably by incineration. It is possible to treat them with formalin, although this itself is rather a dangerous chemical. The virus can persist in the environment for a month or more, so at least three months should elapse before another kitten is obtained. An older, fully vaccinated cat can be obtained sooner, since it should be protected against the infection.

The peritoneum, the lining of the abdominal cavity and its contents, is affected by the condition known as feline infectious peritonitis. This is another serious viral disease for which there is no vaccine and no hope of recovery once symptoms are apparent. Unlike feline panleucopaenia, however, the virus itself does not survive long in the environment, but is especially likely to be spread in catteries and other localities where a number of animals are housed in close proximity. For this reason, reputable catteries will want to see proof of vaccination.

Young cats are again particularly susceptible, and the incubation period may range from 36 hours up to four months. Appetite declines and an intermittent fever is present for a period of time. Accumulation of fluid in the abdomen, referred to as ascites, occurs in the latter stages of the disease; if the covering (pleura) of the lungs are affected, then progressive difficulty in breathing may become evident. The nervous system can also be involved, leading to a loss of balance and convulsions; there may also be impairment of vision. Once the disease is confirmed, it will only be a matter of weeks before death occurs; it may well be kinder in the latter stages to have the cat painlessly put to sleep by the veterinarian.

Urinary tract disorders

Feline urolithasis, also referred to as feline urological syndrome (FUS) is, in practical terms, a blockage which results from an obstruction in the urinary tract. It is most common and serious in male cats because of the structure of their urethras. The urethra is the route by which urine leaves the bladder to be voided from the body and the passage is relatively narrow, particularly in neutered toms. If a plug of material builds up here, the cat will have difficulty in urinating and will usually refuse to squat down low as normal. It is also likely to be reluctant to leave its dirt box and any urine which is passed may contain signs of blood. Cystitis, or inflammation of the bladder, can also be associated with urolithasis, but is seen especially in female cats. Actual bladder stones are relatively rare in cats, especially toms.

The underlying trigger for urolithasis is not clearly understood, although several predisposing factors have been implicated. It occurs more commonly in neutered obese cats fed a high proportion of dry food in their diets. Infections, perhaps surprisingly, do not often occur in conjunction with urolithasis. It is, nevertheless, a serious condition and needs rapid treatment. Severe illness resulting from the build up of toxic chemicals in the body and dehydration will be noticeable within 24 hours of the obstruction developing.

The veterinarian may have to give the cat an anaesthetic, in order to insert a draining tube, or catheter, up through the urethra into the bladder, cautiously breaking down the obstruction in the process. Pressure on the bladder itself has to be exerted extremely carefully because of the risk of rupturing it. In severe cases where catheterization is not possible, the bladder may have to be emptied directly.

Intravenous correction of the dehydration which accompanies the obstruction is likely to be necessary; subsequently, the cat should be encouraged to drink as much as possible. Salt can be sprinkled on food but it may promote diarrhoea in some cats. Gravy is another possible alternative; it is also sensible to change the diet to canned and fresh food, both of which have a relatively high water content. A veterinarian may also recommend a urinary acidifier such as ammonium chloride, although this is unpalatable to many cats. By increasing the acidity of the urine, these chemicals will make the compounds responsible for the blockage more soluble and less likely to crystallize out in the urethra.

Circulatory disorders
Heart disease is relatively rare in cats but certain developmental defects, such as hole-in-the-heart, are occasionally encountered in kittens. Valvular problems, often arising from bacterial infections, do not produce severe symptoms, which is probably as well because treatment is difficult. Digitalis, commonly used in other species, produces toxic effects including vomiting at very low dosage levels in cats.

Arterial thrombosis usually affects cats in middle age with the thrombi, or clots, occurring on the heart valves, perhaps as a sequel to infection, rather than in the coronary arteries supplying the heart as in humans. Pieces of such clots are liable to break off and are then carried to other parts of the circulatory system. In the cat these emboli often lodge in the terminal part of the aorta, blocking the branches known as the iliac arteries, which are responsible for supplying blood to the hindlimbs. When this happens, the cat's hindlegs suddenly fail for no apparent reason and they feel cold, while a pulse is very hard to detect.

Spontaneous recovery may occur if the blood supply is restored by alternative channels or forces its way past the clot. Local damage resulting from the interruption to the blood supply is likely to persist, however, and the limb may well remain weak. Kidney damage can also be associated with this condition. Unfortunately, recurrences are not uncommon; the use of anticoagulents as preventive therapy, apart from being hazardous, is not always successful. Euthanasia may be necessary if the cat appears very distressed.

The most significant blood disorder seen in cats is feline leukemia, a cancer caused by a virus — FeLV or feline leukemia virus. Anaemia, which results from the decrease in the number of red cells, can occur independently of leukemia. FeLV also causes the disease called lymphosarcomatosis, by far the most common cancer encountered in cats, which produces tumours at various sites in the body. The virus responsible can be present in the saliva, milk and urine, apart from the blood of infected cats, but does not survive well in the environment generally, lasting a maximum of three days. Spread is therefore most noticeable in areas where cats are kept together in a confined environment.

After exposure to the virus, 60 to 70 percent of cats will recover without problems, either because they are naturally resistant or because they develop effective antibodies. The remainder of infected cats are unable to overcome the virus and these are likely to succumb to its effects, especially leukemia and lymphosarcomatosis. The cat's resistance to other infections will also be lowered. The incubation period before the onset of symptoms is very variable and may be as long as several years. The tumours associated with the disease most commonly affect the intestine and kidneys in the abdomen, while the thymus gland in the neck is a common site in younger cats. The symptoms vary according to the organs affected. In the case of a tumour affecting the thymus, the cat may have difficulty in swallowing and breathing because of pressure on the nearby oesophagus and trachea, and a cough.

Lymph nodes are often enlarged in this condition and this will help a veterinarian to diagnose the disease. A blood test is useful for diagnosis. The disease can then be confirmed by removing a small section from a lymph node for study under a microscope, which will show that the normal structure of the node is lost.

There are various sites around the body where blood can be taken but most commonly a sample is collected from the cephalic vein running down the front of each forelimb. The area concerned is clipped of fur and swabbed and the vein is raised in order to insert the needle. Many cats do not resent this procedure, although if they have been upset by the journey or by waiting in the veterinary surgery, they may not prove very cooperative.

Show cats in particular are often given routine blood tests for FeLV and when a positive result is recorded, even though no symptoms are apparent, the cat should be kept in strict isolation for several months. The test will have to be repeated; if it is negative, the cat has overcome the infection and is immune. A second positive test indicates that the cat is still infective and is also likely to succumb to the disease.

There is no cure for feline leukemia virus or its associated tumours, although certain drugs can be used to obtain some remission. If a cat is diagnosed as suffering from FeLV it is better to have it painlessly destroyed, rather than allowing it to remain a source of infection for others. Research is continuing to produce a vaccine. There is no evidence to suggest that FeLV can be transmitted to humans but sensible precautions should be taken when handling such cats, if only because they represent a potential hazard to others.

Respiratory infection
Cats are very susceptible to certain viral infections affecting the respiratory tract and these are often complicated by the presence of secondary bacterial invaders. The two most important diseases are feline viral rhinotracheitis (FVR) and feline calicivirus infection, which account for 80 percent of cases of respiratory infection worldwide. These two infections are often labelled as 'cat flu', a term also used to describe FIE. A similar infection, caused by the feline chlamydial agent, an organism with certain characteristics of both a virus and a bacterium, is regarded as being a major cause of respiratory disease in cats in North America, but may only produce mild symptoms such as conjunctivitis, characterized by weepy eyes. Unlike viruses, this infection will respond to antibiotic therapy.

The incubation period of FVR depends largely on the dose of virus received by the cat and extends between two and 10 days. The virus can only survive outside the body for a maximum period of 18 hours and is readily destroyed by disinfectants such as cetrimide. Infection can be spread by various means, either directly from the resulting discharges from the eyes and nose, or from urine and faeces, where it is present in small amounts. Cats may also pick up the virus from contaminated food bowls or dirt boxes. Sneezing is another route of spread, as infective droplets can carry a distance of up to nearly 7ft (2m).

The first signs of infection are likely to be depression and loss of appetite, followed by repeated attacks of sneezing. The discharge from the eyes and nose will appear clear at first, turning yellowish and cloudy once bacteria are present. Small, elongated ulcers will be apparent in the mouth, especially on the upper surface of the tongue, and make eating painful. Young cats are especially susceptible to FVR and can show signs of infection for up to six weeks in bad cases, coupled with severe weight loss. In pregnant queens, abortion may well result from infection.

Calicivirus (FCV) can also lead to ulceration of the mouth, but is less severe than FVR. It is important to persuade an affected cat to continue eating if possible; strong-smelling foods, such as sardines or pilchards in tomato sauce, may prove acceptable. These can be broken up with a fork so they are less painful to swallow and do not require much chewing.

There is no real treatment for either FVR or FCV, but antibiotics should help to prevent serious bacterial complications. With effective vaccines available against these infections, all cats should really be protected, but sadly this is not the case. Very occasionally, the vaccine itself proves unreliable. Particular sites for spread of such respiratory infections are places where cats congregate, such as shows and boarding kennels. When an outbreak does occur in kennels, rigorous disinfection with cetrimide, good ventilation, ensuring approximately 12 changes of air in the room per hour, and spacing the cats as far apart as possible is recommended.

Even after recovery, cats can continue excreting the virus and infecting others for up to 11 months. While FVR virus is excreted intermittently, especially after periods of stress such as a move, FCV will be constantly passed into the cat's environment. Care must be taken to ensure that susceptible individuals are not exposed to infection by this means.

One of the most serious complications associated with such infections is chronic rhinitis (runny nose) and related problems, such as sinusitis and blocked nostrils. These cases can be be very difficult to clear up successfully and require weeks of antibiotic therapy, rather than days as is normal. The veterinarian may take a swab of any discharge for culture purposes. The swab is carefully wiped over the surface of a special media in a dish and this is then incubated. The resulting bacteria can be assessed for their reaction to various antibiotics to discover which is likely to prove most effective.

Nervous disorders

RABIES Rabies affects cats, as well as all other warm-blooded creatures, and there is no treatment for this dreaded disease when symptoms are apparent. Humans face an appalling death if they are bitten by an infected animal or even if saliva containing the virus enters the body via a cut. The fear of water, or hydrophobia, typically associated with the latter stages of the human infection does not occur in animals. The incubation period for this disease is quite variable; it may be as long as six months before symptoms become evident. The virus travels up the peripheral nervous system to the brain; if it is introduced to the body close to the head, symptoms will appear shortly.

In the early stages particularly, rabies does not produce any clear-cut diagnostic signs. There may be a change in the cat's character at first, followed by aggressive behaviour and a lack of response to painful stimuli. Excessive drooling from the mouth, resulting from an inability to swallow even saliva, may be noticeable, while an alteration to the sound of the voice can also become apparent. Paralysis will develop, followed by a coma and then death. Symptoms may be evident over a two to 10 day period on average, but the cat will actually be infective before it starts to exhibit clinical signs.

Rabies is an insidious disease; in many parts of the world, such as North America where infection is endemic in the wildlife, cats can be routinely vaccinated against the disease. Britain is currently free of rabies and has very strict controls on the import of cats and other mammals to maintain this status. Vaccination here is not normally permitted unless the cat concerned is being sent abroad to an area where rabies occurs, and must be authorized by the Ministry of Agriculture, Fisheries and Food.

Any animal suspected of being infected should not be handled if at all possible. Veterinary advice must be sought immediately. When approaching such an animal, protective clothing, including gloves, will be necessary. If there is any likelihood of human infection, the wound should be washed out at once, preferably with ethanol, or else water, followed by application of a tincture of iodine solution. A doctor must, of course, be contacted at once.

KEY-GASKELL SYNDROME An apparently new disease affecting the nervous system of cats was identified in Britain in 1982 and appears to be quite widespread. It has become known as the Key-Gaskell Syndrome, after the two workers at the Bristol Veterinary School who first recognized the disorder. All cats seem to be susceptible, although a higher incidence of disease has been noted in young shorthairs. The illness can strike kittens as young as 10 weeks old and there is no difference between the sexes in susceptibility. The disease may not be infectious, since often only one cat in a multi-cat household will develop symptoms and those living permanently indoors on their own can also be affected.

Two forms of the illness are recognized. In one type, the cat appears quite normal with a healthy appetite during the evening, but then starts vomiting at night. It loses its appetite, and the pupils of the eyes are noticeably dilated. Diarrhoea may also be apparent; in the more protracted cases, constipation is likely to be noted. Symptoms may at first resemble an upper respiratory tract infection, with sneezing being evident. Weakness of the hindlimbs or more generalized loss of mobility is also observed in many cases.

The disease exerts its effects on the autonomic nervous system. The ganglia, where the nerve cells link together, show characteristic changes. Since the actual cause of the Key-Gaskell Syndrome has not been discovered yet, treatment is restricted to alleviating the symptoms. Fluid drips to counteract the dehydration and stimulation of tear and mouth secretions by appropriate drugs all have a part to play, but cannot repair the damage to the nervous system. Cats should be showing an improvement within three weeks, if they are likely to recover successfully. Those which continue vomiting will probably not overcome the effects of the disease.

Research into the Key-Gaskell Syndrome is continuing. The possible role of fleas and their control has been a focus of attention, with one suggestion being that the disease may be linked as a sequel to treatment, but this has not yet been confirmed and the most recent work tends to dismiss this theory. When a case is diagnosed, it is probably sensible to keep the cat isolated and disinfect its environment thoroughly, in case the illness could prove infectious to others.

Age

The lifespan of cats varies widely. Those living wild as strays may only survive for two years or so while individuals kept as pets are often likely to live well into their teens. As with all creatures, cats tend to become less active as they grow older and it will be normal for them to spend relatively long periods sleeping, choosing comfortable locations near a radiator or fire in winter, lazing in warm spots during the summer. They are more susceptible to extremes of temperature in old age and may not want to wander outside on cold days. They will often be reluctant to go out if it is wet and a dirt box indoors will be necessary.

Changes in the lifestyle of an older cat are gradual and often insidious, linked to failing health. The teeth, after many years of use, are likely to be showing signs of wear; dental care is often needed to keep an elderly cat eating. If a veterinarian has to extract teeth, softer foods should be provided. The appetite of older cats is likely to decline with the decrease in their activity and some become relatively finicky eaters. Their diet will need to be adapted accordingly. Sardines in oil once or twice a week will help to prevent constipation, a condition to which elderly cats are prone. Beef mince, rolled in bran, is also palatable and will add fibre to the diet.

Constipation may also arise in conjunction with a decrease in fluid intake; the faeces will be relatively dry and harder to void. In most cases the underlying cause is likely to be a decrease in muscle tone of the intestines, so that the passage of their contents is slowed down. In a severe case of constipation the use of a laxative, as recommended for fur balls, should prove effective.

More specific signs of old age include changes in the coat. Fur around the muzzle tends to become paler, while the hair is likely to be thinner and dryer overall. Progressive deafness may also be noted, along with failing eyesight, although both conditions are quite rare in cats.

Regular veterinary checks, every nine months or so depending on the cat's state of health, are advisable. With age, the cat will be less able to sharpen its own claws, and these may become overgrown. Arthritis is not a severe problem in cats but degenerative changes in the joints may result in intermittent lameness, typically after a period of rest. If the cat does become noticeably handicapped, veterinary advice must be sought. Under no circumstances should human treatments be administered as they are likely to prove toxic. The choice of drugs available to

alleviate these symptoms is rather restricted because of the cat's inability to metabolize many drugs successfully. This task is largely undertaken by the liver whose functioning ability also declines with age, so relatively small doses will be necessary to prevent a toxic reaction.

The most significant problem with old cats is, however, progressive kidney failure. The condition is reflected by an increased fluid intake and a correspondingly raised urine output. Incontinence may also occur, while appetite will be reduced, leading to weight loss over a period of time. There is also increased loss of the water-soluble B vitamins and so a net deficiency may well result. It is always worth

Cats left to fend for themselves or abandoned by inconsiderate owners have a much shorter lifespan than those kept as pets. A farm cat will usually survive well, however, living off rodent populations and sheltering in barns and outhouses (RIGHT). It is quite common to see colonies of cats living wild in derelict areas of towns and cities (BELOW and BELOW RIGHT). Despite the efforts of animal welfare organizations and concerned individuals, the increased risk of disease and injury, the effects of ill health brought on by an inadequate diet and simple exposure to the elements will all lessen chances of survival (FAR RIGHT).

supplementing the intake of these particular vitamins in an elderly cat. Vitamin B12 appears to act as an appetite stimulant and may be given in the form of an injection by a veterinarian, to assist the overall condition of a geriatric cat.

If the cat has bad breath, this could indicate teething problems perhaps with gingivitis, which is inflammation of the gums, or kidney failure or a combination of both factors. When consulting a veterinarian, it is worth taking a fresh urine sample obtained from the cat, in a clean sealed jar. This can be tested immediately using a narrow strip impregnated with suitable chemical compounds, which

may help to reveal characteristic changes notably in the protein and sugar levels of the urine.

The sample can be most easily collected by lining the dirt box with clean metallic foil and then carefully pouring the urine into the jar. Alternatively, a smaller piece of foil with raised edges may be slid under the cat when it is in the process of urinating. This may disturb it but only a relatively small amount of urine is required. It is absolutely vital, however, that the container used for the sample is thoroughly clean; deposits of sugar for example, will ensure a false reading.

Where kidney failure is suspected, the veterinarian is also

likely to palpate the cat's kidneys directly. It is relatively easy to feel the kidneys either side of the vertebrae in the abdomen; when these have shrunk and have a pitted surface, they are not functioning effectively. There is no curative treatment for kidney failure in an elderly cat, but it can be possible to stabilize the condition by medical means and dietary changes. The latter may not always be practical; reducing the cat's protein intake when its appetite is already in decline might serve to worsen the situation and a compromise over food is likely to be necessary.

The kidneys, along with other body organs, may be sites for tumours in later life. Another relatively common site in cats is the oesophagus. The symptoms associated with tumours vary according to their location, in this instance, repeated regurgitation of food is likely to be indicative of a malignancy. It is possible to confirm the presence of such obstructions in the gullet by means of radiology. A contrast medium, typically barium, serves to highlight the tumour on the resulting X-ray.

Euthanasia

There comes a time when it is no longer fair to keep the cat alive. This is always a fraught decision and one which must ultimately be taken by the owner, although a veterinarian will be able to advise and discuss the matter beforehand. Once any cat has reached the point where it appears to be suffering — constantly vomiting its food or persistently refusing to eat, for example — then euthanasia must be seriously considered if no hope of treatment remains.

While many owners prefer their pet to end its days in home surroundings, it is often better to make the final gesture of farewell and take the cat to the veterinary surgery. There is no need to be present at the end and the cat itself will probably be less distressed if left on its own. An emotionally charged atmosphere is likely to be detected by the cat and will serve to upset it unnecessarily.

The task itself will be quickly and efficiently performed by the veterinarian, with the assistance of a nurse. The most widely used method consists of injecting a measured overdose of barbiturate, usually into one of the leg veins. The cat then quietly passes away in a matter of seconds with no signs of distress. The procedure is identical to that carried out for anaesthetic purposes except that the barbiturate solution used for euthanasia is much stronger. Another means of euthanasia involves the use of a halothane mask, normally reserved for anaesthetic purposes.

Afterwards, some owners prefer to bury their pets in the garden, although this is not permitted in all areas. A deep hole, preferably at least 2ft (60cm) should be dug; it is now possible to obtain a coffin of appropriate dimensions if required. Another alternative may be a neighbourhood pet cemetery, where even headstones are available and the plot is kept neat and tidy for an annual fee. Veterinarians can also arrange disposal of the body by cremation or the local authority waste collection service.

Cat Diseases and Human Health

Zoonoses — diseases which can be passed from animals to humans — have attracted much attention over the past few years. No cat disease presents a significant danger to human health in the average household, however, unless children are allowed close, unsupervised contact. Ringworm is perhaps the most common zoonosis and may produce no clear-cut signs in the cat itself. To combat other diseases regular worming and rapid hygienic disposal of cat faeces will be necessary. The risk of toxoplasmosis is immediately removed by such simple precautions in the home.

Cat bites and scratches can be unpleasant, and must be washed thoroughly at once, using hot water and a suitable antiseptic. In the same way that a bite may lead to an abscess in another cat, so a similar infection can develop in humans. Providing the wound is kept clean and dabbed with antiseptic cream, it should heal without problems. If an abscess does develop, causing a painful swelling at the site of the injury, antibiotic treatment and medical advice will be required. In all such cases, if the person bitten has not received a tetanus vaccination for the previous three years, then it is sensible to contact a doctor, especially since a cat's bite can be fairly deep. The bacteria which cause tetanus develop best under such conditions, where their immediate environment contains little oxygen. If rabies is endemic in the area, a doctor must be consulted at once.

A rare illness typically associated with cat scratches may result in a mild, febrile condition in humans. The lymph nodes of the body become noticeably swollen, although this symptom is associated with many other diseases; the person will also feel very weak. The disease is referred to as Japanese cat scratch fever and is thought to be caused by a virus but is not confined exclusively to Japan. Blood tests may be useful in diagnosing the illness, although recovery is generally uneventful. Cats will rarely scratch or bite unless frightened or in pain themselves.

In a home where very young children are present close supervision of cats is essential. Various cases of suffocation have resulted from a cat lying over a baby's face. Although death may not occur, there can still be serious and permanent brain damage. One such instance reported in the *British Medical Journal* in 1982 concerned a five-week-old baby girl, previously quite healthy. She was discovered with the cat positioned across her face, had turned blue because of a lack of oxygen and was having difficulty in breathing. Although this baby appeared to recover after a short period of time following artificial resuscitation, other disorders soon became evident, including convulsions. It was obvious that her nervous system had been impaired; when she died at eight months, it was discovered that her brain showed the typical signs of oxygen deprivation. While positive confirmation that the cat was directly responsible for the baby's handicap was not possible, the risk is obvious.

Providing parents are aware of this potential threat, similar tragedies will not occur and a cat can be kept safely in the same household as a baby. Great care must be taken to close doors and windows as necessary, so the location of the cat in relation to the baby is always known. Older children, as well as visitors, should be advised of the danger, so they themselves can take care to exclude the cat from the baby's room. The warmth of the body of a young child and its soft surroundings will attract the cat, which is really only seeking a comfortable bed itself.

Human allergies to cats are not uncommon. These give runny eyes and noses, repeated sneezing and even difficulty in breathing in severe cases. The symptoms are similar to other allergies such as those to pollen or household dust; confirmation can only be obtained after a simple, painless skin test carried out by a doctor. The fur and possibly the skin debris of the cat will give rise to such allergies, most commonly associated with longhaired breeds.

While cat diseases do not present a significant danger to human health in the average household, sensible precautions should be taken to minimize the risk. Ringworm, a skin disease caused by a fungus and transmitted by cats, is one of the most common problems particularly as the cat itself may have no obvious symptoms. Children should not be allowed close contact with cats unless supervised by an adult; this will help to reduce the chances of the cat scratching or biting due to incorrect handling *(LEFT)*. Babies should never be left alone in a room with a cat: cats like soft, warm places and may accidentally smother a young child in its cot. Pregnant women should never clean litter trays or come into contact with cat faeces. Toxoplasmosis, a parasitical infection transmitted by this means, can affect unborn children.

Mouse Colour English

Bed Fellers of Kittens

Reproduction

Cats are by nature highly sexed animals. This trait is shared by wild felids; lionesses on heat mate every quarter-hour during the three-day period, and a pair of leopards were once recorded mating 100 times in 11 hours. Even if owners do not want their cats to breed, an understanding of the way the cat's reproductive cycle works is important.

Thousands of unwanted cats are born each year; many of these are destroyed or live for only a brief time as strays — finding good homes for crossbred kittens often proves extremely difficult. It is part of the responsibility of every cat owner not to add to the numbers of these abandoned animals. Neutering not only prevents unwanted kittens, but also serves to eliminate certain unwelcome aspects of behaviour and make the cat more adapted to life in domestic surroundings.

Care and nurturing of kittens is almost exclusively the concern of the female cat: this is true in the domestic species *(TOP)* and in the case of wild felids, such as the lion *(FAR LEFT)*. For the first three weeks, the mother (dam) will devote all of her time and energies to her kittens, rarely leaving the nest. Kittens are born blind and virtually helpless and spend most of their early days suckling *(LEFT)*. By about the third week, they acquire a measure of independence and begin to explore the world outside their nest *(ABOVE)*. At this stage, the mother will often refuse to suckle them on demand and will leave the nest herself for longer periods.

The Reproductive System of the Male

The reproductive anatomy of the male cat is not very different from that of other mammals, in spite of its internal penis. This organ deposits semen in the female's reproductive tract, and swells with blood during periods of sexual excitement to facilitate penetration of the vagina. The penis of the cat, however, is barbed with small spines around the tip, or glans. These may serve to keep the erect penis in position, but also appear to stimulate ovulation in the female.

The testes, where the semen is produced, are located outside the body because body temperature is too high for spermatozoa to mature successfully. Prior to birth, the testes develop first in the abdomen of the kitten and then descend into the scrotal sac. On some occasions this may not occur and one or, rarely, both testes are retained in the body. Such cats are known as cryptorchids. The testicle will need to be removed surgically if it has not descended by the age of eight months. Castration alone is not recommended because the cat will continue to display the typical signs of male behaviour, including spraying.

In the testes, semen is produced in the seminiferous tubules, while the neighbouring interstitial cells are responsible for producing the sex hormone testosterone. This is sometimes known as the 'male' hormone, but can also be detected in females, who correspondingly possess relatively higher levels of oestrogen, the 'female' hormone, than males. Testosterone is responsible for the development and maintenance of the secondary sexual characteristics which, in the case of the cat, include the presence of thicker skin in the region of the neck, and prominent jowls around the face.

The Reproductive System of the Female

The uterus of the female cat has two relatively long 'horns' which connect to the ovaries by tubes known as oviducts. The horns meet to form the body of the uterus which terminates in the cervix and connects to the vagina, or birth canal, where the male inserts his penis. The reproductive cycle in the queen cat differs from that of the human female

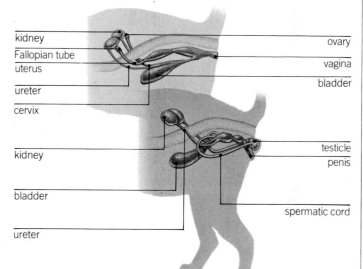

Cou[...]
violen[...]
not ac[...]
LEFT). M[...]
brief pro[...]
repeated [...]. ro
show her w[...].. ́o mate, the
female will r[...] and display to
the male stalking around her (1).
Prior to mating, the female will
adopt a characteristic posture,
known as lordosis, raising her
hindquarters to the male and
displaying her vulva (2). The
male will mount her, often
grabbing the scruff of her neck;
sometimes biting (3). Ovulation is
brought on by the act of mating
(4). The reproductive systems of
the male and female cat are
broadly similar to those of other
mammals (BELOW).

kidney
Fallopian tube
uterus
ureter
cervix
kidney
bladder
ureter
ovary
vagina
bladder
testicle
penis
spermatic cord

and indeed most mammals, in several fundamental respects. The most important of these is the fact that the actual release of eggs, or ovulation, is brought about by mating.

Ovulation, as with other reproductive processes, is mediated by hormones released under the control of part of the brain called the hypothalamus. It triggers an adjoining region, known as the anterior pituitary, which in turn then produces and liberates follicle stimulating hormone (FSH) into the circulation. The hormone acts on the ovaries, stimulating the development of fluid-filled follicles containing ova. The ovaries contain masses of minute ova from birth, but only a relatively small proportion of these will develop and be released during the individual's lifetime. Oestrogen is produced within the follicles and this produces characteristic signs of 'heat' or sexual activity, as well as preparing the uterus to receive the fertilized ova.

The process of fertilization, when a male sperm fuses with an ovum, normally occurs in the uterine horns, with the sperm swimming up through the cervix from the vagina. The number of ova released will determine the maximum number of kittens which can be born; this number is usually between three and six. The fertilized ovum then moves down into the uterine horns where the process of implantation, or attachment to the uterine wall, occurs, giving rise to the development of a placenta.

Although only one sperm can fertilize an ovum, it is possible for a queen to bear kittens by different sires in one litter if matings occur very closely together. Certain queens will also mate while pregnant and can even conceive during this period, although such behaviour is unusual. The second set of kittens may be born prematurely at the same time as those from the initial mating. Under controlled conditions such events are not likely to occur.

The Breeding Period and Mating

The female cat may start having oestrus cycles when only three and a half months old, although this is quite unusual. Seven months is more likely, perhaps even later in the case of some longhairs. Siamese as a general rule mature early,

but other factors, such as climate, can also be significant. Kittens born in a spring which precedes a cold summer may not start their cycles until they are one year old. Tom cats are unlikely to be mature before one year and in some instances may not reach puberty until their second year.

The breeding period, during which time a queen may cycle continuously, extends over the greater part of the year, from the end of December until the beginning of the following September. Most kittens are born during July and August, although later litters are not unknown if the weather remains mild. When in oestrus, the queen is said to be 'calling'. This description results from the noise made by certain cats, notably Siamese, during this period. Reliance on calling alone to detect oestrus is not reliable in all cases. Many foreign breeds, such as the Russian Blue, may not be noticeably vocal. It is also difficult to detect oestrus by changes in the vulval region, as only a very slight swelling may be evident around the vulval lips. Other behavioural signs are much more helpful. Queens on heat become restless and often abnormally affectionate; they also rub and lick the area around their vulvas repeatedly.

The oestrus period in the cat supposedly lasts for three weeks, but signs of oestrus will be particularly noticeable for one week. Several males will make advances before one is finally accepted. This stage lasts from 12 hours to four days as a rule, during which time the queen, if she is allowed out, may not return home. Once the female has decided on a mate, repeated episodes of copulation over a day or so usually occur. The protracted courtship is thought to bring the ovarian follicles up to the point of rupture, when the enclosed ova are liberated and can then be fertilized.

Mating itself is a relatively brief procedure, with the male stalking around the female as ⟨ moves and displays to him. Matin ⟨ the female's cooperation, as ⟨ hindquarters to a virtually horizon ⟨ her vulva to the male. He will grab t ⟨ his mouth and may actually bite her ⟨

There is no 'tie', or locking, as occu⟨ ⟨ ⟨ ⟨ ⟨ une spines on the male's penis prove traur ⟨ ⟨e vaginal walls, especially on withdrawal. The si ⟨ ⟨icance of these spines is not completely understood, but they may serve to stimulate the release of luternizing hormone (LH) from the pituitary of the female, which in turn ensures that the follicles rupture. At these sites structures known as corpora lutea develop, and begin secreting progesterone. This hormone ensures that the uterus will be ready to accept the fertilized ova and, with declining levels of oestrogen in the circulation, the queen's sexual drive diminishes accordingly. Releasing ova in response to coitus appears to have particular benefits for creatures which are only drawn together for mating purposes. Regular release of ova, as occurs monthly in human females, provides no guarantee for solitary creatures that a male would be in the vicinity to effect fertilization when the ova are released, and thus the future of the next generation would be threatened.

Stud mating

For the ordinary owner, there is rarely any financial benefit to be gained from keeping and breeding from a pedigree queen — bloodlines are only established over a period of years, with considerable work and effort. Many owners, however, prefer to pay a stud fee to have their cats mated to another pedigree, particularly if any of the kittens are to be

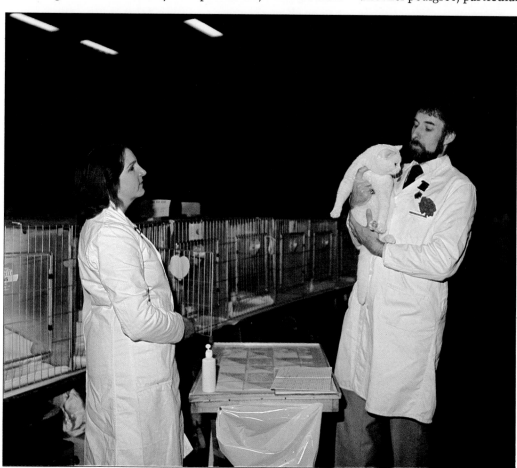

Choosing the right stud cat is an important decision for the pedigree breeder. Visiting cat shows is a good way of studying the characteristics of a particular breed, noting type and colour of regular winners and making contact with other breeders *(RIGHT)*. Pedigree studs are advertised in cat magazines; before selecting a particular stud, it is useful to visit the breeder's premises to see the particular tom and inspect the quarters. The premises should be clean, with all the cats in good health. At this stage, the fee should be decided, together with any other contractual conditions. Many breeders will also advise on the selection of the stud cat. A good stud tom should complement the queen, not reinforce her strengths and weaknesses *(FAR LEFT)*. The resulting kittens should then show an overall improvement on both parents.

DEVELOPMENT OF THE FETUS In the first stage, known as implantation, a connection is made with the uterine wall about two weeks after mating (1). The embryo is nourished by a yolk sac until the placental connection is fully operational and the umbilical cord has developed (2, 3). This is achieved by day 22 of pregnancy; at the same time the head and limbs are becoming apparent (4). At four weeks old, the fetus is about 1in (2.5cm) in length and its organ systems are fully formed (5). Five weeks after mating the fetuses will be causing a swelling of their mother's abdomen. The fetus may double in size within a week, reaching its final size of about 5in (12.5cm)(6).

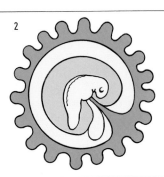

kept. If an intact pedigree queen is allowed to roam free, the litters will almost certainly be crossbred.

The advice of an experienced breeder is invaluable when selecting a stud or a queen for breeding purposes. The stud tom should complement the particular queen, balancing out her own strengths and weaknesses so that the kittens show improvement overall. Visits to shows will give opportunities to assess type and bloodlines and cat magazines can be studied to keep in touch with regular winners.

Championship winners are not often for sale but most breeders are prepared to part with kittens with good pedigrees. When starting a stud, breeders often begin with one or two queens and increase numbers as the stud develops around the kittens. Indeed, it is often more satisfactory to obtain young cats as breeding stock, rather than buying a mature individual, unless its past history is known. Such cats often prove liabilities and may turn out to be poor mothers. Kittens from a relatively large litter are sought by many breeders because it appears that they, in turn, may produce slightly more offspring per litter than is average for the breed concerned.

It is usual practice to mate a queen at her second, rather than first heat, although problems can arise with precocious breeds. Siamese may commence calling before four months of age, but should not really be mated until eight months, preferably later. Unfortunately, the follicles on the ovaries may develop into cysts if the cat is not allowed to mate. Veterinary advice will be necessary to deal with this condition if the cat fails to mate or conceive.

Visiting the stud gives an opportunity to see the tom and view the premises. The stud quarters should be kept extremely clean and thoroughly disinfected between queens. It is also important to establish the stud fee; this will be influenced by the status of the male, with championship winners commanding correspondingly higher fees. There is no guarantee that mating will produce any kittens and some owners will permit a second mating period free of charge in the event of an initial failure.

When the queen starts calling, an appointment can be confirmed by telephone with the stud owner. The queen should then be taken to the stud with minimum disturbance, especially in the case of an uninitiated cat. Relevant papers must also be taken: the queen's pedigree, and vaccination certificates both for feline infectious enteritis and respiratory viruses are likely to be required, possibly together with the result of screening for feline leukemia virus. Many stud owners also like a diet sheet for the queen, as she will remain in residence for several days.

It is quite normal for the stud owner to examine the incoming queen for any signs of illness and even to take her temperature. This is often slightly raised as a result of the journey. If the queen appears at all off-colour, it is preferable from all points of view to defer mating until a later date.

Mating quarters consist of adjacent pens with a connecting door. The queen, still in her box, is introduced on one side of the partition and then released. The tom will already be on the opposite side; at first the door between the two will be kept closed. Some queens become very wild at the scent of a male and may scratch and struggle violently; they should never be carried free into the enclosure for this reason.

After a period adjusting to her environment, the queen will begin to acknowledge the male by rubbing along the bars to attract his attention. On rare occasions, the journey may have disturbed a queen so much that mating will have to be postponed until the next period of oestrus. The time taken to settle down in breeding quarters will vary greatly, largely according to the experience of the female; with previously unmated animals, it may take eight hours or so before they feel comfortable in their surroundings.

Once the signs of wanting to mate are evident, the cats can be allowed to mix together. After mating, the queen is likely to strike out at her mate and he must be allowed sufficient space to withdraw a safe distance. A shelf is often provided in stud quarters for this reason. The female's apparent resentment is normally brief; subsequently, mating may take place again.

The violent episodes which can occur during mating necessitate the constant yet discreet presence of the stud owner. Difficulties are especially likely to arise with inexperienced cats of either sex; pairings are usually arranged so that at least one partner knows the routine.

The queen is normally separated after one mating. Once she has settled down, she will be reintroduced to the tom for further matings. This procedure is carried out daily and should ensure successful fertilization of her ova. Most studs keep queens for at least three days and often longer, if the queen is left for a short period with the tom following the third mating.

Pregnancy
Signs
On her return home, the female cat should be kept isolated from other cats if possible and not allowed outside in case mating with another sire takes place. The follicles rupture about a day after coitus and, once the ova are fertilized, they reach the uterus within five days. Implantation occurs about two weeks after mating. The placentae, or 'after-births' develop; these provide the kittens with oxygen and nourishment via the blood and remove toxic waste products by the same route.

The gestation period is approximately 63 to 66 days following mating. Survival of kittens born prematurely — a

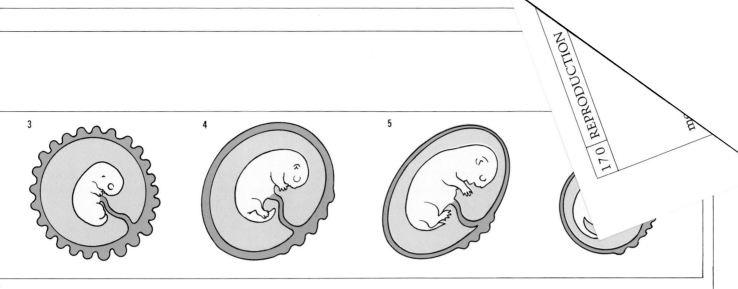

week or more early — is rare. Like human babies, such kittens will be unable to inflate their lungs and breathe atmospheric air.

It may be possible for an experienced breeder or veterinarian to detect the developing fetuses by gentle palpation of the abdomen about three weeks after mating. This should not be undertaken by the inexperienced; unintentional injury, either to the dam or the kittens, may result.

An external indication of pregnancy which appears about the same time is the development of the nipples, especially in cats giving birth for the first time. They enlarge and turn pink; this change is sometimes referred to as 'pinking up'. Three weeks after mating, the fetuses are about the size of peas, but will be causing a noticeable distension of their mother's abdomen a fortnight later. From day 49 of the pregnancy, it is possible to feel the distinct outline of the kittens in the uterus, although the actual number present is hard to detect accurately. Their developing skeletal systems will also appear on X-rays from this stage onwards, although unnecessary exposure to such radiation should be avoided if possible. The major period of the kittens' physical growth of the kittens takes place during the last third of pregnancy.

Care

The queen will not require significantly increased amounts of food until the kittens rapidly increase in size, from about six weeks onwards. She can be fed to appetite and in the latter stages may be taking twice her usual amount of food. This should be offered as three or four meals a day, while milk, a good source of calcium and other minerals, must also be freely available. For cats which cannot digest even goat's milk, alternative sources of calcium will need to be provided. Comprehensive supplements for all queens can be obtained from a veterinarian.

There is no need to restrict the activity of a pregnant cat, although she will need to be handled with extra care during the latter stages of pregnancy. The kittens, each weighing perhaps ¼lb (0.55kg), will be a considerable burden on a creature that normally only weighs 10lb (5kg) or so. About a week before the kittens are due, it is sensible to worm the queen so that she will be less likely to act as a source of infection. Treatment should be continued every week through the suckling phase.

At least 10 days before the kittens are due, cardboard boxes lined with paper towelling should be distributed in various warm, secure locations around the home. One side of each box should be cut away to allow easy access; later it can be taped back to prevent the kittens from walking off unsupervised. Paper towelling is preferable for bedding purposes because it can be easily discarded when soiled and

there will be no risk of young kittens being accidentally smothered. The queen will probably investigate all the boxes, before concentrating on one or two. As the time of birth approaches, she should be encouraged to select a suitable site by closing her in the room concerned; otherwise she may wander away or even adopt a bed for the purpose.

Birth

Cats do not normally have difficulty in giving birth, but it is advisable to notify the veterinarian of the likely date of the kittens' arrival, in case problems do arise. Immediately before giving birth, the contractions of the uterus will be visible against the cat's flanks and she will probably appear anxious and restless. However, even queens of the same breed can vary greatly in their reaction to giving birth. Once the movements in her sides are apparent, she must be confined to the room where the chosen box is located. Signs of a discharge in the vulval region may be evident; she will also start treading the paper to form a bed.

After the first stage of labour, the cat will then actively strain and may cry out. This is quite usual and not a cause for concern. She should be left without interference throughout the whole birth process unless difficulties arise. The period of straining before the first kitten is born can vary, and is often longer in cats giving birth for the first time, but will normally be about 30 to 45 minutes. The kittens should be presented (born) head first; occasionally breech presentations, with the hindquarters emerging first, are encountered. This can be dangerous, since the head may become stuck; the kitten concerned is likely to start breathing while still in the vagina and may choke as a result. Careful manipulation, using a clean towel or piece of cotton sheeting, will be necessary to free the kitten. It must be handled gently, preferably as close to the shoulders as possible, as that the risk of injury is minimized.

The third or final stage of labour entails the passing of the placentae, one for each kitten. This may be interspersed with the birth of subsequent kittens, but more commonly the young cat emerges still attached to its placenta. The connecting umbilical cord should be cut by the queen and she may then eat the afterbirth. This behaviour is quite normal, but it is perhaps preferable to remove the placentae if she shows no interest in them. Most litters consist of about four kittens but larger or smaller numbers are not uncommon. The kittens are usually born at intervals of between 10 minutes and an hour.

If the queen is very tired after giving birth, she might not cut the cord or break the amniotic sac enveloping the kitten. Without rapid assistance the young cat is likely to die. In such an emergency the sac can be broken with clean fingers and then, most importantly, the kitten's nose and mouth must be wiped clear of any debris, which may otherwise stop it breathing. Opening the jaws slightly with a finger should stimulate inflation of the lungs. If the kitten still does not respond after having been held upside down, its rib-cage should be rubbed repeatedly. Applying pressure to the chest is not recommended in case internal organs are damaged. The remaining alternative is artificial resuscitation.

If the cord has not been cut by the queen, a piece of cotton, previously boiled in water, should be tightly knotted around the cord about 1in (2.5cm) from the body. Hands should be washed thoroughly in cetrimide before performing this operation. Cut the cord on the side of the knot furthest from the body. A few drops of blood may appear but this is no cause for alarm if the cord is tied off adequately. The kitten should then be returned to its mother so that it can start suckling. The remains of the cord will eventually dry up and drop off.

After giving birth to all her kittens, the queen usually settles down and starts cleaning them while they suckle. Only now is she likely to take a drink to refresh herself; some queens stay with their offspring constantly for the first day. In rare cases, after the queen appears to have finished giving birth and everything is proceeding normally she may show signs of second-stage labour again up to a day later and produce more kittens.

Complications

There are several instances when veterinary assistance will be required. The first indication that all is not well will be if no kittens appear after the queen has been straining for an hour or more. The first kitten is probably in an incorrect position with its head causing an obstruction. Unfortunately, the birth canal of the cat is too small for a major manual correction of presentation. A Caesarean section may be required; providing surgery is begun without undue delay, there is usually a good prognosis for both mother and kittens. In some cases, such as a female with a fractured pelvis, the veterinarian may recommend simultaneous spaying, removing both kittens and uterus via an incision made in the abdominal wall. Abnormally large kittens, giving rise to the condition described as 'fetal oversize', are not common, but can sometimes be the case of a hold-up in the birth process.

It is important to check that the number of afterbirths passed corresponds to the number of kittens. If any are retained within the body, the cat is likely to become ill. They can be detached by suitable drugs, often given in the form of an injection. Any signs of a brownish discharge from the vagina, coupled with a raised temperature, must also be treated seriously. The cat will appear sick and dull and rapidly lose interest in her kittens. Antibiotic therapy will prove effective in most cases.

Once the kittens are suckling, the mammary glands should be observed for any signs of mastitis. The glands most commonly involved are those nearest the tail, but often only one will be affected. It will appear painful, hot and swollen, as a result of the accumulation of pus within and the queen will resent any kittens attempting to suckle from it. Apart from antibiotic treatment, some protection

Determining the sex of kittens can be difficult *(LEFT)*. Both have two openings, the female's anal and genital openings closer together (1) than the male's (2). The umbilical cord dries up soon after birth, leaving the belly button or umbilicus *(RIGHT)*. An orphan kitten is best fostered, but if there is no alternative to hand-rearing, a milk substitute should be given. Encourage the kitten to suck by only releasing small amounts at a time *(BELOW)*.

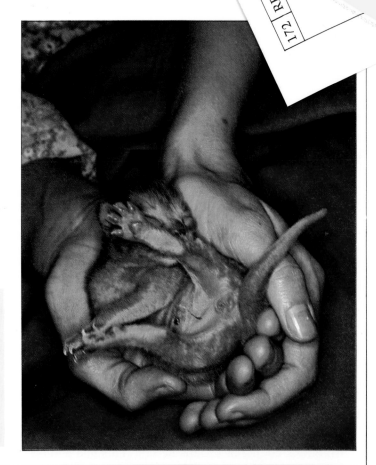

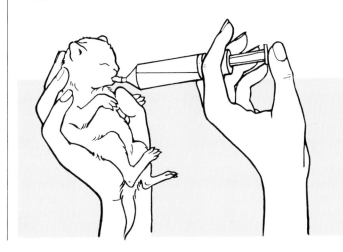

LABOUR Cats normally give birth without any difficulty. The first signs that a queen is about to give birth include general restlessness and heaving movements of her flanks, indicating that contractions have begun. At this point, she should be confined to the room where the nesting box is located (1). After a period of straining, the first kitten will appear as a protrusion from the vagina. Once the kitten is born, the mother will free it from any retaining membranes and rupture the umbilical cord (2). More kittens will be born at regular intervals (3) and each one will be licked vigorously to encourage it to breathe (4). After each kitten is born, its placenta or afterbirth will be passed and the mother may eat it if it is not taken away (5). It is important to check that one afterbirth has been passed for each kitten. The kittens may begin suckling before the last of the litter is born (6); once all the kittens have arrived, the mother will settle and clean them thoroughly while they feed (7). Most litters consist of about four kittens.

must be given to the gland itself to minimize discomfort.

Of the other conditions that affect a cat which has recently given birth, perhaps the most serious is prolapse of the uterus where the uterus is expressed through the vagina. This is typically associated with a prolonged birth cycle or excessive straining; the uterus will hang out as a red, inflamed mass of tissue. Rapid veterinary attention is required to clean the uterus and reinsert it back in the abdominal cavity.

One of the most disturbing disorders of the lactating queen is lactation tetany or milk fever, seen predominantly in cats nursing large litters. Shaking, muscle tremors and collapse typically occur, but rapid treatment with calcium borogluconate, given by a veterinarian, will lead to a spectacular recovery. It is also advisable to reduce the number of kittens being suckled by placing a few with a foster mother, but they should remain with their mother for the first few days in order to obtain the 'first milk', or colostrum, a fluid containing vital antibodies.

Care of Kittens
Hand-rearing

If kittens are orphaned the use of a foster mother is to be recommended if at all possible; rearing kittens by hand is an extremely time-consuming, albeit rewarding, task especially during the early weeks. Cats will readily foster other kittens alongside their own without difficulties, providing their litter is relatively small. One or two kittens from a large litter could be transferred usefully to a queen with only a couple of kittens herself. This is a potential advantage of having two cats expecting litters at approximately the same time. A vet may be able to help find a foster mother.

If a foster mother cannot be found, the necessary milk substitute powder can be obtained from a vet. Complete products which correspond exactly to the queen's milk are now available; alternatively, other general rearing foods sold in pet stores can be used. Cow's milk alone is inadequate because it contains insufficient protein to support the growing kittens. Special feeding bottles for kittens are also produced but in an emergency a simple eye-dropper or a 5ml syringe without a needle can be used.

Good hygiene plays a very important part in successful rearing. Feeding bottles must always be kept scrupulously clean, and should be thoroughly washed and rinsed between feeds. The milk powder should be mixed fresh each time according to the instructions and offered at a temperature of 100°F (38°C). It is vital never to rush a feed; otherwise there is a significant risk of choking the kitten. Fluid entering the lungs is likely to lead to the development of inhalation pneumonia, with serious, often fatal, consequences. Kittens rapidly learn to suck and the feeding mixture should only be given a drop or so at a time.

Young kittens take small quantities of fluid at first, perhaps only 3ml per feed, and must be fed every two hours around the clock. Their food intake should have doubled by the age of a week and four-hourly feeds, certainly through the night, should then prove adequate. At three weeks old, they can be offered a little solid food on a spoon, such as a finely chopped boiled fish mixed with gravy. As soon as the kitten starts to lap, feeding will become much easier.

Kittens need to be kept warm, at a temperature of about 86°F (30°C) at first, which can then be lowered carefully in stages to 70°F (21°C) by the age of six weeks. A hot-water bottle in the bed will encourage the kitten to snuggle up, as it would to its mother, while an infrared lamp should be suspended above the box. Models specifically produced for use with livestock, which emit predominently heat rather than light, should be used if possible. The temperature on the surface of the bedding should be monitored with a thermometer; it is possible to overheat the kitten if the lamp is placed too close.

In order to stimulate the mother's habit of licking her kittens after they have fed, they should be wiped over with a damp cloth wetted with warm water. This in turn will encourage them to urinate and defecate, and their bedding will then have to be changed.

Normal development

Kittens normally start suckling soon after birth. Each will adopt a particular nipple. Any which appear to be having difficulty in suckling should be examined for the presence of a cleft palate. This is a developmental abnormality affecting the roof of the mouth and is often shown up by milk running down the nostrils. In such cases, no treatment is really possible, and the kitten will have to be painlessly destroyed by a veterinarian.

After a few days in her box, the queen may decide to move her litter to another location, carrying each kitten in turn by the scruff of its neck. The box should be transferred accordingly, although there is no guarantee that she may not decide to move on again. The kittens are likely to be growing at the rate of ½oz (15g) daily, which puts a considerable burden on the mother, who needs to be fed accordingly. She is likely to drink more when lactating, because of the loss of fluid in her milk. Mineral and vitamin supplementation may be advisable, depending on the diet concerned, and advice on this should be obtained from a veterinarian. Food must be offered three or four times a day during this period, to prevent the queen having to draw on her own body reserves to nourish the kittens.

The kittens, born blind, start to open their eyes from five days onwards depending on the breed; Siamese, as always, are precocious in this respect. This is a gradual process extending over several days; gentle bathing using cottonwool soaked in warm water may be necessary to remove any discharge. If the eyes become sealed again, they may be infected and an antibiotic ophthalmic preparation will be required to prevent any serious and lasting damage.

At the age of three weeks, the kittens will have begun to take their first tentative steps and weaning can start in earnest about a week later. There are now complete canned foods produced especially for kittens and these should be used if possible. Other palatable items for young cats include finely chopped mince and boiled fish. Milk, or a suitable substitute, should also be freely available. Kittens will often eat more readily at first from a plate rather than a bowl. Feeding periods should be supervised to ensure that one or two individuals do not dominate at the expense of their littermates, nor must their mother be allowed to eat all the food. By five weeks old, each kitten should be consuming about 3oz (70g) of food, as well as milk, spread over four daily sittings.

The litter will be virtually independent of their dam when two months old, although certain longhairs, such as Persians, may need to be left with their mother for another month. The queen's milk will dry up naturally once the kittens stop suckling. She must be kept separate from toms thoughout the whole kittening period; it is not unknown for queens to conceive again about 10 days after giving birth. During this period calling is often not obvious and courtship will only be brief if she mates while caring for kittens.

Vaccination and registration
The first vaccination is normally given at about nine weeks of age, followed by another three weeks later. Worming around the same time is also to be recommended. No further vaccinations are generally likely to be required for a further year.

Pedigree kittens should be registered at around six weeks of age, once their sexes are known. The registration procedure varies according to the association concerned. It may be advantageous to register them with more than one organization, especially in the United States where there are nine major associations. The entire litter can simply be registered or each kitten separately. In the former instance, the individuals may then be registered independently for new owners.

The purpose of registration is to ensure that any particular member of the breed could be traced at a later date, and for this reason all registered cats must have a unique name. Most breeders have a prefix, usually relating to their stud, which they register for their own exclusive use. All kittens bred by them are then listed with this description, followed by another name. Advice on such matters should be sought from the organization concerned prior to submitting a formal registration application. Pedigrees trace the bloodline of a specific cat back over at least four generations, showing the ancestry of both parents. When a cat changes hands, it may be possible to add the suffix of the new owner, but there can be no confusion as to who initially bred the cat in question.

Reproductive Problems
Female cats allowed to roam free will often disappear while in oestrus and may not return home for a few days, until after mating. Toms stay out for longer periods and suffer particularly during the latter part of the breeding season, often reappearing in very poor condition during August. They have usually lost considerable weight and their relatively large kidneys may be evident as swellings in the abdominal region, either side of the vertebral column. They should, however, respond well to good feeding, and soon put on weight again.

Spontaneous abortion is very rare in cats, although it can occur in conjunction with FeLV infection. This is more likely to cause resorption of the fetuses before they have developed to maturity. Repeated small litters are usually indicative of the same problem. Another possible cause could be endometritis, or inflammation of the lining of the uterus, which is often linked with a vaginal discharge. If the uterus becomes full of pus, the condition is referred to as pyometra. This is more commonly seen in older cats, 14 or 15 years old, which are not actually breeding yet still cycling regularly. The only treatment for pyometra is a rapid ovarohysterectomy (spaying), and providing surgery is carried out without delay, then the chances of recovery are likely to be good.

Neutering
Such surgery is not only carried out to prevent unwanted kittens, but also serves to facilita[…] kept solely as a pet into domesti[…] wandering of mature tom cats[…] troublesome habits. The sensible ow[…] to overcome such difficulties, givin[…] stressful existence. Neutered indivi[…] than their intact counterparts and obesity [… li]kely to be a significant side-effect of the operation, particularly if the diet is controlled accordingly.

In the case of the male cat, surgery, referred to as castration, can be carried out at virtually any time, although five months is perhaps the best age. At this stage, the blood supply to the testes is relatively small and the risk of post-operative haemorrhage is significantly reduced. Some pedigree breeds, such as the Abyssinian may need to be left intact until they are slightly older. Signs of masculinization of the head will be apparent if the operation is deferred for several months, as some owners prefer, but spraying of urine around the home will have already begun.

Castration, even in young cats, necessitates the use of an anaesthetic. This may be given either as an injection or in the form of gas. Recovery from gaseous anaesthetic is invariably quicker than recovery from the intravenous method — as cats can often be conscious again within 10 minutes after gas — but other factors will also influence the veterinarian's decision in this regard. It is preferable to castrate an adult cat outside the breeding season, between September and December. The operation will be less traumatic then, both psychologically and physically, since blood flow to the testes will be reduced at this time. After castration, sexual drive will be lost but the cat's hunting instinct will not be affected. The risk of abscesses resulting from fights is also significantly reduced. Sexual alopecia, or hair loss, may result from the loss of testosterone from the circulation, but can be corrected by implants if necessary.

Spaying, or ovarohysterectomy, entailing both removal of the ovaries and uterus, is to be recommended for all queens not kept for breeding purposes. While there is a risk of sexual alopecia developing, spaying removes the threat of ovarian cysts and pyometra in later life. Surgery is normally carried out at the age of four and a half months before kittens are likely to be sexually mature, and so is less complex. In older cats showing signs of oestrus, spaying is not recommended until a later date. The hormonal changes resulting from oestrus mean that the tissue is receiving a larger blood supply and the uterus itself is more fragile and prone to rupture.

The operation can either be carried out through an incision in the flank, or via the mid-line of the abdomen, underneath the body. The area has to be clipped of fur to ensure a sterile environment around the site of the incision, and the fur may grow back paler, particularly in the case of Siamese. For this reason, providing there are no veterinary objections, owners often prefer to have their cat spayed via the mid-line where the change will be less noticeable.

It is routine for cats to be kept overnight by the veterinarian after surgery. Very few complications result from spaying. Occasionally the cat may take out the sutures (stitches) from its wound and these will need to be replaced. The sutures are always removed about a week after surgery, by which time the site of the incision should be healing well. For the first few days at home the cat should be kept indoors.

SPAYING AND PREVENTING OESTRUS

Spaying is the removal of both ovaries and uterus in a female cat, preventing breeding. This operation, best carried out at the age of four and a half months, is recommended for all queens not kept for breeding purposes. Spaying only prevents unwanted kittens, but also serves to integrate the cat better into a domestic environment. Before surgery, the area where the incision is to be made is shaved of fur and thoroughly cleaned to give a sterile site for the operation (1). The veterinarian will then administer an anaesthetic, usually intravenously or by gas (2). An incision is made, either in the flank or along the mid-line of the abdomen and the organs are exposed (3). The ovaries, Fallopian tubes and uterus are removed (4) and the wound is then closed with sutures, or stitches (5). Stitches are removed about a week after the operation, by which time the wound should be healing.

If the owner wants the cat to breed, but it has begun calling prematurely, there are chemical means of inhibiting oestrus. Progesterone analogues, in tablet or injection form, have been used for contraceptive purposes for some time, but can lead to weight gain. Newer drugs with fewer side-effects, such as the gonadotrophin inhibitors, are now becoming available. These act by preventing the release of FSH from the pituitary, the hormone which initiates the oestrus cycle. No chemical inhibitor of oestrus is recommended for use on a permanent basis.

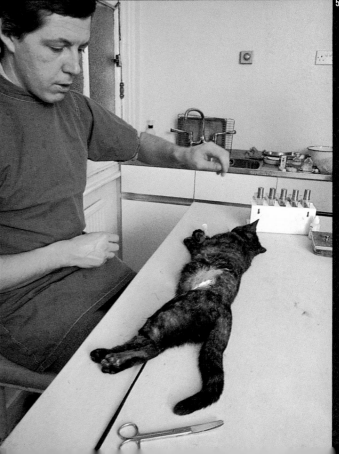

The Wild Cats

Cats comprise the distinct family Felidae; within this grouping there are now three recognized genera. The large cats such as the lion, leopard and tiger are included in the genus *Panthera*, while the cheetah is classified on its own as the sole member of the *Acinonyx* genus. It differs in several respects from other cats; it has, for example, non-retractable claws. The domestic cat is classified under the description of *Felis catus*, and the remaining members of the family are usually grouped together in the same genus *Felis*. There are 37 recognized species of wild cat, all of which are described in this chapter. They are listed in alphabetical order by their common names, within broad geographical groups. Where species occur both in Africa and Asia, such as the lion, they are classified under the former heading.

Many of these animals have been extensively hunted, often for their fur, and are now threatened with extinction. Wildlife reserves and protection areas have been set up in recent years in an attempt to increase numbers in the wild, while strict import controls have been enforced in an effort to regulate trade. Although some wild cats, notably the ocelot which tames easily, have been kept as pets, none of these animals are really suitable for the ordinary domestic environment, and in most countries special permits are now required to keep such animals.

AFRICAN CATS Wild cats native to the continent of Africa include the lion (1), the leopard (2), the cheetah (3), the caracal (4), the sand-dune cat (5) and the serval (6) *(LEFT)*. The cheetah *(Acinonyx jubatus) (RIGHT)* is thought to have originated in Asia, where it is now extremely scarce, and then spread into Africa. No fossilized remains have been discovered in the latter continent. The cheetah's markings include two black lines which run from the corners of the eyes to the corners of the mouth, giving it a sad expression. Female cheetahs look after their cubs until they are two years old.

African Cats

African Wild Cat (*Felis lybica*)
Weight: up to 18lb (8kg)

The African wild cat is the species most closely related to the domestic cat, and is regarded as its nearest ancestor. These animals range over the whole African continent, apart from areas of dense equatorial rain forest and the arid deserts. They feed largely on small mammals, but have also been known to eat insects such as crickets and even snakes when other food is in short supply. They are shy by nature, but youngsters taken by natives soon settle down to a domesticated existence, hunting vermin around the settlements. Their gestation period extends up to 60 days which closely approximates to that of the domestic cat.

Black-footed Cat (*Felis nigripes*)
Weight: up to 4½lb (2kg)

Black-footed cats inhabit the relatively arid regions that occur through the southern part of the continent, but in contrast to other cats living in similar conditions, this species is prominently marked. These cats are the smallest of the wild felids, but are considered to be among the fiercest. Folklore credits them with attacks on giraffes in which the giraffes are seized by the neck and bitten through the jugular vein. The black-footed cat is solitary by nature, mating quickly with little prior contact. Although the resulting offpsring grow more quickly than their domestic counterparts, they take nearly two years to become sexually mature. The kittens are taught to hunt by their mothers. Despite interesting habits, for example, they appear to dig readily and may cover large distances in their search for prey, they remain one of the least-studied of the wild cats. The black-footed cat has been crossed successfully under captive conditions with the domestic cat.

Caracal (Caracal Lynx) (*Felis (Caracal) caracal*)
Weight: up to 50lb (23kg)

This cat appears to be related to both the leopard and the lynx. Its name is derived from the Turkish word *karakal* which means 'black-eared'. As well as occurring in Asia, the caracal is widespread through much of the drier regions of Africa, but is never found under true desert conditions. They often prey on birds, using their speed and agility to catch them feeding on the ground, and sometimes leaping into the air to paw them down. Caracals may withdraw with their catch to a convenient tree, where it can be consumed without interference from other carnivores. There would appear to be a distinct breeding season, depending on the locality, and the young live alongside their dam for a year or more. Caracals have been kept for 18 years in captivity.

Cheetah (Hunting Leopard) (*Acinonyx jubatus*)
Weight: up to 110lb (50kg)

The cheetah is unique among cats; its ancestors evolved separately from other felids from the Pliocene Period, at least three million years ago, onwards. They have been kept for hunting puproses since about 3000 BC and this tradition was maintained virtually up to the eighteenth century. According to the writings of Marco Polo, 1,000 hunting cheetahs were housed at the court of the Great Khan, while later in Europe they were used to catch hares and roe-deer. The speed of the cheetah enables it to close on prey at about 65mph (90kph) over short distances.

The range of these cats has been markedly reduced over recent years and its numbers have declined severely in many areas. The population in Africa is estimated at a maximum of 25,000 individuals, and could be as low as 8,000. Although now given protection throughout the continent, apart from South Africa, the high value of its fur has attracted poachers and adequate protective measures cannot be effectively enforced. The cheetah is now virtually extinct in Asia; none have been sighted in India since 1951. Its last remaining strongholds appear to be in the vicinity of the Afghanistan-Russian border and in eastern Iran, where perhaps 300 still survive in their wild state.

The lifespan of the cheetah is fairly short in the wild, because as soon as its speed starts to falter, so does its ability to catch prey. It cannot stalk like other cats and, being solitary, cannot rely on another's kill as do many lions. Often, having achieved a kill, cheetahs are robbed by other carnivores such as lions. When pregnant, female cheetahs are particularly vulnerable to starvation and attacks from lions, while up to half their offspring may be lost by predation. They are not generally aggressive towards humans, but are difficult to breed in captivity.

Golden Cat (*Felis (Profelis) aurata*)
Weight: up to 40lb (18kg)
One of the least-known of the wild cats, this species is believed to possess mystical powers by the tribes which live within the belt of central Africa where it occurs. They keep its locations secret from outsiders, but it is known to live in forests at high altitude and is predominantly nocturnal in its habits. Pygmies believe the tail of the gold cat gives good fortune, especially to elephant hunters.

Leopard (Panther) (*Panthera pardus*)
Weight: up to 150lb (70kg)
Leopards used to exist in Europe during the Pleistocene Period, approximately one million years ago, but their range is now restricted to parts of Africa and Asia, extending into China and Siberia. They often live at high altitudes, and have been found at up to 15,000ft (4,572m). These cats live and hunt alone, stalking prey determinedly with maximum stealth before pouncing and killing their victims by suffocation. They can leap 22ft (6.6m) in exceptional circumstances, and clear 10ft (3m) without difficulty.

When chasing baboons, leopards can themselves occasionally fall victim to an attack from other members of the baboon troop. Packs of hunting dogs will also kill a leopard if it cannot escape up a nearby tree. Under captive conditions leopards can live for two decades or more. Black forms of the leopard are not uncommon, especially in Asia, and result from an increase in the black pigmentation of the coat, although the dark markings themselves remain unaffected. Such leopards occur most commonly in forested regions through the range. Occasional pale-coated individuals with blue eyes have also been recorded.

Lion (*Panthera leo*)
Weight: up to 750lb (340kg)
The lion is the best-known member of the family of wild cats. It breeds freely in captivity, to the extent that, in many zoos, contraceptives are given to lions to keep numbers down. The lion is another cat which extends from Africa into Asia, although the latter population is now confined to a reserve of 450 square miles (1,200sq km) in area, at Gir in the western region of India. There may be fewer than 200 individuals still remaining in this locality. Only a very small number of this subspecies, *persica*, are in zoos.

The mature male lion with its long flowing mane has long been a symbol of nobility and power; in reality, this is a misconception. Lions are sociable cats, living in groups known as prides, which can be comprised of as many as 35 females overseen by a dominant male. The task of providing food for the whole pride falls to the lionesses, with the male generally being content to feed from their kills. He may consume 60lb (27kg) at one time and then will fast for several days. Lions are found in grassy areas often near

plains, away from dense forest. The male cubs leave the pride by the age of three years to establish territories.

Sand-dune Cat (Sand Cat) (*Felis margarita*)
Weight: up to 6lb (2.5kg)
The sand-dune cat gained its scientific name from Commandant Margueritte, who led the expedition to the Sahara in 1856 when these cats were first discovered. They occur in predominantly arid areas and are also found in the eastern region of Saudia Arabia and western parts of Asia. Sand-dune cats have hair mats which protect their feet against slipping on loose surfaces or burning on hot rocks. These animals are mainly nocturnal, emerging from their burrows when it is cool to hunt for rodents and insects.

Serval (*Felis (Leptailurus) serval*)
Weight: up to 40lb (18kg)
The serval lives in bush country through much of western and central Africa, although its distribution has declined during recent years. It is hunted in certain areas for food, while its coat is valued by some tribes to make a cloak or *karrosses*. Although the serval resembles the caracal, it is not as aggressive, and can purr like a domestic cat. Odd black individuals have been reported, especially in certain areas such as the Aberdare Mountains, at an altitude of about 9,800 ft (300m).

The caracal *(Felis caracal) (ABOVE)* is characterized by its relatively long legs and ear tufts, which resemble the tufts on the ears of lynxes. It occurs in Asia as well as Africa. In certain areas of Asia, contests have been organized in which caracals are set against each other to determine which is best at catching birds. Temminck's golden cat *(Felis temmincki) (LEFT)* is believed to be a close relative of the African golden cat *(Felis aurata)* and is somewhat similar in appearance. The African species has a coat of even colouring, showing no trace of spots or stripes, whereas Temminck's golden cat has striking markings on the face and legs, and is also slightly larger. Both species are rare, the African golden cat being rarely seen by outsiders to its native area. It is believed to possess magic powers by the tribes which live where it occurs.

The lion is probably the best-known of all the wild cats and is found south of the Sahara ranging over most types of terrain. Today, only a very small number are left in Asia, in the western region of India. Lions are essentially nocturnal hunters and spend much of the day resting. They often congregate around waterholes (TOP), not only to drink, but also to catch prey unawares. Antelope and zebra are favoured catches. The mane of the male lion (RIGHT), around the head and shoulders, is quite variable in colour; sometimes it is even black. The length of the mane also varies. It starts developing in young males from their third year on. White lions attracted much attention when they were first seen in the mid-1970s. Two were born in

October 1975, in a pride being studied by a wildlife researcher, Chris McBride. The private reserve where this occurred is known as Timbavati, and is located in the Transvaal close to the Kruger National Park. Unlike the albino lion, previously described from studies made in the same region, these white lions had yellow eyes like ordinary lions. Another African cat, the serval *(Felis serval)* *(ABOVE)* is sufficiently agile to catch birds flying 6ft (1.8m) off the ground. The coat of the serval is normally light brown with dark spots; when the coat is speckled, these cats are sometimes referred to as Servaline cats.

ASIAN CATS There are many species of wild cat native to Asia. These include the tiger (1), the clouded leopard (2), the jungle cat (3), the flat-headed cat (4), the snow leopard (5) and Temminck's golden cat (6) *(LEFT)*. The clouded leopard *(Panthera nebulosa) (RIGHT)* hunts on the ground, often during the day. Prey is normally knocked off balance and then killed by a bite on the neck. Cubs are taught this hunting routine from the age of about three months on, by their mothers. Clouded leopards spend much of their time in trees and are rarely spotted in the dense forests where they live.

Asian Cats

Asiatic Steppe Wild Cat (Indian Desert Cat) (*Felis ornata*)
Weight: up to 9lb (4kg)
Closely related to the African wild cat, this species inhabits arid land ranging from northwest India and Afghanistan eastwards to Mongolia and China. It sometimes takes over disused badger setts and feeds predominantly on small mammals, although berries are also consumed occasionally. The Asiatic steppe wild cat is solitary and nocturnal and about the same size as its domestic counterpart. The gestation period is believed to be about nine weeks; up to five kittens are born in a litter, one more than the average number for the domestic cat.

Bornean Red Cat (Bay Cat) (*Felis (Profelis) badia*)
Weight: up to 7lb (3kg)
The Bornean red cat closely resembles Temminck's cat, although it is much smaller. Very little is known of its habits, but it is thought to be a rare species, living in dense jungle. At its name suggests, the Bornean red cat is confined to the island of Borneo.

Chinese Desert Cat (Pale Desert Cat) (*Felis bieti*)
Weight: up to 12lb (5.5kg)
The discovery of this species came about by chance, when the expedition of Prince Henri d'Orleans was forbidden entry to the city of Lhasa, in Tibet, in 1889. As the party turned eastwards, an alert zoologist noticed two unusual skins in local fur markets. No other trace of the Chinese desert cat was found until 1925, when a skull was discovered. This species is now thought to be closely related to the Asiatic steppe wild cat and is probably confined to a region near the borders of western China and eastern Tibet. In spite of its name, the Chinese desert cat has generally been sighted in steppe landscapes or forested mountainsides.

Clouded Leopard (*Panthera (Neofelis) nebulosa*)
Weight: up to 66lb (30kg)
The clouded leopard was first described by Sir Stamford

Raffles during the nineteenth century, and he adopted the local Malay term *rimaudaham*, meaning 'tree tiger', for this cat. The Chinese refer to it as the 'mint leopard' because of its leaf-like markings, distinguishing it from the leopard itself, which is known as 'golden cash'. Clouded leopards extend through Nepal into China and southwards to Sumatra and Borneo. These cats live in forests, spending much of their time in trees, lying with their feet either side of a convenient branch, but are shy and rarely seen.

The relationship of the clouded leopard to other members of the cat family is unclear. In common with the smaller cats it cannot roar, and yet its pupils can contract to form vertical slits, which is characteristic of big cats. Its dentition is unusual, as the upper canines are slightly elongated and there is also an increased gap from the canines to the premolars.

Fishing Cat (*Felis (Prionailurus) viverrina*)
Weight: up to 18lb (8kg)
This species, as its name suggests, occurs close to water, frequenting marshland areas throughout much of southeast Asia. It is said to dive into water to catch fish but also feeds on crustaceans and molluscs, as well as land mammals. Its claws are much longer than those of other cats and appear to be adapted for scooping fish out of the water. There is a documented case of a male fishing cat killing a female leopard twice its size, but other accounts seem to contradict this report, referring to these cats as being easily tamed.

Flat-headed Cat (*Felis (Prionailurus) planiceps*)
Weight: up to 18lb (8kg)
The appearance of this cat might suggest at first that it is more closely linked with creatures such as otter and mink than with other cats. The species is found through Malaya to Borneo and Sumatra, occurring especially in lowland areas. It appears to consume fruit and frequently digs in plantations for sweet potatoes, according to a report of 1893. More recent information, however, suggests that the flat-headed cat is nocturnal and eats fish.

Iriomote Cat *(Felis (Mayailurus) iriom otensis)*
Weight: about 12lb (5.5kg)
The discovery of this cat in 1967 generated a great deal of scientific interest. A Japanese naturalist called Tagawa had heard rumours of its existence while on the island of Okinawa and set out to Iriomote, a small island located at the southern tip of the Kyukyu chain, about 124 miles (200km) east of Taiwan, in an attempt to locate the species. The cat has a very limited distribution since Iriomote is only 113 square miles (292 sq km) in area. The island's natives prized these cats for their meat before they were given protected status. Subsequent studies suggest that it is related to the leopard cat, living in forest areas. Only 100 individuals are thought to be in existence.

Jungle Cat (Reed Cat) *(Felis (Chaus) chaus)*
Weight: up to 30lb (15.5kg)
The jungle cat was known to the Egyptians, who kept it for hunting wildfowl. It has a wide distribution through the Middle East and Afghanistan, extending into parts of western China. This cat appears to be a common and adaptable species, often being seen in many parts of its range during daylight hours. Jungle cats prey on a wide variety of small mammals and birds, even killing porcupines. They are not adverse to taking chickens around human settlements, typically lurking in reedy areas for most of the time. Females can have two litters a year, and the kittens are mature by the age of 18 months.

Leopard Cat *(Felis (Prionailurus) bengalensis)*
Weight: up to 12lb (7kg)
A very adaptable species, the leopard cat occurs throughout southeast Asia, extending northwards into Siberia, and is even encountered on some of the Philippine Islands, as well as Bali. It appears to be solitary, although a number of males come together to court a female at breeding time. The average litter consists of three kittens. Like the jungle cat, the leopard cat roams close to human habitation and may take domestic livestock, especially chickens.

Marbled Cat *(Felis (Pardofelis) marmorata)*
Weight: about 12lb (5.5kg)
Another of the little-known smaller species, the marbled cat is thought never to have been photographed. Skins, skeletal remains and sketches provide the basis of scientific knowledge about this cat. It appears to frequent remote

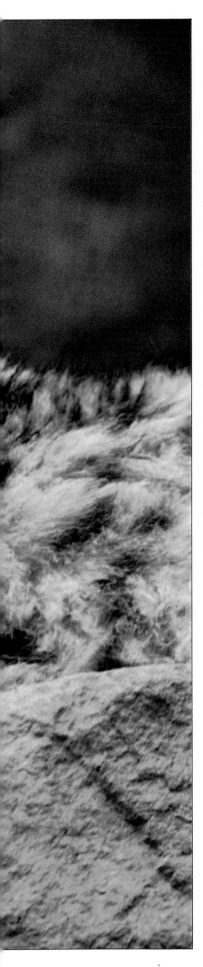

The snow leopard (Panthera uncia) (FAR LEFT) occurs in some of the most remote areas of central Asia. The pale, thick coat, with dark irregular spots and streaks, enables the snow leopard to blend into its surroundings and remain largely undetected when hunting. Like other subspecies of the leopard, the melanistic (black) form (Panthera pardus) (LEFT) is graceful and can climb and swim with ease. This type of leopard is more common in Asia than Africa. Another cat native to Asia is the jungle cat (Felis chaus) (ABOVE). This cat has a reputation for being a fearless hunter and is thought to have spread across from the Middle East to Asia. It now ranges over a very wide area. The coat of the jungle cat is sandy brown.

The numbers of tigers in the wild have declined dramatically over recent years. They will breed quite well in captivity, however; ultimately reserves may be their only hope of survival. Although there is only one species, tigers differ quite significantly in their appearance. Siberian tigers *(ABOVE)* have a relatively long, pale-coloured coat, with few stripes. Tigers from the Indian subcontinent *(FAR RIGHT)* have shorter fur and more striking coat patterning. They are not well adapted to hot conditions and may cool themselves by lying in water, seeking shade during the warmest parts of the day.

areas through Nepal and Assam to Indochina, Sumatra and Borneo. Birds are thought to be its chief prey, and it spends long periods in trees, according to observers in India. Marbled cats in Borneo, however, are believed to be largely terrestrial, as well as nocturnal.

Pallas's Cat (Manul) *(Felis (Otocolobus) manul)*
Weight: up to 11lb (5kg)
A native of the frozen wastelands of central Asia, Pallas's cat is rare in many parts of its range. It is secretive by nature and not easy to observe, usually only becoming active at night and hiding in a suitable burrow during the day. The coats of these cats are unusually thick and evolved as protection from the cold. Pallas's cat lacks the graceful morphology associated with other cats, possessing a broad head with flat ears and eyes positioned high in the skull, and short, stocky legs. Living in an environment where there is little vegetative cover it has adapted to observe without being seen itself. Pallas's cat has been kept in a semi-domestic state in parts of its range, and is said to have been used in the development of the Turkish Angora breed, but this is not generally accepted.

Rusty-spotted Cat *(Felis (Prionailurus) rubiginosus)*
Weight: up to 4½lb (2kg)
The rusty-spotted cat is localized to the area of southern India and Sri Lanka (formerly Ceylon). On the mainland, it is most commonly encountered in grassy areas rather than true jungle, but in Sri Lanka it occurs in the wet mountainous forested region to the south of the island. These cats are largely nocturnal, and feed on small mammals as well as birds. Kittens can become quite tame if obtained at an early age, although very little appears to be recorded about their breeding behaviour.

Snow Leopard (Ounce) *(Panthera uncia)*
Weight: up to 150lb (70kg)
The snow leopard is known to occur at high altitudes in central Asia, although formerly it may have ranged into Iran and down to northern India. It is typically found in mountainous regions, between 9,800 to 19,700 ft (3,000 to 6,000m), coming down to lower levels during the winter. Here it feeds on deer, gazelles and even wild boar. Other prey may include ibex, argali, various birds and even domestic animals.

Pairs come together for mating, with the resulting offspring remaining with their dam for up to two years. The average litter appears to consist of three cubs, born after a gestation period of 100 days. Snow leopards are little studied in the wild since they live in inhospitable and relatively inaccessible areas, ranging widely over their territories in search of prey. Their numbers are therefore largely a matter for conjecture, but they are hunted because they prey on domestic animals and for their coat. A ban on the use of the snow leopard's fur was agreed in 1971 by members of the International Fur Trade Federation.

Temminck's (Asiatic) Golden Cat (*Felis (Profelis) temmincki*)
Weight: up to 24lb (11kg)
This species is thought to be a close relative of the African golden cat, although it is slightly larger in size. It also prefers forested surroundings broken with tracts of stony ground, giving rise to its Chinese name of *shilului* or 'rock cat'. Temminck's golden cat will take a wide variety of prey, ranging from birds to water buffalo calves. It has a fierce reputation but several youngsters have been tamed without

difficulty from an early age. Dark examples are known; one was once kept at Basel Zoo, Switzerland.

Tiger (*Panthera tigris*)
Weight: up to 800lb (360kg)
The tiger has been known and feared in Europe since the time of the ancient Greeks. It is the largest member of the cat family, weighing on average 400lb (190kg), while the biggest individuals may be twice as heavy. The powerful jaws and muscular body have made the tiger a lethal hunter, and it will take prey even larger than itself. Females mature at the age of about four years, producing up to four cubs in a litter, although breeding only occurs every other year.

Tigers are found in India and southeast Asia, ranging up to an altitude of 7,900ft (2,400m), and often stay close to water where they like to bathe. The decline in the number of tigers since the Second World War has, however, been dramatic and, out of eight recognized subspecies, some, such as the Chinese form, are already virtually extinct. In India alone, where the tiger population was estimated to be around 40,000 in 1930, the numbers have fallen to only 5,000 individuals.

Uncontrolled yet ruthless hunting, coupled with deforestation which has destroyed much of its habitat, are the major causes of the tiger's demise. Despite protection measures through many parts of its range, the threats to the tiger's existence still remain and, under the auspices of the World Wildlife Fund, special reserves are being established for these magnificent beasts. They are easy to breed in captivity and often exceed their average lifespan in the wild — about 15 years — under these conditions. A well-organized captive breeding project, linked with secure reserves in the wild, would afford the best opportunity of saving the endangered subspecies of the tiger, which have been threatened with extinction by over-zealous hunting for sport.

Reports of black tigers have never been authenticated, but various white forms are fairly well known. Some are genuine albinos, pure white with pink eyes, while others have a pale body colour and lighter markings than normal. In the Rewa State of India, one white tiger was caught alive and photographed in 1915. Others were subsequently seen and in 1951 the Maharaja of Rema started a breeding programme, with some of the resulting white progeny being sent to zoos at Bristol in Britain, and Washington DC in the United States.

American Cats

Bobcat (Bay lynx) *(Felis (Lynx) rufus)*
Weight: up to 35lb (16kg)
The bobcat is confined to northern parts of North America, occurring in both Canada and the United States. It mainly eats small mammals, but will take deer occasionally. The mating period extends from February to June and the kittens are born about seven weeks later, in a secure den. They first venture out when they are approximately five weeks old, but do not start hunting with their dam until the age of at least three months. Bobcats may wander long distances in search of new territory after becoming fully independent at about nine months old. They have a reputation for being savage and yet in turn are quite liable to fall victim to any pumas within their range. Bobcats are hardy and survive well under difficult conditions.

AMERICAN AND EUROPEAN CATS
These cats include the puma (1), the margay (2), the bobcat (3), the European wild cat (4), the ocelot (5), the lynx (6), the jaguar (7) *(LEFT)*. Lynx have only 28 teeth, compared with 30 in related cats. Their tails are short and they have tufted ears. The Spanish lynx *(Felis pardellus)* *(ABOVE)* is one of the most striking members of this group, but it is now an endangered species. The bobcat *(Felis rufus)* *(RIGHT)* is capable of surviving under the harsh winter conditions of its native territory, northern areas of the United States and Canada.

The jaguar (Panthera onca) (ABOVE) is the most ferocious of all the South American carnivores and can even pose a danger to humans. These cats frequent rivers and pools where they catch fish. Jaguars are either yellowish-brown with clusters of dark spots, or dark brown, almost black. Geoffroy's cat (Felis tigrina) (RIGHT) is about the same size as a domestic cat, but is much more vicious. This cat is named after the zoologist Geoffroy Saint-Hilaire. The margay (Felis wiedii) (FAR RIGHT) resembles the ocelot (Panthera pardalis) so closely that it is often difficult to distinguish between the two species when they are kittens. When fully grown, the margay is smaller than the ocelot, its tail is longer and its eyes bigger. These cats have sometimes been kept as pets but they do not settle well into a domestic environment, like all of the wild cats, and remain wild all of their lives. The margay is a particularly energetic climber; in the wild it is adept at catching birds.

Geoffroy's Cat (Geoffroy's Ocelot) (*Felis (Oncifelis) tigrina*)
Weight: up to 8lb (3.5kg)
This cat is found in South America, ranging from Bolivia and Argentina into Brazil and Uruguay. It is known as the *gato montes* (mountain cat) in Argentina, occurring in relatively open country and feeding on birds and small mammals. Only two or three kittens are born in a litter. Geoffroy's cat is nocturnal and appears to be quite aggressive; one kept with domestic cats turned on them and killed them all.

Jaguar (*Panthera onca*)
Weight: up to 300lb (135kg)
The jaguar and its various subspecies apparently developed in the northern American continent and spread southwards along with other cats. In South America, it is regarded as a symbol of male potency; its name was corrupted from the Tupi-Guarani term *yaguara* which translates as 'the beast which overcomes its prey by a leap'. In areas where Spanish is the prevalent tongue, the jaguar is known as *el tigre*.

At the peak of its distribution, the range of this cat extended down to the borders of Patagonia, but did not actually stretch into this region. During the present century, it has become extinct in Uruguay and has nearly disappeared from Argentina. The demand for skins for fur coats has been largely responsible for its demise. Just prior to protective legislation being introduced in 1970, over 7,000 skins were sent to the United States alone, over an eight-month period.

The jaguar is rarely found far from water and apart from eating mammals will also prey on reptiles. Numbers used to congregate at turtle breeding grounds, feeding on the reptiles themselves as well as digging for their eggs. Such is the power of their jaws that jaguars can break open the shells of these turtles and other similarly protected creatures such as armadillos without difficulty. They will also catch fish, and tales that they lure them within reach are widespread through many parts of South America. Jaguars wade into shallow areas of water to take heavy fish such as the pirarcu, which can weigh 450lb (200kg) and grow up to 13ft (4m) in length. There have been rare sightings of black jaguars, while pale-coloured individuals are also known.

Jaguarundi (*Felis (Herpailurus) yagouarundi*)
Weight: up to 22lb (10kg)
The jaguarundi resembles a weasel or badger more than a cat, yet closer study reveals its true links. Its nearest relative is either the mountain cat or the puma. The range of the jaguarundi extends south from Arizona to northern parts of Argentina.

It lives predominantly in forest areas, resting in its den during the warmest part of the day. The jaguarundi has acquired a reputation for stealing domestic fowl from human settlements. Its short legs help to conceal its presence when stalking prey in an area where there is little cover. These cats can become quite friendly and were apparently kept by South American Indians to prey on rodents around their communities, although they never lose their hunting instinct for birds.

Kodkod (Huina) (*Felis (Oncifelis) guigna*)
Weight: up to 7lb (3kg)
The kodkod is a rarely seen species from South America, occurring in Chile and parts of Argentina. It was first recorded during the eighteenth century by the naturalist Juan Molina, in his book on Chilean wildlife. These cats appear to be nocturnal, and live in dense forests. They prey on chickens if the opportunity arises.

Margay (Tree Ocelot) (*Felis (Leopardus) wiedii*)
Weight: up to 18lb (8kg)
Only one margay has been seen in the United States, at the Eagle Pass on the Rio Grande in Texas. The major part of its range is believed to extend south from Mexico to northern Argentina. Margays are thought to spend long periods in trees, where they feed largely on birds. The elusive habits of the margay make any assessment of its numbers difficult.

Mountain Cat (Andean Highland Cat) (*Felis (Oreailurus) jacobita*)
Weight: up to 15lb (7kg)
The mountain cat is virtually unknown, although it is thought to occur through the relatively high Andean regions, Chile and Peru, extending to parts of Bolivia and Argentina. The anatomy of its skull is unique and this feature has led some taxonomists to classify it in a separate genus, *Oreailurus*. The prey of the mountain cat is believed mainly to consist of mammals such as viscachas.

Ocelot (*Leopardus pardalis*)
Weight: up to 30lb (13.5kg)
The ocelot is another species which has been hunted remorselessly for its fur during modern times and its distribution has declined as a result. Formerly occurring throughout much of North America, it is now found only in the southernmost region of Texas and parts of Mexico. The population in South America has been less severely affected, and here it ranges down to northern Argentina. Ocelots live in varying habitats, from equatorial rain forest to areas of dry scrubland.

Pairs stay together in a distinct territory throughout the year and hunt at night, often communicating by means of mewing calls. Another unusual feature of the ocelot is its relatively tame nature, with hand-reared specimens in particular becoming quite docile.

Oncilla (Tiger Cat; Little Spotted Cat) (*Leopardus tigrinus*)
Weight: up to 8lb (3.5kg)
The oncilla was initially thought to be related to Geoffroy's cat but a closer affinity to the margay has now been proven. It is a forest-dweller, ranging from Costa Rica south to Argentina and Paraguay. Males become very aggressive at breeding time. One or two kittens are born after a gestation period of about 75 days. They develop slowly, being 17 days old when they open their eyes and nearly eight weeks before taking solid nourishment. The oncilla has been crossed with the domestic cat, but barely half of the resulting kittens were born alive.

Pampas Cat (*Felis (Lynchailurus) colocolo*)
Weight: up to 14lb (5kg)
The pampas cat is confined to South America, living in the grassland of Argentina and moving into forest further north. It is nocturnal, feeding on small mammals and also birds, especially tinamous and domestic chickens. These cats appear to be quite common in certain parts of their range such as Chile, but are reputed to be aggressive and wild, resisting all attempts to tame them.

The ocelot *(Panthera pardalis)* *(LEFT)* is one of the least aggressive of the wild cats. It spends much of its time close to the ground, although it will retreat to a suitable branch when sleeping. Ocelots are good swimmers, even though they tend to avoid water. These cats are rarely found in open country. Usually there are only two kittens in a litter. The spotted and striped coat has been highly prized and ruthless hunting of these animals for their fur has meant that they are now in danger as a species.

Puma (Mountain Lion; Cougar) (*Felis (Puma) concolor*)
Weight: up to 130lb (60kg)
These cats are found over a wide area of the Americas. Despite their size, however, they are not related to other big cats. Pumas purr and groom their coats by licking in the same way as a domestic cat; they cannot roar like a lion. They wander over large areas in search of prey but do not present a great hazard to humans, although sporadic attacks have been verified.

During the breeding season the female remains on heat for nine days, and is courted by several potential mates. The gestation period is approximately 13 weeks and up to six kittens are produced. They grow rapidly and are suckled for at least three months, although they start to take meat from six weeks onwards. Pumas live for 12 years or so, until their ability to hunt and catch prey is lost. They are then particularly at risk from the packs of hunting dogs used to pursue them. Their meat is a popular dish in certain areas and tastes like veal. Pumas breed well under captive conditions, while rare black specimens from the southern parts of their range have been recorded.

European Cats
European Wild Cat (Forest Wild Cat) (*Felis silvestris*)
Weight: up to 24lb (11kg)
The wild cat used to be found throughout Britain, but by the First World War it had been driven back to remote areas of Scotland. Its numbers in this region have subsequently increased and it has spread back into other counties north of the border. Wild cats still occur in much of southern Europe, as well as parts of Russia and neighbouring countries.

These cats remain wild even if hand-reared from kittenhood, although they have been crossed successfully

with domestic cats. The resulting offspring more closely resemble their wild ancestors.

Under natural conditions the young are born in a den and only emerge when about a month old. They are taught to hunt by their mother from three months of age onwards and become fully independent about eight weeks later. Although their prey varies according to the area concerned, rodents feature prominently in their diet, but a few individuals take large animals, including fawns and even lambs. In areas where wild cats occur alongside lynxes, they often fall victim to their larger relatives.

Lynx (Northern Lynx) (*Felis (Lynx) lynx*)
Weight: up to 64lb (29kg)
The lynx in Europe has suffered badly as a result of human persecution over the course of centuries and its range has been reduced accordingly. It no longer occurs in most of western Europe, apart from Spain and Portugal, but still extends into Scandinavia and other northern areas except Denmark, spreading also into Russia and neighbouring countries including Czechoslovakia. In areas where it has been afforded protection, the lynx's numbers have risen.

This cat is named after Linceus who piloted the Argonauts, which gives an indication of its powerful eyesight. Lynxes can recognize a mouse at a distance of 250ft (75m) and deer over 1,650ft (500m) away. The characteristic tufts on their ears are thought to assist in pinpointing sounds accurately, while the extensive covering of fur extending over the feet protects against severe cold and enables these cats to walk on freezing ground. Females seek out their mates; about ten weeks later, up to four kittens will be born. Males become mature at three years, approximately 12 months after females. Lynxes live 14 years on average in the wild.

The puma or cougar *(Felis concolor) (LEFT)* can be a ruthless killer. One individual is reported to have slaughtered 50 sheep in just one night. There are persistent reports of escaped pumas living wild in remote parts of Britain, but these have not been verified. The puma is naturally found over wide areas of North and South America, the widest distribution of any American wild cat. They have, however, become quite scarce in areas of Canada and the United States.

GLOSSARY

ACA American Cat Association

ACFA American Cat Fanciers' Association

Agouti Colour between bands, particularly associated with Tabbies and Abyssinians

Ailurophile/Ailurophobe A person who loves/hates cats

Alter Neuter or spay

Angora Old term used for Persians, now reserved for Turkish breed

AOC Any other colour

AOV Any other variety

Back-cross Mating back of offspring to a parent

Blaze Forehead marking, often white, always distinct

Bloodline Cats which are related to each other, through various generations

Break Alteration to nose profile

Brindling Hairs of incorrect colour/type in wrong locality

Brush Tail, especially in connection with Longhairs (Persians)

Calling Behaviour of female during oestrus

Carry Genetic expression, relating to the presence of a gene which is not actually evident in the appearance of a particular individual

Castration Neutering of a male cat

Cat Fancy Selective breeding and exhibiting of cats

CCA Canadian Cat Association

CFA Cat Fanciers' Association (USA)

CFF Cat Fanciers' Federation (USA)

Cobby Sturdy, short-legged type; stocky appearance as exemplified by British Shorthairs

Cross-breeding Mating of two (usually pedigree) varieties together

Cryptorchidism Failure of testicles to descend in male cat

Dam Mother cat

Doctoring Neutering

Entire Unneutered

FCV Feline calici virus (linked with FVR)

FeLV Feline leukemia virus

Feral Reversion to the wild, after domestication

FIA Feline infectious anaemia

FIE Feline infectious enteritis

FiFe Fédération Internationale Féline

FIP Feline infectious peritonitis

Foreign Description applied to cats with a lithe, fine-boned body, as exemplified by the Siamese

FPL Feline panleucopaenia (alternative name for FIE)

Frill Ruff around the face

FSH Follicle stimulating hormone

FUS Feline urological syndrome

FVR Feline viral rhinotracheitis

GCCF Governing Council of the Cat Fancy (Britain)

Ghost markings Faint tabby pattern seen in young kittens which soon disappears

Haw 'Third eyelid'; nictitating membrane

Heat Female's period of oestrus

Heterozygous Possessing a pair of different genes, with one from each parent, on opposing positions, on a pair of chromosomes

Homozygous As above, but the genes in question correspond

Hot Reddish tinge which is a fault on cream cats, seen especially along their backs

Hybrid Offspring resulting from parents of different breeds, or species

ICF Independent Cat Federation (USA)

In-breeding Crossing of closely related cats, eg brother to sister pairing

Jowls Prominent cheek folds, seen especially in male cats

Kink Malformation, typically of the tail

Line-breeding Crossing of members of a related group, such as mother to son; father to daughter. The relationship is not as close as for in-breeding

Locket Patch, usually white, contrasting with the coat under the chin

LH Luteinizing hormone

Malocclusion Failure of the jaws, and thus the teeth, to meet correctly

Mongrel Cat with no fixed pedigree

Muzzle Jaws and nose

NCFA National Cat Fanciers' Association (USA)

Neuter Castrated male or spayed female

Nictitating membrane Membrane present at the side of each eye nearest the nose, which usually becomes apparent in cases of illness and debility when it partially extends across the eye

Nose leather Skin across the nose

NZCF New Zealand Cat Fancy

Odd-eyed Having two eyes of a different colour

Oestrus Breeding period of the female

Oriental Used in association, or interchangeably with foreign to denote type

Pads The leathery undersides of the feet

Pencilling Thin markings reminiscent of pencils, on the face of a Tabby

Phenotype The appearance of the cat, such as its colour or hair length, as a reflection of its genotype (genetic make-up)

Pinking up Expression used for the development of the pregnant queen's nipples

Points Coloured regions of the body, typically associated with Siamese

Prefix Chosen name used exclusively by breeder for own-bred kittens

Queen Unneutered female, usually kept specifically for breeding purposes

Recognition Approval by a governing body or association

Registration The recording of a kitten's birth, giving appropriate details such as its ancestry, with a governing body

Rumpy Description used for a Manx, which has no tail

Self Coat of one even colour

Sex linkage Genetic trait associated with the sex chromosomes

Spaying Neutering of female cat/kitten

Spraying Habit of males, serving to mark their territory with urine

Squint Deformation, causing the eyes to stare intently at the nose, hence giving a cross-eyed appearance

Standard of points Points scale to which exhibition cats are judged

Stud Male cat kept for breeding, or breeding premises themselves

Stumpy Remnants of a tail in the Manx

Tabby Markings, either striped, spotted or blotched

TICA The Independent Cat Association (TICA)

Ticking Banding seen on the hairs of Abyssinians

Tipped Ends of individual hairs of a different colour to that at the base

Tom Intact male cat

Type The appearance of the cat (or breed)

UCF United Cat Fanciers (USA)

Variety Specifically colour form or other characteristic within a breed, but often may be used in place of breed itself

Vibrissae Whiskers around the head

Wedge Refers to head shape, especially significant in Siamese

Whip tail Thin, long tail tapering to a point at its end

FURTHER READING

Ashford, A and Pond, G.
Rex, Abyssinian And Turkish Cats (John Gifford, 1972)

Brearley, J.M.
All about Himalayan Cats (TFH Publications, 1976)

Dunnill, M.
The Siamese Cat Owner's Encyclopaedia (Pelham, 1974)

Ewer, R.F.
The Carnivores (Weidenfeld and Nicolson, 1973)

Guggisberg, C.A.W.
The Wild Cats of the World (David and Charles, 1975)

Johnson, N.H. with Galin, S.
The Complete Kitten and Cat Book (Robert Hale, 1979)

Joshua, J.O.
Cat Owners' Encyclopaedia of Veterinary Medicine
(TFH Publications, 1979)

McBride, C.
The White Lions of Timbavati (Paddington Press, 1977)

McBride, C.
Operation White Lion (Collins and Harvill Press, 1981)

Pond, G. (editor)
The Complete Cat Encyclopaedia (Heinemann, 1972; Crown, NY, 1972)

Pond, G. and Calder, M.
The Long-haired Cat (Batsford, 1974)

Pond, G. and Raleigh, I. (general editors)
A Standard Guide to Cat Breeds (Macmillan, 1979; McGraw Hill, NY, 1979)

Richards, D.S. *et al*
The Burmese Cat (Batsford, 1975)

Richards, D.S.
A Handbook of Pedigree Cat Breeding (Batsford, 1977)

Robinson, R.
Genetics for Cat Breeders (Pergamon Press, 1977)

Simpson, F.
The Book of the Cat (Cassell, 1903)

Tottenham, K.
Looking after your Cat (Ward Lock, 1981)

Wilson, M.D.
Encyclopaedia of American Cat Breeds (TFH Publications, 1978)

Wright, M. and Walters, S. (editors)
The Book of the Cat (Pan Books, 1980)

USEFUL ADDRESSES

The following is a list of the main cat fancy organizations throughout the world. It is usually appreciated if you enclose a stamped, addressed envelope when writing for information.

American Cat Association,
10065 Foothill Boulevard,
Lakeview Terrace,
California 91342,
USA

American Cat Fanciers'
Association (CFA),
PO Box 203,
Point Lookout,
Missouri 65726,
USA

American Feline Society,
41 Union Square W,
New York,
NY 10003,
USA

Canadian Cat Association,
14 Nelson Street West (Suite 5),
Brampton,
Ontario L6X 1BY,
CANADA

Cat Fanciers' Association,
PO Box 430,
Red Bank,
New Jersey 07701,
USA

Cat Fanciers' Federation,
2013 Elizabeth Street,
Schenectady,
NY 12303,
USA

Crown Cat Fanciers'
Association,
1379 Tyler Park Drive,
Louisville,
Kentucky 40204,
USA

Feline Association of South
Australia,
7 Athelney Avenue,
Brighton,
South Australia 5048,
AUSTRALIA

Fédération Internationale,
Féline (FIFe),
Friedrichstrasse 48,
6200 Wiesbaden,
WEST GERMANY

Governing Council of the
Cat Fancy (GCCF),
Dovefields,
Petworth Road,
Witley,
Surrey GU8 5QU
ENGLAND

National Cat Club,
The Laurels,
Chesham Lane,
Wendover,
Buckinghamshire,
ENGLAND

Kensington Kitten and
Neuter Cat Club,
Fairmont,
78 Highfield Avenue,
Aldershot,
Hampshire,
ENGLAND

Long Island Ocelot Club,
PO Box 99542,
Tacoma,
Washington 98499
USA

New Zealand Cat Fancy Inc,
PO Box 3167,
Richmond,
Nelson,
NEW ZEALAND

The Independent Cat
Association,
211 East Olive (Suite 201),
Burbank,
California 91502,
USA

United Cat Federation,
6621 Thornwood Street,
San Diego,
California 92111,
USA

Western Province Cat Club,
PO Box 3600,
Cape Town 8000,
SOUTH AFRICA

GENERAL ADDRESSES

American Human
Association,
5351 S Roslyn Street,
Englewood,
Colorado 80111,
USA

American Society for the
Prevention of Cruelty to
Animals,
441 East 92nd Street,
New York,
NY 10028,
USA

Canadian Society for the
Prevention of Cruelty to
Animals (CSPCA),
5214 Jean-Talon Street West,
Montreal, Quebec H4P 1X4,
CANADA

Cat Action Trust (CAT),
The Crippetts,
Jordens,
Beaconsfield,
Buckinghamshire,
ENGLAND

Cat Plan Insurance,
Pet Plan Ltd,
32 Wood Lane,
London W12 7DU,
ENGLAND

Cats Protection League,
20 North Street,
Horsham,
West Sussex RH12 1BN,
ENGLAND

Cat Survival Trust,
Marlind Centre,
Codicote Road,
Welwyn,
Hertfordshire AL6 9TV,
ENGLAND

Feline Advisory Bureau,
6 Woodthorpe Road,
London SW15 6UQ,
ENGLAND

Pedigree Petfoods·
Education Centre,
Waltham-on-the-Wolds,
Melton Mowbray,
Leicestershire LE14 4RS,
ENGLAND

People's Dispensary for
Sick Animals (PDSA),
PDSA House,
South Street,
Dorking,
Surrey RH4 2LB,
ENGLAND

Petcare Information and
Advisory Service,
254 George Street,
Sydney,
New South Wales,
AUSTRALIA

Pet Health Council,
Walter House (4th Floor),
418-422 The Strand,
London WC2R 0PL,
ENGLAND

Royal Society for the
Prevention of Cruelty to
Animals (RSPCA),
The Manor House,
Causeway,
Horsham,
West Sussex RH12 1HG,
ENGLAND

RSPCA (Australia),
Colter Road,
Canberra ACT 2600,
AUSTRALIA

Society for the Prevention
of Cruelty to Animals
(SPCA),
Wellington,
NEW ZEALAND

SPCA (South Africa),
P.O. Box 38035,
Johannesburg 2000,
SOUTH AFRICA

Spillers Pet Advisory
Service,
New Malden House,
1 Blagden Road,
New Malden,
Surrey KT3 4TB,
ENGLAND

INDEX

Page numbers in *italic* refer to the illustrations and captions.

ACKNOWLEDGEMENTS

The pictures on these pages were reproduced by kind courtesy of the following:
2-3 The Bridgeman Art Library, courtesy of the Gavin Graham Gallery, London; **7** The Bridgeman Art Library, courtesy of the Guildhall, City of London; **8, 9** Trustees of the British Museum; **13** Victoria and Albert Museum; **15** Mary Evans Picture Library; **17, 22** Michael Freeman; **37** Mary Evans Picture Library; **38, 39** Animals Unlimited; **40** Creszentia Allen; **42, 46** Animals Unlimited; **47, 49** Creszentia Allen; **50, 51, 53, 54, 55** Animals Unlimited; **56** Creszentia Allen; **58, 59, 62, 63, 64, 66** Animals Unlimited; **67**(al, ar) Creszentia Allen, (b) Animals Unlimited; **69** Animals Unlimited; **70**(al, ac, ar) Creszentia Allen, (b) Animals Unlimited; **71** Creszentia Allen; **73** (a) Creszentia Allen, (b) Animals Unlimited; **74** Creszentia Allen; **75** Animals Unlimited; **77** (a) Animals Unlimited, (b) Creszentia Allen; **78, 79** Animals Unlimited; **81** (a) Animals Unlimited, (b) Creszentia Allen; **82, 83, 86** Animals Unlimited; **87**(a, c, br) Animals Unlimited, (bl) Creszentia Allen; **90** Animals Unlimited; **91**(a, cr, br, bl) Animals Unlimited, (cl) Creszentia Allen; **93** Mary Evans Picture Library; **98, 99** Animals Unlimited; **111** Mary Evans Picture Library; **114** Michael Freeman; **122**(c,b), **123** Animals Unlimited; **131**(tl, tr, c) James Marks; **137** Mary Evans Picture Library; **140** Animals Unlimited; **161** Mary Evans Picture Library; **162** Michael Freeman; **166, 167, 174, 175** Animals Unlimited; **177** Mary Evans Picture Library; **179** Ardea London (photo: Clem Haagner); **181**(a) Ardea London (photo: Clem Haagner), (b) Ardea London (photo: Richard Waller); **182**(b) Ardea London (photo: Ian Beames); **183** Ardea London (photo: Arthus-Bertrand); **185, 186** Ardea London (photo: Kenneth W. Fink); **187**(a) Ardea London (photo: Dr Charles McDougal), (b) Ardea London (photo: W. Weisser); **188** Ardea London (photo: P. Morris); **189** Ardea London (photo: Dr Charles McDougal); **190** Ardea London (photo: Jean-Paul Ferrero); **191** Ardea London (photo: Tom Willock); **192**(a) Ardea London (photo: Kenneth W. Fink), (b) Ardea London (photo: Francois Gohier); **193** Ardea London (photo: Francois Gohier); **195** Ardea London (photo: Adrian Warren); **196-7** Ardea London (photo: Kenneth W. Fink).

All other photographs property of Quarto Publishing Limited.

KEY: (a) above; (b) below; (l) left; (r) right; (t) top; (c) centre